STUDIES IN MEDIEVAL AND RENAISSANCE HISTORY

Volume X

(Old Series, Volume XX)

STUDIES IN
Medieval and Renaissance
History

Volume X
(Old Series, Volume XX)

EDITORS:

J. A. S. EVANS

R. W. UNGER

AMS PRESS
New York

AMS PRESS, INC.
56 EAST 13th STREET

ISBN 0081-8224
ISBN 0-404-62850-8 (Set)
ISBN 0-404-62860-5 (Vol. X)

Library of Congress Catalog Card Number 63-22098

Manufactured in the United States of America

CONTENTS

Introduction   vi

The Angevin Economy, 960–1060
   Ancient or Feudal?
                         Bernard S. Bachrach   1

Chivalric Romances in the Italian
   Renaissance.
                         Paul F. Grendler   59

A Tale of Two Princes:
Politics, Text and Ideology
in a Carolingian Annal.
                         Janet L. Nelson   103

Index   141

Contents of Previous Volumes   151

INTRODUCTION

Studies in Medieval and Renaissance History is a series designed for original major articles in all fields of medieval and renaissance history. Volumes will appear approximately once a year.

    Studies in Medieval and Renaissance History was formerly published by the University of Nebraska Press, and the impetus for the creation of the series came from the belief that there was a need for a publication that would accommodate the study that was too long to be included regularly in scholarly journals, but too short to appear as a book. The editors will consider articles in all areas of history from approximately the third to the sixteenth centuries—economic, social and demographic, political, intellectual and cultural, and studies that do not fit neatly into a single traditional category of historical investigation.

    While the series is devoted primarily to the publication of major studies, it contains occasional bibliographic essays, and briefer articles dealing with unpublished archival and manuscript resources. The *Studies* also makes available in translation original articles by scholars who do not write in English or French.

    Studies in Medieval and Renaissance History is published by AMS Press for the Committee for Medieval Studies at the University of British Columbia, and the editors welcome submissions from all scholars doing research in medieval and renaissance fields, including those whose interests are not strictly historical.

J. A. S. Evans

THE ANGEVIN ECONOMY, 960–1060: ANCIENT OR FEUDAL?

Bernard S. Bachrach
University of Minnesota

THE ANGEVIN ECONOMY, 960–1060: ANCIENT OR FEUDAL?*

In a finely nuanced and stimulating article recently published in *Past and Present*, Chris Wickham set out through the use of a Marxist problematic to illuminate what in economic terms underlies the end of the ancient world. It is unnecessary here to rehearse Wickham's detailed arguments for an Althusserian approach as modified by the theories of Hindess and Hirst with a copious debt to Finley, some influences of Amin and other revisions for which Wickham appears willing to take the credit or stand the blame. It suffices to make clear, perhaps at the risk of some simplification, that Wickham sees the "ancient" mode as one in which the dominant source of surplus extraction is tax and not rent. The "feudal" mode, i.e. rent taking, Wickham frequently reminds us, was very much present in the ancient world but it did not dominate it. When rent is seen to surpass tax—and Wickham vigorously cautions that a simple though obviously unattainable quantitative measure is too mechanistic to be a viable criterion—it may be concluded that the "feudal" mode has become dominant. As Wickham emphasizes, "the heaviness of taxation is not its absolute weight, together with a calculation of what harm this did to the productiveness of the economy . . . but what the relative weight of taxation to rent paying was." Thus Wickham concludes that when society is "dominated by the feudal mode of production, the 'feudal social formation,' . . . western states were feudal, not just their economies. . . ."[1]

It is not my intent here to quibble with Wickham's conceptualization of the problem since as he correctly observes: "Modes of production are ideal constructs, .the justification for particular definitions, as long as they have an internal logic and thus make sense, must be their usefulness. . . ."[2] However, as a medievalist I was particularly struck by Wickham's assertion: "Each of the numerous

3

tiny political units of the post-Carolingian period. . . . By the definitions used in this article, all were feudal. . . ."[3] This conclusion is unsupported by basic research, and Wickman's references to a collection of articles, *Structures féodales et féodalisme dans l'occident méditerranéen,* cannot sustain his very broad-gauged generalizations. Wickham's other references in support of his "all were feudal" claim are to the classic work on *principautés* by Dhondt and Bloch's *Feudal Society.* These studies simply cannot bear the weight that they are made to carry; "all" covers a very broad horizon.[4] Indeed, I know of *no* thorough examination of the economic structure of any state which emerged in the tenth century from the collapse of the Carolingian empire that has been carried out within useful range of the definitions that have been developed by Wickham and which he has applied in such a stimulating manner to the problem of the end of the ancient world. For example, the magisterial *Les Hommes et la terre* volumes that have been produced in France since the Second World War in response largely to Marc Bloch's 1936 suggestions for future research, are conceptualized so differently from Wickham's Marxist problematic that they do not provide even the basic information needed to address the relative role of tax and rent in terms of the fundamental economic structure of the post-Carolingian states of the tenth and eleventh centuries.[5]

It should be made clear from the outset that if the "ancient" mode dominated any of the economies of post-Carolingian states, Wickham's general thesis regarding the transition from the ancient world would not be significantly effected. The post-Carolingian polities of *Francia occidentalis* which are the subject of Wickham's generalization were quite small and if by some chance an "ancient" economy or two in particular regions survived even into the tenth or eleventh centuries it would have to be proven that these represented more than very local phenomena. However, if such a late example of an "ancient" economy were merely a new creation as is more likely, this might discomfort a few very traditional Marxists who insist upon history moving in a one–way progress from "ancient" to "feudal" to "capitalist." Wickham certainly is not one of these, and such traditionalists could simply deny the validity of Wickham's construct because he failed to include slavery or they could parry with a "theological" argument and point out that, traditionally, dialectical materialism does not recognize historical tergiversation.[6]

Aside from pointing out that Wickham made a sweeping, though unsupported generalization, what would be the purpose of expending extensive effort to ascertain whether the economy of one or another post-Carolingian state was dominated by tax or rent? There is, of course, the cliché about the value of knowledge for its own sake, but more importantly from a Marxist perspective an understanding of the history of the small states in the post-Carolingian West must be based upon an accurate description of the nature of their economic structures. Once the economic base has been identified it is the essential of Marxist theory that the resulting superstructures such as the family, politics, religion, ideology, and the state itself can be properly understood.[7]

The current state of research does not permit a broadly-gauged survey of the economies that flourished in the many post-Carolingian states in the West.[8] Rather, we are at a stage where the basic research on the particular states still remains to be done.[9] Therefore, in this paper I will examine the economic base of the Angevin state which was built upon the ruins of the Carolingian empire in a small part of *Francia occidentalis* following the devastation wrought by the civil wars and Viking invasions of the ninth and early tenth centuries. For the period from 960 to 1060, i.e. the century encompassed by the reigns of Geoffrey Greymantle (960–987), Fulk Nerra (987–1040), and Geoffrey Martel (1040–1060), an effort will be made to ascertain whether the dominant source of surplus extraction in the Angevin economy was tax or rent, i.e., was the economy "ancient" or "feudal"?[10]

THE ANGEVIN SYSTEM OF TAXATION

During the period under consideration here the Angevin counts administered a complex system of taxation in which a wide variety of imposts were levied directly and indirectly by the government on immoveables, moveables, and persons.[11] On occasion it would seem that we are able to catch more than a glimpse of direct taxes levied on the land itself, although it is difficult to ascertain if these were vestiges of a system that most scholars believe was already in decay during the Carolingian era or Angevin attempts at something new.[12] The land taxes of the later Roman empire *(capitatio terrena, iugatio)* became the *tributa, functiones,* and *census* of the Merovingian era and the *census regius* or *census regalis* of the Carolingian system.[13] In the Angevin state the *census* seems to have been focused upon alodial land although not exclusively. Thus, for example, an alod is normally seen to be subject to the *census* owed to the count but there were also special alods that were by definition exempt from the *census* and were thus treated "as a royal alod," i.e., "ut regale alodium."[14] The point need hardly be made that this *census* cannot be considered a rent since an alod was real estate held in full property during this period in the west of France.[15]

Other examples of the *census* as a land tax can be glimpsed at the stronghold of Château-Gontier where the land within the *castrum* was subject to this impost.[16] At what would appear to be another extreme we can find small pieces of land *(reicules)* subject to the *census* where this levy is clearly described as one of the comital taxes *(consuetudines comitales)*, i.e., these are royal taxes that had devolved upon the comital government. It is also perhaps of some interest that this census on the *reicules* was assessed annually; it is described as a *taxatio annualis*.[17] Another tax on small holdings was that levied by the government on houses located within fortifications.[18] The term *terra censuales* also on occasion can be shown to refer to lands subject to a land tax, but when the text which provides such terminology is ambiguous it is perhaps safer and certainly less controversial to think of such lands as held at a rent.[19]

Whether these examples of a direct tax on land were continuous developments from the Carolingian era or more modern impositions cannot be ascertained. By contrast, it is clear that the *terragium* was a new direct tax on land, i.e., a levy collected by the state which first appears in the territory of the erstwhile Carolingian empire in 980.[20] From the Angevin evidence the *terragium* appears primarily to have been levied on assarts and it was an additional tax, i.e., it was in addition to the full range of comital *consuetudines* that were levied on all reclaimed lands. Indeed, not even the greatest landholders in the Angevin state could undertake the project of assarting forests or waste in their own possession without a comital license.[21]

It would be highly imprudent in light of the fragmentary and often ambiguous nature of the evidence to give too much weight to the direct taxes on the land itself as part of the mix of revenues collected by the Angevin state.[22] Clearly of more importance were those taxes generally called *consuetudines* that were levied directly on the productivity of the land or other forms of production.[23] At harvest time the count's agents went into the countryside and assessed the *consuetudo* on various crops: *avenagium* on the crop of oats,[24] *fenagium* on the hay,[25] and *frumentagium* on the grain.[26] The "crop" of animals was also taxed: the *friscingagium* was levied on suckling pigs,[27] *multonagium* on yearling rams that were castrated so that they might be more easily fattened for the slaughter,[28] the *bribigium* on new lambs,[29] and the *vaccagium* on the calves.[30] In addition, direct taxes were also collected on the production of bread in ovens *(furnaticum)*,[31] on the production of wine *(vinagium)*,[33] and on the flour ground in mills *(molinagium)*.[33]

Not only did the tax collectors go out into the countryside to collect these direct imposts, but the taxpayers were responsible for paying the expenses of these governmental officials while they were on the job. Thus, for example, in a particularly forthcoming text dating from 1040 we learn that when the count's *servientes* went to collect the *vinagium* at the villa of Saint-Georges-sur-Layon which belonged to the monastery of Saint Florent de Saumur, one of the greatest landowners in Anjou, each of these tax collectors was to receive a daily ration of one *denarius* worth of bread, one *denarius* worth of meat, and a *sextarius* either of wine or of flavored wine *(mustus)*.[34] As will be seen below these payments were not ungenerous and likely served as the bulk of the daily pay for these government agents.

Unlike the *consuetudines* discussed above which were levied on productivity, usually at a rate of 10 percent, i.e., a *decima*, of the total in the "field" and occasionally at a higher, even a much higher, percentage of the gross, there was a congeries of interrelated imposts more directly mandated to sustain the functioning of the state in war and peace.[35] These obligations fell more broadly on the society as a whole and were not as explicitly tied to productivity. Among the taxes in this latter group upon which scholars have focused considerable attention is the *fodrum*. This levy was originally intended to provide fodder for the animals used by the army and it was assessed as needed.[36] The burdensome nature of this impost which was limited only by what was available to fill the government's needs is frequently attested in the Angevin sources as the count's officials appear to have found various creative ways to meet the requirements of the state. The burdensomeness of the *fodrum* in Anjou during this period may have been occasioned, at least in part, by the fact that fodder and related supplies for the men were sought not only when the Angevin army or component parts of the armed forces were *in hoste* or *in expeditione* and also *sine hoste,* i.e., at times when the military was not actually on campaign.[37]

Closely connected to the *fodrum,* which in peacetime would appear on occasion as "hospitium equorum," were levies of all types of foodstuffs for the army.[38] The obligation to provide food for the army did not fall only on producers but also on *burgenses.* In recognition of the fact that *burgenses* generally were not engaged in agriculture it was permitted for them to pay this tax in money rather than in kind.[39] In peacetime, moreover, efforts appear to have been made to limit the tax called the *abergementum* to sustaining the count and his officials, i.e., the men of the count's military household who travelled with him at all times. The *abergementum* encompassed not only the basics of food (including wine) and lodging for the men and appropriate supplies for the horses, but even stipulated that such detailed requirements as blankets or bedding *(culcitura)* be provided for the itinerant comital household.[40]

In order to obtain the means to transport the supplies needed by the army in time of war and for the government in peacetime the Angevin count imposed the *angaria* on all those who owned wagons, carts, oxen, and asses.[41] Actually, the *angaria* not only included hauling service which at times is called the *carragum,*[42] but also a messenger service called the *cavaugadum* which was imposed upon all those who owned horses.[43] It is not exactly clear how this "post service" worked and what, if any, relation it may have had to the Carolingian system which itself was based upon the Roman *tractoria.*[44] Parenthetically, it may be noted that fishermen who plied their trade in boats on the major rivers of Anjou such as the Loire, and they did so only by government license, were responsible for the *evectio;* this encompassed transport services for the count's household which included his military following as well as more general hauling obligations and the carrying of messages.[45]

More thoroughly military in nature was the general obligation for all those under the jurisdiction of the Angevin government to perform the *bidamnum.* This was a service due annually that apparently was owed by all landholders, free and unfree alike, which generally entailed fifteen days of labor and was focused upon the building or the repair of fortifications that were located either firmly within the Angevin state or on the frontiers.[46] Those who found such service inconvenient or perhaps demeaning were permitted to find substitutes; as one text puts it: "hoc bidamnum tale erat ut omnes qui in hac possessione terram tenebant, aut ipsi aut laetati [sic] eorum . . .

pergerent. . . ."[47] These *laeti* obviously would then do two tours of service. Although lords were often eager to have their dependents avoid this burdensome public service, the counts rarely granted immunities.[48] They did, however, permit commutations of this tax *(consuetudo)* for regular payments in money.[49] Apparently more general than the *bidamnum* were *corvadae* that were imposed by government officials such as the *vicarius* or someone exercising the vicarial power in his place on dependents of various lords in order to carry out public works.[50]

A lengthy theoretical discussion is not required in order to classify as taxes the labor services performed for the government. This should seem especially obvious when such services were at least on occasion commuted for payments in money as noted above with regard to the *bidamnum*. Without debating the endless ramifications of a "labor theory of value," it should be sufficient to make clear that medievalists traditionally have categorized the labor services performed or perhaps more accurately "paid" by agricultural dependents to their *seniores* as "rents" and thus such labor services levied by and "paid" to the government as a public obligation may reasonably be considered a tax. Indeed, a direct tax![51]

In this vein it is exceptionally important that the obligation to perform military service—both for local defense and for operations beyond the frontiers—was universal in the Angevin state.[52] Thus, for example, the count's *satellites*, i.e., his *vassi* and *fideles*, were required not only to answer the *submonitio*, i.e., the call to arms themselves, but they were required to bring their *rustici*, i.e., their agricultural dependents, along with them.[53] Also, the *villani*, both those who were dependents of a lord such as the *rustici* mentioned above or the lowly *famuli* of a great *senior* as well as those who were not dependents, were required to answer the comital *submonitio* "pro praelio publico" under the leadership of a government official such as the *vicarius* or under the command of their lord or his substitute in cases where the *senior* was an ecclesiastic.[54] Even those who held but small plots of land, the *ruricolae*, owed military service as did those who were inhabitants of the *burgi*, i.e., the *burgenses*. The latter, whose wealth more than likely was not in land and whose livelihood was probably earned through trade and commerce or as artisans, are explicitly warned that for "nullam causu mercedis" will they be exempt from military service.[55]

It is clear that not all of those who were called up for service beyond the frontiers were to be used as combat troops. Some men were employed in the provision of logistic support on campaign by

driving wagons and similar useful services while others were explicitly
designated to carry out the building of fortifications and defensible
encampments in enemy territory.[56] This, of course, was fully consistent with Angevin military policy of gaining control of neighboring
territories, in part, through the establishment of strategically located
strongholds.[57]

A further sense of the sophistication of Angevin military
organization in drawing on all strata of society can be glimpsed from
an arrangement made by the count to assure the smooth functioning
of his offensive capability while at the same time protecting his frontier. In what was likely to have been a common type of arrangement,
the castellan of a frontier stronghold, in this case Montreuil-Bellay,
was instructed by the count's *submonitio* to lead the *caballarii* who
garrisoned this fortification to the count's army in order to carry out
military operations beyond the frontier. At the same time that the
castellan received his orders, the *vicarius*, whose administrative district
included not only the *castellaria* of Montreuil-Bellay but a considerably larger area, also received a *submonitio* from the count. In the
particular case under discussion here, the *vicarius* customarily called
up the *homines* living at the villa of Méron, which was under the
lordship of the monastery of Saint Aubin, and then led these men to
Montreuil-Bellay where they served as a temporary garrison until the
castellan returned with the *caballarii* to take up their normal duties
once again.[58]

Additional direct revenues were paid to the comital government relating to the use of public lands and waters ostensibly in the
same manner and for the same reasons that earlier they had been
collected by the Carolingian kings. A broad spectrum of rights were
held by the count on all "wooded land" whether privately held by his
subjects as *sylva* or belonging to the comital fisc and called *foresta*.
Thus it was required that the count's subjects purchase licenses or
obtain immunities, if, for example, they would hunt, chop down oak
trees for building, or carry out general land clearing for the purpose
of developing arable, i.e., assarting.[59] Licenses, of course, were also
required if anyone wished to hunt or chop down oaks in the forests of
the comital fisc or to fish on the major rivers such as the Loire for
commercial purposes.[60]

We may now turn from the complex of direct taxes imposed
and collected by the Angevin government to those imposts that may
be classified as indirect levies. These taxes may be divided into two

groups. The first group we can classify as tolls which were levied at the frontiers and internally on the circulation of merchandise. The term *theloneum* is often used in a general manner to describe this impost but in a more specialized context it appears to refer primarily to the toll paid by ships that carried merchandise up and down the Loire as well as on the lesser rivers of Anjou.[61] Other specialized terminology can be discerned such as the *pedaticum* that was imposed upon all those who carried vendable or potentially vendable goods, i.e., merchants and non-merchants alike,[62] the *rotaticum* or wheel tax which identifies the vehicle carrying the goods for taxation along with a smaller tax for goods carried on pack horses.[63] There are also mentions of the *pontaticum* that was paid for crossing a bridge. The bridges were used in addition as toll stations where the *theloneum* was collected from boats that passed beneath the span.[64] Moorage charges and port charges, the *ripaticum*[65] and *portaticum*[66] respectively, appear less frequently in the Angevin documents. The same is true for the *pulveraticum* as a general term denoting a toll.[67]

The second group of indirect taxes which would seem significantly to have contributed to the revenues collected by the government were levies on sales (*vendae* and *venditiones*). It is very important with regard to these imposts to emphasize that all sales, retail and wholesale alike, whenever they were made and by whomever they were executed, both free men and dependents alike, were subject to sales taxes. These taxes were not imposed only on those "qui vivunt mercatore."[68] Despite the army of minor government officials who are seen in the documents doing their duty, often with great zeal and officiousness (see below), it would have been impossible to collect taxes on every sale that took place. Yet, before concluding that these government officials operated solely in the markets and fairs where they normally did collect all of the sales taxes, it should be emphasized that they went at least as far as collecting taxes on the retail sales of wine in taverns (*cauponae*).[69]

The profits of justice were yet another source of government revenues collected by the Angevins. The system that prevailed in the Angevin state was a modified version of that which had functioned in the Carolingian empire. Under this system the counts had received one-third of all the fines paid in the local court over which he or his subordinates presided. One-third of these fines went to the king.[70] However, with the collapse of royal control over local administration it is arguable that the king's portion of the fines or *freda* went to the

Angevin counts and thus the next lower range of government func-
tionary was positioned to received what earlier had been the count's
portion. The importance of the income generated from these fines
may perhaps be gauged, in part, by the government's policy of not
permitting its subjects to obtain the profits of justice from the three
major crimes: i.e., homicide, arson, and theft, and of only very rarely
giving the income earned from lesser crimes as gifts or rewards for
service. The vigorous efforts undertaken by some of the count's most
influential subjects to obtain access to these profits, coupled with the
production of forged documents to secure mere "crumbs", would
appear to be additional indices of the value with which this income
was perceived.[71]

   Of particular importance in sustaining what had been Carolingian royal prerogatives were the count's efforts to secure the profits from enforcing the ban. Most visible in this context is the elaborate
system of enforcement of the *heribannum,* i.e., the fine levied upon
those who failed to answer the count's *submonitio* to perform military
service either as a combat effective or in support of operations.[72]
Another example of the Carolingian *bannum* that fell to the Angevin
state was control over minting and money changing along with the
fines that were imposed upon violators.[73]

   We have already seen that in consonance with the traditions
of the Carolingian empire the Angevin government maintained the
foresta with its concomitant revenues even in those woodlands that had
never been or no longer were a part of the comital fisc. In addition,
there were revenues that were collected only from woodlands that
belonged to the comital fisc; these included fees paid by those persons
who wished to pasture pigs, collect wax, or gather nuts. Also various
revenues came to the count for granting fishing rights on waters that
belonged to the fisc.[74] The landholdings of the Angevin government
were considerably greater, at least during this period, than those of
any of its subjects. Therefore, in light of the neo-Althusserian model
under consideration here, it would appear to be of some moment
whether one considers these revenues as well as those in service, kind,
and money remitted by tenants who dwelled on lands of the comital
fisc to be rents.

   An argument certainly could be formulated to sustain the
notion that the count as head of the Angevin government had access
to these revenues because he was a *Landesherr* rather than as a result
of *Grundherrschaft.* By contrast, a scenario might be conceptualized in
which it would be illuminating to consider as rent the vast income that

came to the Roman emperor from the lands of the imperial fisc. To my way of thinking, however, these overly rigid approaches are unhelpful because the uses to which the revenues from comital and, indeed, earlier from imperial lands were put ostensibly were the same as those to which "true" taxes were put, i.e., the sustention of the state.[75]

Several points concerning the complex tax system that has been described above require emphasis. First, it is of importance that the foregoing reconstruction was not based upon a constumnal or handbook of the types that were compiled later in the Middle Ages and which often provided information of antiquarian interest about institutions that were no longer viable. Rather, as the notes indicate the system described above has been reconstructed from contemporary documents which depict vital institutional structures at work.

The second point that requires emphasis is that the ensemble of taxes levied by the Angevin state constituted a very heavy burden. This weight is evidenced in many ways. For example, there are laments by great lords such as the abbot of Saint Florent who is seen to complain that with "ingravescentibus exactionibus . . . pressi afflictionibus." It is emphasized in another context that as a result of the count's *malae exactiones* "fundi eius gloriosi sancti vastati erat ac deserti." The fear of government tax collectors *(procuratores)* is voiced and their zeal in doing their job is seen to threaten the economic viability of the land.[76] References in the Angevin texts to these kinds of laments can be greatly multiplied, although a not very long list of references regarding the existence of poverty can be generated; it would seem, however, that complaint about the burdens of taxation and the existence of poverty are ubiquitous in Western civilization.[77]

In order to address the neo-Althusserian model under consideration here, it is not sufficient to demonstrate merely that the tax burden was great but to ascertain its weight relative to the burden imposed by rent. This calculation can be made in a very rough manner quantitatively—precise statistics no more survive from eleventh-century Anjou than from the Roman empire in the fifth or sixth century—and with great nuance qualitatively, i.e., in the respective impact of tax and rent on social structures. The effect, as Wickham has correctly observed, "was certainly not purely a quantitative one, that of the relative weight of tax and rent; such a claim would be extremely mechanistic, reducing a whole system to a reflection of a set of [undiscoverable] statistical relationships."[78]

ANGEVIN RENTS

Initially, let us look at what may perhaps be considered quantitative evidence. In the Angevin state, as we have seen, taxes were levied on everyone—free and unfree, lay and ecclesiastical, alike. Many taxpayers, however, paid no rents. Among these we must include small allodial landowners whose number in the Angevin state probably should not be underestimated since allodial lands are frequently mentioned in the documents. A particularly startling example comes from the *Livre noir de Saint-Florent,* a cartulary that was compiled toward the end of the eleventh century in order to put in manageable condition and assure the safety of 271 documents of which most were issued during the prior 150 years. Here, of the sixteen documents recorded in roughly chronological order in folios 13r.-19v., thirteen are concerned with allodial holdings.[79]

Like allodial landowners, the merchants, clerics, and artisans of the Angevin state are also likely to have paid few if any rents. Thus it is to the great landowners, lay and ecclesiastical alike, and more particularly to their agricultural dependents, who surely comprised a substantial element of the population (although the percentage is undiscoverable), that it is necessary to look in order to ascertain some quantitative sense of the relation between tax and rent. At the outset it should be emphasized that although the direct tax on land in the Angevin state was very probably of relatively little significance in the total mix of tax income as compared with the returns brought to the Roman government by the imperial *annona,* the products of the land were taxed. Thus it is crucial to underscore the fact the the great landowners paid taxes on what their resources, i.e., lands, mills, and ovens produced, at a rate of 10 percent of the gross, but, in general, they did not pay rents. Ostensibly, rents were paid only by dependent cultivators who, of course, were also burdened by the Angevin state with a full range of taxes.[80]

How much rent dependent cultivators could pay even in a best case situation consisted of what was left over from their resources, i.e., income and laboring capacity, after their subsistence needs and tax levies were met. One basic structure that conditioned the peasants' resources was the manner in which the land was distributed. Unlike the *latifundia* of the late antique and early medieval Mediterranean world which many contemporary scholars believe were morselled up by their owners into parcels of land populated by a

rent paying peasantry,[81] the great estates of Anjou in the era 960–
1060 were structured in the classic bipartite manner that was common
to the region between the Loire and the Rhine at least from the later
eighth century and very probably from an even earlier period.[82] In
this system based upon the *villa* about one-third to one-half of the
arable land was held *indominicatum* while the remainder was parcelled
out in small units, often called *mansi*, to dependent cultivators who
paid rent for this land with payments in kind, labor on the lord's
demesne, and sometimes with payments in money. The total landed
resources at the command of the dependent cultivators from which
rent could be paid were at best only slightly greater than the landed
resources dominated directly by the landlords who paid no rent.[83]

  We can gain further insight into the upper limits of the rent
paying capacity of the dependent cultivators from some very gross
data on agricultural productivity. Mediavalists have developed a frag-
ile consensus that in the region between the Loire and Rhine, at least
through the eleventh century, an average return on seed of $2:1$
prevailed in the production of cereal grains which were the basic
crops.[84] Without oxen a peasant could cultivate about fifteen acres of
arable in the course of an agricultural year of about 250 days.[85] From
this arable the peasant could produce approximately 1,900 kgs. of
wheat.[86] After setting aside 950 kgs. as seed for the next year's
planting, subtracting approximately 750 kgs. which was required to
provide the wheat equivalent calories to sustain himself for a year at a
rate of slightly more than 2 kgs. of unmilled wheat per day,[87] and
paying a tax to the Angevin government of 190 kgs., a mere 30 kgs of
wheat remained at a maximum to be used by the peasant to pay rent
to his landlord. The ratio of tax to rent thus may be put at about $6:1$.

  This calculation, while perhaps having some heuristic value
as an indicator of the general pattern of distribution of the dependent
cultivator's resources is, of course, highly schematic; many other
variables need to be taken into consideration. During the period
960–1060 there is an abundance of evidence to indicate substantial
demographic growth in this region.[88] This population growth could
not have been based upon an average family size of less than four.[89]
After one takes into consideration variations in caloric needs due to
age and sex with regard to distribution in the population structure it
is not unfair to conclude that it was necessary for a peasant family to
have had available for consumption double the wheat equivalent
calories provided by fifteen acres of arable with a productivity ratio of

$2:1.$[90] This doubling or more than doubling of the caloric income of the peasant family was very probably accomplished in a highly varied manner by means such as hunting small game, gathering wild fruits, berries and roots, gardening, and perhaps by day work for wages in either money or kind.[91] It is important to emphasize that a varied diet, i.e., one that included not only a balance of carbohydrates and proteins but also vitamins and minerals, was needed for survival. The increased levels of fertility that were required in order to sustain Angevin population growth also testify to a "satisfactory" diet. In short, an unrelieved regimen of cold wheat gruel was nutritionally impossible for an extended period of time to feed the growing population of Anjou in the period under consideration here.[92]

In terms of evaluating the productive capacity of the family unit of dependent cultivators it is clear that the more that was produced in untaxed income from its "hunting and gathering" activities in the course of a year the greater total resources it possessed from which rent could be taken by the landlord. The upper limit here is conditioned by the labor available to the family unit combined with opportunity. In all likelihood the peasant family unit was far more productive than our documents and speculations based upon those documents indicate; this is especially likely in the context of substantial population growth which must be undergirded by a pattern of growth in the food supply. Thus it is probably safe to conclude that the approximately $6:1$ ratio of tax to rent suggested by the gross calculations above was in reality much smaller, i.e., the landlord could take more of the peasant's grain because all of the 750 kgs. of grain set aside in the calculations made above was not required by the family for subsistence as their total needs were met by more informal sources of supply.

Despite these more flexible conditions, rents do not seem to have been very high. From a corpus of data developed by using bits and pieces of scattered information found in contemporary documents it seems that a *junctum* of arable land (70 percent of an acre) rented on average for about 4 *denarii* per year.[93] An *aripennis* of vineyards (about 37 percent of an acre) with a productive capacity of about 100 gallons of wine rented for an average of about 5.5 *denarii* per year.[94] In one text we find a *junctum* of land with a stone house on it renting for 6 *denarii*.[95] Since these data cluster largely from the early part of the period under consideration here, it is not impossible that rents increased toward the middle third of the eleventh century.

However, it should be emphasized that we find no forthright complaints at all about the burdensomeness of rent and the few inferences
concerning the possible burden of rent that might be drawn from an
occasional document fade into utter insignificance went compared
with the ubiquitous complaints about taxes.[96] The leniency of the
system of rent-taking on land is evidenced in part by a customary
formula from the region that reads: "If this same rent they [the rent
payers] will have been found to be late or negligent in paying let every
effort be made to amend the situation, but let them not lose the land
that they are seen to hold as a result."[97] When compared to the vigor
if not indeed the brutality of the government's tax collectors, rent
taking appears innocuous.

    The suggestion that these rents were not high may perhaps
be provided with support by a comparison with some few prices that
appear in the documents of the period. For example, we find on two
occasions an entire *mansus* being sold for 120 *solidi*.[98] Serfs seem to be
worth between 20 and 30 *solidi* each.[99] By contrast, the average price
for a war horse was about 40 *solidi*.[100] One is reminded by these prices
of the case of Isanhard who in 761 sold his ancestral lands and a slave
for a horse and a sword.[101] True, prices rose. For example, the war
horse went from 12 *solidi* ca. 800 to 40 *solidi*,[102] but a rough parallel-
ism of values seems to have prevailed from the Carolingian era to the
mid-eleventh century.

    The second major resource with which rent was paid by
dependent cultivators was their labor. The amount of labor service a
landlord might obtain from his peasants was limited, like the rents in
kind, by what the dependent required to sustain himself and his
family and by what the government took in taxes. Some of the ex-
actions imposed by the state upon the time and labor of its subjects,
free and unfree alike, were for a fixed period of time and these would
appear, at least upon cursory examination, to have been not overly
burdensome. For example, the *bidamnum,* as we have seen, was usually exacted for a continuous period of fifteen days of labor on an
annual basis for the purpose of building or repairing fortifications
within the Angevin state. The fifteen-day period of work did not
include travel time to and from the taxpayer's home and the place
where the required labor with "pick and shovel" was to be carried
out.[103] Thus perhaps on average another two or three days might be
added for travel to the fifteen days of actual labor.[104] Yet, despite the
apparently mild burden imposed by this tax in labor, we do find

efforts by lords to purchase commutations for those living on their estates. The abbot of Saint Florent, for example, arranged to pay 200 *solidi* on a yearly basis to have commuted the *bidamnum* owed by those who dwelled at the *villa* of Saint Georges; this despite the fact that their obligation was only for eight days as contrasted to the normal fifteen.[105] With such a sum of money the government could purchase at least seven war horses in order to supply the requirements of the count's military household.[106]

Other services demanded by the government such as the *corvadae* for road repair and more importantly military service which had no fixed limits are likely to have required more time and labor from the peasants and, indeed, from others than did the *bidamnum*. Military obligations such as that imposed upon the *villani* at Méron to garrison the stronghold of Montreuil-Bellay when the regular garrison of *caballarii* rode off beyond the frontier would last at least a few weeks but might perhaps extend for a few months.[107] Although the Angevin government was almost constantly involved in military operations during the period from 960–1060, not all campaigns were of long duration. However, some were quite long such as Fulk Nerra's operations against Nantes in 992 which lasted for about three months; the same count's campaign against Tours that culminated in the battle of Pontlevoy in 1016, his operations in 1026, and in 1033 each lasted well over a month. Geoffrey Martel also had several long campaigns far from home. Indeed, he invaded Normandy twice and frequently operated in Maine.[108] The campaigns carried out by the armies of the Angevin state were not as lengthy as those of the armies of the Carolingian empire which ultimately led to the impoverishment of much of the middle range of free landowners.[109] It can be concluded, however, that the amount of time and labor, not to mention expense incurred by both free and unfree alike either as combat effectives or as support troops, was not inconsiderable.

Whatever time the dependent cultivator had available to expend as rent in the form of labor service on his landlord's demesne after securing the subsistence required for himself and his family and after meeting his tax obligations to the state could not have been very great. Since oxen were used extensively for plowing—indeed, the Angevin government maintained special facilities as part of the fisc for breeding these draft animals and arable was occasionally identified in terms of the number of oxen needed for plowing[110]—more land could be cultivated with less labor than if oxen had not been available. Horses were not used for plowing.[111] However heavy labor services to the lord may have been in the Angevin state, they are highly unlikely to have been as great as those performed by the peasants on the great estates of the Carolingian era whose obligations are described so elaborately, for example, in the polyptych of Saint-Germain-des-Près which was drawn up at the order of Abbot Irmino ca. 820.[112] The dependent cultivators of the Carolingian empire were not directly liable to the state for military service as were those in the Angevin state. Rather, about 50 percent of the so-called "rents" paid or performed by peasants on Abbot Irmino's estates were, in fact, "taxes" that went either directly or indirectly to sustain the Carolingian government's constant military operations.[113]

A glimpse of the Carolingian peasant's obligations in terms of labor services can be instructive in helping us to understand the upper limits of what might be obtained in rent from dependent cultivators on the *villae* in the Angevine state who carried out their military obligations directly. A good example of what might be considered an average obligation of labor service can be obtained from an examination of the often-studied *brevis* from the polyptych of Saint-Germain-des-Près regarding Palaiseau. There in the course of a year the typical manse-holder was responsible for cultivating 6 perches of arable, i.e., 23 furlongs each slightly more than 2 feet in width. Four perches were plowed in winter ("ad hibernaticum") and two perches in summer ("ad tremissem").[114] Although there are variations throughout the polypytch in the quantity of fixed service owed by the dependent cultivators and, on occasion, there are references to manses inhabited by more than one family, it was the general labor (*corvadae*), cartage (*carropera*), handiwork (*manopera*), and wood cutting (*caplin*) which were performed at the will of the lord ("quantum ei jubetur"), where the potential to extract relatively large amounts of labor service was most probably located.[115] In the Angevin situation, by contrast, the vast array of government demands combined with the requirements of subsistence severely limited how much labor the dependent cultivator could possibly perform at the order of his landlord. Whereas the Carolingian peasant paid much of what he owed to sustain the government's military operations as a "rent" to his landlord, the dependent cultivator in the Angevin state was taxed directly in labor and kind to support the army.

It is clear that any effort to draw up a balance sheet on the basis of the available but often intractable and fragmentary quantitative data examined above for the purpose of ascertaining the putative relation of tax to rent in the Angevin economy is a risky business. Nevertheless, the impression that taxes were heavy in the ensemble is manifest. There is no need to dwell upon excessive levies such as the 50 percent tax, or more accurately a maximum tax of 50 percent, that the government could and occasionally did impose on the crops produced from assarts.[116] Nor is it necessary to emphasize the heaviness of various tolls such as the yearly rate of one *denarius* per horse, ox, or cow, that was charged to a herder for regularly crossing a public bridge with his herds. Indeed, contemporaries conservatively estimated that the bridge at Saumur earned a yearly average revenue after expenses of 2,000 *solidi*.[117] In short, the direct taxes on production, the indirect levies in the form of sales taxes, tolls, and the profits of justice, and perhaps most importantly the demands in labor service, kind, and money to sustain the military fell on everyone free and unfree, but rents ostensibly were paid largely by the latter.

However, by contrast with the resources of the government, of the great lay and ecclesiastical lords, the small allodialists, the merchants, and the artisans, the peasants surely did not command the lion's share of the assets in the Angevin state with which to pay both the taxes they owed and rent. The natural limitations imposed upon a peasant class that may have possessed more than half the arable in the Angevin state but surely less than half the total land, were such that its rents could not possibly have matched the ensemble of taxes that it paid and that everyone else paid as well. To sustain this tentative conclusion it remains to be seen whether the superstructural elements of Angevin society as seen in light of Wickham's neo-Althusserian problematic reflect an economy in which the surplus extraction was dominated by tax rather than by rent.

SUPERSTRUCTURAL REFLECTIONS

Within Angevin society little of importance seems to have escaped domination by the state. For example, virtually all ecclesiastical building of consequence was controlled and supported by the government.[118] Not only were new important foundations such as the convent of Ronceray and the monasteries of Beaulieu, Saint Nicholas and Trinity of Vendôme established by the count, but they were built on lands of the fisc and supported from government resources that ranged from income-producing estates to tax exemptions.[119] Any accounting of the financial base of these religious institutions makes clear that the contributions directed to them by the state executive were far greater than the contributions made by all others combined.[120]

While the surplus extraction controlled by the state played the major role in providing both for the revival of the church and for the economic survival of Angevin religious institutions, monastic and ecclesiastical resources were used as a matter of course by the state to help sustain government policies.[121] The highest officers of the Angevin church were generally chosen by the count.[122] The few abbots who seem to have been "freely elected" appear only during the last decade of our period and then in the wake of the papal reform movement that gradually began to take hold after the Council of Rheims in 1049.[123] Not only was the ecclesiastical hierarchy within the Angevin state dominated by the government but this was true as well in the client states, i.e. those *comtés* that recognized Angevin domination.[124] In the historical perspective of the present study these dependent polities are the analogues of Rome's vassal kings.[125]

Monks and priests traditionally served as scribes and clerks in transacting those aspects of government business that required a modicum of education.[126] In fact, the cathedral school at Angers likely succeeded because of government encouragement.[127] At higher levels of responsibility abbots served as negotiators and ambassadors for the government.[128] Other even more worldly types of service were also traditionally demanded from the state's ecclesiastical servants. For example, when Theoderic became abbot of Saint Aubin in 1056, but "before he received the solemn gift of the pastoral staff *in capitulum* [from the count] . . . he asked the brothers if the count had any violent *consuetudines* that imperiled their souls. They answered in the affirmative because the late Count Fulk had earlier imposed upon them the *custodia* of the *castra* on the borders. . . ."[129] Bishop Hubert of Angers (1007–1047) was known to lead Angevin military forces in the field under the count's orders.[130]

However great the government's utilization of the surplus extraction available in the Angevin state may have been for the building and sustaining of religious institutions, the resources expended by the state in the construction and maintenance of fortifications was even greater. During the period from 992 to 1039, for example, Fulk Nerra, who earned from historians the sobriquet "le grand bâtisseur," built at least thirty-five strongholds, most of stone, within the Angevin state and on its borders.[131] Among these "public works" a small stronghold such as Langeais which was built hurriedly nevertheless took almost two years to complete at a minimum cost of providing the sustenance-equivalent for more than 50,000 worker-days in the course of a year.[132] If we were to consider the case at Langeais as the norm simply for the purposes of this study, although obviously it represents very close to a cheapest case scenario, the construction of thirty-five strongholds of this type in a period of forty-seven years averages out to the utilization by the state of more than 37,000 worker-days each year in surplus extraction to carry out its building program for major fortifications. These figures do not include maintenance of the fortifications.[133] They also do not include the construction of curtain walls which were common, the digging of moats, and other refinements that could properly be considered aspects of construction rather than of maintenance.

The great cost of military construction makes it clear that a substantial portion of the surplus extraction controlled by the Angevin government was expended in order to sustain the state's "defense" interests. Another index of such expenditure can be identified by an examination of the cost of feeding war horses which generally were about 15 to 16 hands tall and weighed between 1,300 and 1,500 pounds.[135] With a return on seed grain of 2 : 1 it required the surplus (i.e., the total crop minus seed and grain equivalent calories needed to sustain the worker who grew the crop) produced by eight men each working fifteen acres of arable to provide sufficient grain (oats, barley, or spelt) to meet the grain needs of a single war horse in the course of a year.[136] These figures do not include the cost of providing 2,200 kgs. of hay grown on 1.25 acres of meadow or about 650 kgs. of straw required for bedding.[137]

For the Angevin government to have had available for service on an annual basis a mere 2,000 horsemen—if only ten *caballarii*, a very small number, were stationed in each of fifty Angevin strongholds, and there were many more than fifty fortifications in the Angevin state, 25 percent of this figure for mounted troops would be attained only by listing garrison troops—then the state required the use of a minimum of about 900 tons of feed grain and hay from the total surplus extraction.[138] In order to haul this fodder obtained through the *fodrum*-tax levied by the government,[139] 1,800 carts each pulled by two oxen had to be levied by means of the *angaria* which as we have seen was taken by the Angevin state as needed from those who had the necessary animals and equipment.[140] The length of time that these carts, the oxen, and drivers might be required to serve depended in part upon the distances that had to be traversed. Since oxen travel only ten miles in the course of a day under good conditions, whether their carts are loaded or empty, it requires little work and less imagination to estimate how long these units might have had to have served on campaigns that saw the army's line of march go from Angers to Nantes or from Angers to Tours.[141]

Through this brief examination of the *fodrum* and the *angaria* we have been able to obtain some insight into how government domination of the surplus extraction through taxes supported elements of the military superstructure. However, these taxes as well as the *bidamnum* and other means used to sustain the construction and maintenance of fortifications, the supplying of mounted troops and also perhaps of non-mounted levies that served the state do not constitute a complete picture of the military superstructure. Of particular interest in the present context is the practice by the Angevin government of hiring mercenaries.[142] Here we see evidence for control of surplus extraction that provided the state with a superstructural capacity to coerce those landlords who might try to withhold their taxes or endeavor to subvert for personal use the taxes owed by their dependents. Regarding the state's coercive capability, it is of importance that the Angevin government not only imposed the traditional fines upon military levies of all classes who were delinquent in satisfying the *herribannum* but when that delinquent was a dependent his lord was also fined.[143]

The ability of the Angevin state to intervene effectively between the landlords and their peasant dependents not only in the direct collection of taxes but also in securing government service permits the conclusion that the social relations of production were aligned with the interests of the state and not with those of the landlords. Such was also the case during the fourth century in the Roman empire and is regarded by Wickham as an indication of an "ancient" social system resting on an "ancient" economic base.[144] This situation also would seem to indicate control by the state over social relations with the landlords. However, such a state of affairs does not permit the conclusion that the state had control over aristocratic status which according to Wickham's model is fundamental to the superstructure of an economy in which surplus extraction is dominated by tax rather than by rent.[145]

Basic to state control over the aristocracy, according to Wickham's model, is the condition wherein public office was sought not because its value was that it brought land with it but because office brought with it "an intrinsic relationship to the state." This "intrinsic relationship" was based upon the fact that the "exploitative force" in the state was public power to dominate surplus extraction through taxation which in turn meant that those who served the state at the upper levels of officeholding had access to this power and thereby to the resources of taxation.[146] In short, the "feudal" aristocrat is seen to prefer, to seek, and secure possession of land because rent dominated over tax, while the "ancient" aristocrat, who generally also possessed significant lands and may even be seen to have tried to obtain more, nevertheless sought public office because this provided him, through the exploitative power of the state, with access to tax resources which dominated over rent in control of the surplus extraction of an "ancient" economy.

It is clear that the upper aristocracy, however defined,[147] in the Angevin state during the period 960–1060 normally served in public office and did so particularly as castellans.[148] Why these aristocrats rendered such service may be answered provisionally with the banality that they regarded it to be in their self-interest. However, if we ignore the "noise" that is created by competing systems of interpretation with regard to "consciousness" and "false consciousness" a rather tautological proposition may be seen to emerge, i.e., since we have shown that tax dominated the economy of the Angevin state it must be considered "ancient" and since the economic system "determines the ground rules for the whole social function,"[149] the aristocracy, unless overwhelming evidence to the contrary be forthcoming, must also be considered "ancient." The task, however, is not to rest upon the logical assertion that the aristocracy of the Angevin state was "ancient," but to adduce evidence that suggests or perhaps even proves that aristocrats were attracted to public office, not because of the land with its accompanying rents that service to the state brought with it, but, because these offices provided access to tax revenues.

That the Angevin state provided various of its officials from time to time with lands is not at issue here; i.e., no effort is being made to suggest that a "feudal" mode did not co-exist with the "ancient" but only that the latter dominated surplus extraction. It is important, however, that these grants of land by the comital government to various officials appear, in general, to have been rather small, rare, and of limited duration.[150] More to the point is the fact that the right to share in tax revenues seems to dominate as the means by which the state remunerated the holders of public office.

Due to limitations of space four brief examples of such payments will have to suffice to illustrate what was normal practice. Bouchard of Broillay was permitted to succeed his father as castellan of the stronghold of Broillay and, as a result, he received for his service the possession of the church of Saint Marcel and the tax revenues *(consuetudines)* that the government normally collected from the church and its appurtenances.[151] When Leo of Meung-sur-Loire was given the *custodia* of the count's fortified house within the walls of the *castrum* of Amboise, his remuneration was the *commendaticiae* (i.e., the complex of military-related imposts levied on the men and re- sources within a particular jurisdiction) of the forest *(Silva Longa)* in le Blésois up to Romorantim.[152] Renaud who was appointed castellan of Château-Gontier complained that he was not being satisfactorily re- warded because the count had already given to the monastery of Saint Aubin the proceeds of the *census* of the *castrum,* i.e., the revenues of the tax on land within the walls of the fortification, and the *vendae,* i.e., the taxes on all sales made within the *castrum.* Thus the count arranged for the monastery to give Renaud the proceeds of the *census* for as long as he served as castellan.[153] Finally, there is the case of the castellan of Saumur. This *oppidanus* received a share of the vicarial returns that were gathered in the suburb of Saint Hillary outside the walls of Saumur as his payment for service.[154]

Examples of this type drawn from both charters and chroni- cles can be multiplied, but perhaps it would be of more value to see how an official with even greater responsibilities than those of a castellan was rewarded. Lisoius of Bazougers, who had gained sub- stantial acclaim for his military exploits, was given command ca. 1015 by Fulk Nerra of the central sector of the eastern frontier of the Angevin state. Under Lisoius' military jurisdiction were both the *oppidum* of Amboise and *castrum* of Loches although the stone tower at the former and command of the garrison at the latter remained in the hands of Sulpicius of Buzançais and the *praepositus* Arraldus, respec- tively. Lisoius is indicated as having in his service his own personal armed following, i.e., his military household, and as having been delegated the authority to issue the call for military service on his own, i.e., without the count's *submonitio,* to both *nobiles* and *ignobiles* and among the *milites* both those who are termed *majores* and those

who are termed *minores.* For his service, "pro servitio," Fulk gave
Lisoius the *vicaria,* i.e., the rights to do justice with the income therefrom and the right to collect the taxes, *consuetudines,* in the region
between the Indre and the Cher that was called "Champagne." These
tax revenues or at least those left over after Lisoius met his expenses
were his remuneration for government service.[155]

Other government officials from the lowly *servientes* we
noted earlier collecting the *vinagium* at Saint-Georges or foresters to
the prestigious *vicarii* and *praepositii* whose income came in part from
a percentage of the profits of justice all were supported primarily by
surplus extraction in the form of taxes rather than from land rents.[156]
Perhaps even more important in gauging the relative importance of
tax and rent in this context is the behavior of public officials during
the last third of the eleventh century after the central government
had been seriously weakened as a result of the civil war in 1067. These
public officials did not run amok in a frenzied effort to seize the
estates of their neighbors or to lay claim to lands belonging to the state
for the purpose of increasing their rental income. Rather, they continued to collect the vast variety of taxes that previously had been
levied in the areas of their competence including the military service
owed by both free and dependent alike, but now they carried on in
their own interest, not in the interest of the state.[157]

Because of the dominant role played by tax as compared
with rent in commanding the surplus extraction of the Angevin
economy, the state was able through the use of reductions in tax and
immunities from imposts to encourage economic growth. For example, this use of tax policy was undoubtedly at work in the development of large tracts of arable from forest and waste by assarting. In
order to encourage this development the government initially
attracted settlers with easy terms (*v* below). It issued licenses and
required its officials to tax the produce of these new assarts at a rate
sufficiently less than the allowable 50 percent maximum so that the
hospites would flourish. Indeed, when the government, shortsightedly
from the point of view of economic development took the full 50
percent tax, these new settlements failed.[158]

In a similar manner the government encouraged the development of burgs in the environs of strongholds and of religious
foundations by maintaining a liberal policy toward the granting of
licenses for such new foundations. In addition, by the judicious use of
immunities such as from the *bidamnum* or from the tax on selling

wine, the state encouraged people to settle in the burgs and mechants to do business in these places.[159] Indeed, under the leadership of Geoffrey Martel, the state was so eager to encourage economic development that a group of Jewish merchants with their families, probably an element from the long-established community that flourished in the city of le Mans which at this time was under Angevin control, was recruited to settle in the environs of the newly rebuilt stronghold of Durtal.[160]

THE MAKING OF AN ANCIENT ECONOMY

How did it come about that after the passage of more than three centuries in which rent putatively dominated over tax in the economy of the western half of the Roman empire—if Wickham is correct—that in one important region of the west of France an "ancient" economy is seen to appear or to reappear and to flourish for a century or more? We may begin by observing that although this region was hit hard both by the Viking invasions and civil wars of the ninth and early tenth centuries, the remnants of some Carolingian public institutions can be seen to have survived. Among these survivals was recognition by the population, or at least by its articulate spokesmen, of the legitimacy of the state's power to tax. This recognition is explicit in the distinction that is made in various documents between *consuetudines, exactiones,* and *costumae* on the one hand, and *malae* or *novae consuetudines, exactiones,* and *costumae* on the other in complaints that were registered concerning the collection of taxes by the state.[161]

The available evidence suggests that those who were responsible for paying taxes did so, if not happily at least with resignation—there are no complaints about (legitimate) *consuetudines*. The Angevin government surely tried to encourage a sense of futility among those who might try to avoid their obligations to the state. This was done by employing a large corps of officials called in various sources: *advocati, agentes, amici, banarii, custodes, exactores districturae, famuli, famuli comitis, fideles, forestarii, homines, iudices, legati, ministeriales publici, ministri, officii, praepositi, procuratores, servientes, subvicarii, vassi, vassi dominici, venatores, vicarii,* and *viceministeriales.*[162] In short, the *consuetudines* were vigorously enforced by energetic government agents who worked very diligently because, as suggested above, the major source of reward for their service was what was left over from their collection of tax receipts after the needs of the state were met.[163]

In this context it is important not to underestimate either the complexity or the thoroughness of Angevin administration. For example, it is possible that as early as the reign of Geoffrey Greymantle an effort was made by the government to inventory the fiscal holdings of the monasteries and churches of the Angevin state with the purpose of recording half of these assets as available to the government for its use.[164] A reflection of this process may perhaps be seen as early as 966 when Geoffrey Greymantle "reformed" the monastery of Saint Aubin. In the process of this "reform" he required that all of the canons of the monastery and everyone else who held property from Saint Aubin return these estates to the monastic fisc. Then, in the charter by which he disestablished the canons and by which he simultaneously installed monks at Saint Aubin, Geoffrey made it clear that he would be using these fiscal resources to carry on the function of the government as he needed them. Not only did Geoffrey use Saint Aubin's resources but he also used those of other Angevin religious establishments to meet the needs of the state.[165]

A careful examination of the complaints concerning the "bad" and/or "new" imposts levied by the Angevin government between 960 and 1060 casts light on the state's tax policy. For example, sometime between ca. 1017 but before August 1025, i.e., after Fulk Nerra had taken direct control of the *comté* of Vendôme but before he placed his grandson, Bouchard, there as count, the former imposed the *pedagium* and the *minagium* throughout the *pagus*. According to a later contemporary, these taxes previously had not existed in the Vendômois.[166] The *pedagium,* however, had been traditional and ubiquitous throughout the *regnum Francorum* at least since the time of Charlamagne and it is highly unlikely that an entire *pagus* such as the Vendômois had been exempted without leaving any earlier evidence of such a unique immunity.[167] The lack of such an immunity is especially likely in light of the undisputed currency in early eleventh-century Vendômois of a large body of "Carolingian" taxes that were collected by the count and which apparently had survived despite the upheavals of the ninth and early tenth centuries.[168] In short, the government's policy in the case of the *pedagium* was not to impose a "new" tax in the Vendômois but to re-impose an old one that had fallen into disuse. Parenthetically, both of these taxes were indirect in nature (the *pedagium* was a general toll on the transport of merchandise and the *minagium* a special tax on salt which may perhaps have been new) would seem to suggest an increase in trade which thus made such an inherently unpopular action as levying these "new" taxes profitable to the state.

A further survey of complaints against Angevin taxes makes it clear that the *malae* or *novae consuetudienes* generally were not new but rather that they were newly imposed upon a jurisdiction that, according to the complaint, had never been responsible for the levies at issue. Among the more frequent complaints were those concerning the *commenditicia,* i.e., the complex of military-related imposts that were levied upon all subjects of the Angevin counts, and in most of these cases the count or his officials are seen to be demanding these levies in areas newly brought under the direct jurisdiction of the Angevin state.[169] The government's right to levy the *commenditicia* was not challenged in "old" areas of the Angevin state.[170] It is likely, given the correlation between the frequency of complaints and their surfacing in the newly integrated regions, that the authorities which previously had held jurisdiction in these areas did not or had not been able to levy these very burdensome military taxes. It was the policy of the Angevin government to impose the entire corpus of tax burdens on all lands and inhabitants under its control. That really new taxes as contrasted to the reimposition of old and unpopular taxes was not the issue with regard to the *malae* and *novae consuetudines* is suggested by the fact that we find no opposition to the *terragium,* i.e., the tax levied on the production from assarts which was truly a new tax.[171]

Trying to explain how it came about that the Angevin state developed an "ancient" economy during the period 960–1060 is likely to be even more controversial than demonstrating that the economy was "ancient." An examination of the conditions that correlate with these developments may, however, be suggestive in understanding the process at least in part. For example, the reign of Fulk the Good (ca. 942–960) is credited by his posterity with having been the "take off" period for economic growth. As Thomas of Loches, a later chronicler working with oral traditions and no longer extant written evidence, put it:

> Moreover, in his time [i.e., during the reign of Fulk the Good] in *pagus* of Anjou, as said above, when the quiet of peace had been conceded by divine influence, this same count, doing enough to repair the fortifications of the *urbs* and those in the surrounding territory and also the churches, gave his attention to agriculture and animal husbandry, desiring himself and encouraging others

through his example to compensate for the poverty of the past, which lengthy hostilities had brought, with an abundance in the wealth of good things from the earth. Then, indeed, many inhabitants from various foreign and surrounding regions migrated to that *pagus*, called as much by the kind generosity of the *princeps* as by the abundance of the earth. For that land, made fertile through long disuse and the cessation of cultivation, was resplendent and responded with a miraculous fruitfulness of produce and of all good things. Concerning the growth of the woods which were for the most part clothed in foliage there was enough for the *coloni* for cutting and for clearing with very little labor.[172]

Two items are worth calling attention to in this account. First, not only were lands returned to cultivation that had lain vacant for a considerable time, but assarting also was carried out by cutting down of forests. In short, the new settlers would appear to have been sufficiently numerous that the arable that had been cleared before the civil wars and Viking raids was not sufficient to satisfy the needs of the immigrants. The second item is perhaps of even greater importance in trying to gain some insight into the designs of the decision-makers who headed the Angevin government. Here the chronicle's explicit statement is that Fulk the Good encouraged a policy of agricultural development by his "kind generosity"; this surely entailed such benefits as immunities from taxes.[173]

Thomas of Loches's identification of substantial migration into the Angevin *pagus* before 960 left a record in subsequent decades. For example, Geoffrey Greymantle, who succeeded his father Fulk as count in 960 and ruled until 987, found it necessary to expand and extend the walls of the *urbs* of Angers in order to enclose suburbs that required defense. At the *castrum* of Amboise on the Loire River, Geoffrey built Châteauneuf. This was a new suburb that he enclosed with defenses of stone. In addition, Geoffrey supported the building of a burg in the environs of Angers that was connected to the monastery of Saint Serge; the monastery was also restored during his reign. At Loches, Geoffrey built an exceptionally impressive stone tower where the Carolingian defenses had been located earlier and he also restored the church of Saint Mary there. Thus he tried to assure both physical and spiritual protection to the growing population of the town at Loches.[174] These actions by Geoffrey taken together with his support for assarting suggest an integrated policy to deal with population growth and to encourage economic development. Since population development occurs over time its effects are only gradually experienced and then only at some remove from the beginning of the process. Thus Geoffrey's actions strongly support the idea expressed by Thomas of Loches and quoted above that the process of population growth began during the reign of Fulk the Good.

Throughout the reigns of Fulk Nerra and his son Geoffrey Martel we can identify a sustained pattern of population and economic growth. New lands continued to be assarted and put into cultivation at a rapid pace,[175] and these efforts were accompanied by an explosive growth in the number of water-driven mills that were constructed along the Loire River and its affluents.[176] New burgs and new churches were also built in large numbers.[177] Monasteries were founded and provided with substantial endowments.[178] Perhaps of greatest importance, however, were the numerous strongholds, most of stone, that were built by the counts in the Angevin *pagus* and on its frontiers.[179] Thus by the time of Geoffrey Martel's death in 1060, the Angevin economy seems to have been in full bloom—complaints about poverty are very few and far between, hunger is not an issue, and a century of monumental construction testifies to the availability of surplus resources to carry out these building projects under government control.[180]

Fulk the Good's encouragement of migration to Anjou and of agricultural development by permitting the forests to be cleared is characterized by Thomas of Loches as being marked by "kind generosity."[181] However, by the reign of Fulk Nerra and perhaps earlier, a new tax, the *terragium*, had been devised and imposed upon production from assarted lands.[182] This tax, as we saw earlier, permitted the government to take up to 50 percent of the crop from an assart as tax.[183] However, as Abbot Frederick of Saint Florent, a contemporary of Fulk Nerra, makes clear, excessive taxation over even a short period of time could and on rare occasion did result in forcing the *hospites* to abandon their newly assarted land. The Angevin counts also understood these basic economic principles and very rarely taxed assarts to the limit and then only under extraordinary conditions.[184]

Through the use of tax policy and licenses the Angevin counts during the period 960–1060 controlled and encouraged economic development. Very little could be done in the Angevin state without a license from the government. As we have seen, landowners could not assart wooded lands, irrigation ducts could not be built to divert water, mills could not be erected, bridges built, or fortifications constructed without comital *licentiae*.[185] All production as we have seen was subject to taxation and all subjects of the state, free and unfree alike, were liable for one or another type of military service. In addition, indirect taxes were levied on goods being transported across the Angevin frontiers and throughout the *pagus*. All sales were subject to taxes, and this was the case not only at markets and fairs, which existed only by government license, but even on retail sales such as the already-mentioned tax that was collected on wine which was purchased at a tavern.

Through the use of a very broad spectrum of taxes, some of which were of Carolingian vintage if not older and had survived the upheavals of the ninth and early tenth centuries, some of which were new impositions of old taxes that had fallen into disuse, and finally through some that were wholly new levies, the Angevin counts dominated the surplus of the society's resources in produce and labor. A swarm of government officials, many of whom were of very low social status and who were paid in large part from the proceeds of the taxes that they collected, were the means used by the counts to carry out this unpopular aspect of administration.[186] The castellans, whose appointment to the command of fortifications and troops placed them in a propitious position to defy the government, were paid largely with tax revenues and, through a variety of consistently applied methods, were kept by the counts from developing great personal wealth and strong local loyalties.[187]

Correlated with this pattern of behavior are hints that the Angevin counts were not unaware of a rather broad spectrum of public functions that was inherent in government activity within the Western tradition. Aside from the ubiquitous references in the documents to the public roads which undoubtedly were kept in repair, at least marginally, through the use of labor levied by *corvadae*, there appears to have been an even deeper sense of what constituted the public role of the state.[188] For example, a distinction is made in the documents between a war conducted by the count, i.e., the *expeditio publica* or the *bellum publicum*, and non-governmental large-scale armed hostility such as a *tumultus* which lacked legitimacy.[189] Labor service for building government strongholds and the *bidamnum* for repairing fortifications (obligations that were owed by all of the count's subjects to sustain Angevin military policy) are referred to as

publica negotia.[190] The counts saw their actions being taken for the
utilitas of the *res publica*,[191] and government agents are called *ministeriales publici.*[192]

In short, the evidence suggests that those responsible for
administering the government permitted the introduction of a modicum of antique thought into their documents with regard to public
business. How deep this "Romanizing" tendency went may well be a
matter of debate. For example, if one were to use the explosive
development of what we have come to call Romanesque style architec-
ture and painting as an index of the penetration of Roman ideas, it
would be difficult to withstand the conclusion that the Angevin state
in the first half of the eleventh century had become a provincial
center of late imperial culture.[193] When, toward the middle of the
twelfth century, Thomas of Loches pieced together various versions
of the family history of the Angevin rulers from earlier accounts, it is
likely by design that he called his work *Chronica de Gestis Consulum
Andegavorum.*[194] Indeed, Geoffrey Martel had himself styled "consul"
in his official *acta*, and Bishop Eusebius who took office in 1047 was
styled *summus sacerdos*, i.e., "high priest," of the Angevin church.[195]

Fulk Nerra, who was *consul* from 987 to 1040, appears to
have been very much influenced in both his tactical and in his strateg-
ic thinking by the *De Re Militari* which was written ca. 450 by the
Roman military authority Vegetius.[196] Perhaps it is redundant to note
at this point that not only were churches in the Angevin state constructed in the Romanesque style but so were the stone fortifications
built by Geoffrey Greymantle, Fulk Nerra, and Geoffrey Martel.[197] In
addition, Roman imperial military terminology seems to have crept
into official usage. The use in documents of the term *laetus* to denote
a dependent who could be called upon to do more than the normal
bidamnum service and *exactores districturae* to denote those who issued
the *submonitio* for the count to those who owed military service are of
particular interest.[198] In the later Roman empire the *laeti* were semi-
free military colonists while the *exacti* were legionary recording
clerks.[199] The appearance of the terms *legati, vicarii, procuratores,
praepositi*, and *agentes* (perhaps an abbreviated form of *agentes in rebus*)
provide additional Romanesque flavor.[200] The Angevin rulers, like
their later contemporaries in Normandy, would appear to have understood very well that things learned from books could be of value in
gaining an advantage over their adversaries as well as for the im-
provement of their government.[201]

Geoffrey Greymantle, Fulk Nerra, and Geoffrey Martel travelled widely with their household staffs and advisors. There were visits to Rome, southern Italy, and further east with the opportunity for extensive contacts with the Byzantines.[202] There is no reason to believe that the Angevins were less willing to learn from the living model that was provided by their contacts in the East than Geoffrey Martel's contemporary, William the Conqueror, was to learn from the Byzantines.[203] However, living models were not essential since written information was no further away than Holy Scripture which provided much information that indicated the centrality of taxation to government. Certainly, the notorious *publicani* and other analogues among the various peoples of the Bible were a constant reminder of how the ancient state did its business.[204]

By evoking something of the Romanesque cultural and intellectual milieu that flourished in the Angevin state at about the same time that an effective and complex tax system was developed, an effort has been made here to win the reader's sympathy for the acceptance of a cause and effect relationship. Although it must be emphasized that correlation is not in itself cause, when correlations are very numerous a situation is created in which it is inherently unlikely, in a statistical sense, that the closely interrelated governmental structures that complemented each other in such an effective manner for a century resulted from something other than hundreds if not thousands of decisions that were taken within the framework of well-drawn designs that were colored by a tinge of antique or Roman thought. To paraphrase the late J. M. Wallace-Hadrill, the Angevins could live like bararians; but they could learn from the past what was valuable for the operation of a successful state and apply these lessons with surprising results.[205]

At various times during the period 960–1060, the Angevin state brought the Saintonge, Mauges, Nantais, Vendômois, Maine, and Touraine under its domination. The Poitou was a dependency for more than a decade and its northern quarter was permanently incorporated into the Angevin *pagus*. The infrastructure created under the leadership of Geoffrey Greymantle, Fulk Nerra, and Geoffrey Martel provided the resources, which even after a half century of weakened central government, enabled Geoffrey Plantagenet and his son Henry to restore order at home, conquer Normandy and Brittany, reconquer Maine, conquer England, and integrate the duchy of Aquitaine (including the remainder of the Poitou) into an empire that

stretched from Scotland to the Pyrenees with Angers at its center. At
the base was the domination of surplus extraction by tax rather than
by rent.

EPILOGUE

Chris Wickham's neo-Althusserian problematic, when applied in a
consistent manner to the later Roman empire and to eleventh-century
Anjou, results in the identification of an "ancient" economy and an
"ancient" social formation in both. This creates some problems for the
historian in terms of the usefulness of such a classificatory model. For
example, a model such as this which leads us to see the Roman
provinces of Moesia, Pannonia, or Noricum in the early fifth century
as having a fundamental identity with the Angevin state in the mid-
eleventh and which at the same time adumbrates as essentially different the economies of the sixth-century Byzantine Ravennate and her
northern neighbor, the *regnum Francorum* in Burgundy, strikes an
aesthetically discordant note.[206] In short, our sense of proportionality
is violated and it must be asked whether the obvious value of surplus
extraction as an analytic tool is commensurate with overturning traditional lines of periodization.

In this vein the observation by Sir Richard Southern that
Fulk Nerra should be considered "a pioneer in the art of feudal
government" should not be taken lightly.[207] Southern defines "feudal" with considerably less precision than does Wickham and trades
heavily upon the intellectual baggage of the "military feudalism"
construct that traditionally is favored by non-Marxist English and
American medievalists.[208] Nevertheless, he tries to convey some sense
of the tone of a society, a view of the world of Fulk Nerra, that is very
different from that of his mid-fifth century "predecessor" in the
region, Count Paul.[209] In short, basic to both non-Marxist and Marxist orientation is the sense that the medieval world is "feudal" however
defined and the later Roman empire is somehow different and that
difference amounts to being ancient. We may quibble interminably
over the chronological frontiers of these constructs but to stretch
ancient even to the comparatively small limits suggested by Pirenne
created such a high level of unease, a kind of anomie or perhaps even
taxonomic anarchy in historical perspective, that scholars have felt
compelled to debate the thesis for more than half a century.[210] What
is psychologically unsettling for scholars at the research front

amounts to an outright disaster for those of us who must teach broadly-gauged courses in the history of Western Civilization which span a thousand years and more.

Yet, all of this aside, or perhaps more exactly because Wickham has constructed an intriguing vehicle for analysis that has the potential to be unsettling, we should regard it as having exceptional heuristic value at the research front. By focusing upon the relation between tax and rent in the Angevin state from 960 to 1060 and finding the former to dominate, even a non-Marxist can be led to the conclusion that Wickham's paradigm enables us to identify what is likely to have been an important element in providing us a greater understanding of how the Angevin government earned its great success. Although the Marxist approach requires that institutions such as the military and the church be regarded as superstructural social formations that are caused by the prevailing economic base to be what they are, those who do not share this faith can perhaps be satisfied with observing a significant correlation between state domination of surplus extraction through tax and state control of the church and the military. What is important is that Wickham's problematic provides for Marxist and non-Marxist alike an avenue of research that may perhaps help to provide new insight into that era which Marc Bloch called "the first feudal age."

Finally, it should be clear that the vast extension of the term "feudal" as variously understood by different schools of Marxists and non-Marxists alike has greatly prejudiced its usefulness. The term "ancient" seems to be not very much more useful. Thus, in light of the antique Roman or imperial facade that was spread ever so thinly over the Angevin world and more particularly because of the role played by tax in the economy, I would like to suggest that we borrow a term from the historians of art and consider Anjou, 960–1060, a Romanesque society.

NOTES

*Research on this paper was made possible by grants from the American Council of Learned Societies, the Graduate School of the University of Minnesota, and the Bush Sabbatical Grant Program of the University of Minnesota. I want to offer them all my deepest gratitude. I am no less indebted to the staffs of the Bibliothèque Nationale in Paris and to the Archive de Maine-et-Loire in Angers. I want particularly to thank Mlle. Poirier-Coutansais, director of the Archive de Maine-et-Loire, for her many kindnesses.

[1] "The Other Transition: From the Ancient World to Feudalism," *Past and Present*, 103 (1984), 3–36. For the quotations "*v*" pp. 10 and 8, respectively.

[2] Ibid., p. 7.

[3] Ibid., p. 30.

[4] Ibid., n. 32. There seems no need to emphasize that Marc Bloch's, *La société féodale* (Paris, 1939–1940), 2 vols. (translated as *Feudal Society* (London, 1961) by L. A. Manyon, and Jan Dhondt, *Études sur la naissance des principautés territoriales en France, IXe-Xe siècle* (Bruges, 1948), provide no basis for Wickham's generalization. The less well-known collection of essays, *Structures féodales . . . (Xe–XIIIe s.)* published by the École Française de Rome, 1980, does require some discussion. Of the thirty-eight papers published in this volume, only six deal with Carolingian territory north of the Alps and Pyrenees. Of these six, the studies by Bonnassie (pp. 17–56) and Magnou-Nortier (pp. 135–172) demonstrate the continued use of public power at least into the eleventh century, as the former put it, "une longue survie des structures très anciennes". Higounet (pp. 109–117) and Gramain (pp. 119–134), deal with the social structures and populations of fortifications. Giodanengo (pp. 35–107) treats vocabulary in the twelfth and thirteenth centuries. Only Poly (pp. 57–84), whose very thinly documented study deals with the "régime domanial", could be construed to have contributed anything remotely supporting Wickham's generalization. However, Poly is not working with the finely honed problematic developed by Wickham.

[5] The article by Marc Bloch, "Sur le passé de la noblesse française: quelques jalons de recherche," *Annales d'histoire économique et social*, 8 (1936), 366–378, is often thought of as a catalyst that was given added life by Georges Duby, "Une enquête à poursuivre: la noblesse dans la France médiévale," *Revue historique*, 226 (1961), 1–22. A fair sample of these theses in alphabaetical order would include: Michael Bur, *La formation du comté de Champagne, v. 950–v. 1150* (Nancy, 1977); Georges Duby, *La société aux XIe et XIIe siècles dans la région mâconnaise* (Paris, 1953, reprt. with different pagination 1971); Guy Devailly, *Le Berry du Xe siècle au milieu du XIIIe siècle* (Paris, 1973); Robert Fossier, *La terre et les hommes en Picardie jusqu'à la fin du XIIIe siècle* (Paris, 1968), 2 vols.; and Elisabeth Magnou-Nortier *La société laïque et l'église dans la province ecclésiastique de Narbonne (zone cispyrénéenne) de la fin du VIIIe à la fin du XIe Siècle* (Toulouse, 1974). The earlier series of regional volumes as represented by Louis Halphen, *Le comté d'Anjou av XIe siècle* (Paris, 1906); and Robert Latouche, *Histoire du comté du Maine pendant le Xe et le XIe siècle* (Paris, 1910), also do not provide the kind of information required to sustain the conclusions concerning "surplus extraction" in the states of the post-Carolingian era that are drawn by Wickham.

[6] Wickham, "Transition," pp. 5–6, makes clear that he places no faith in the linear progress of the Marxist modes of production.

[7] Ibid., pp. 4, 7, I have paraphrased Wickham on the centrality of the economic base in its relation to the superstructures.

[8] There is no small disagreement among scholars as to "what is a state?" and clearly it is beyond the scope of this paper to find a "solution" that is likely to be universally acceptable. However, it does not seem to me to be fundamentally misleading if we consider the various polities that emerged from the dissolution of the Carolingian empire to be states. For those who would see the background for some of my thinking on the problem, the following works will be of interest: Helmut Quaritsch,

Staat und Souveränität (Frankfurt, 1970), 1, 11–19, stresses some of the difficulties in defining the state; and S. Z. Ehler, "On Applying the Modern Term 'State' to the Middle Ages," in *Medieval Studies Presented by Aubrey Gwynn S. J.*, ed. J. A. Watt, *et al.* (Dublin, 1961), p. 496, provides a broad definition with three basic characteristics: "a territory, a population and an established governmental power." More medieval in focus are the stimulating pieces by F. L. Cheyette, "The Invention of the State," in *Essays on Medieval Civilization*, eds. B. K. Lackner and K. R. Philp (Austin, 1977), 143–178; Walther Kienast, *Studien über die französischen Volksstämme des Frühmittelalters* (Stuttgart, 1968); and J. R. Strayer, *On the Medieval Origins of the Modern State* (Princeton, 1970). Those who would seek areas of usefulness in the traditional views of the state and a Marxist problematic that treats the state as superstructure may find N. Poulantzas, *Political Power and Social Classes*, trans. T. O'Hagan (London, 1973), and P. Anderson, *Passages from Antiquity to Feudalism* (London, 1974), with the literature they cite to be of interest.

[9] *v*, above, n. 5. Wickham, "Transition," pp. 31–33, exaggerates the growth of "manorialism" and the decline of the "free peasantry" in following E. Muller-Mertens, *Karl der grosse, Ludwig der Fromme, und die Freien* (Berlin, 1963).

[10] The basic works on this period are Halphen, *Le comté;* Olivier Guillot, *Le comte d'Anjou et son entourage au XIe siècle* (Paris, 1972), 2 vols; and Bernard S. Bachrach, "Geoffrey Greymantle, Count of the Angevins 960–987: A Study in French Politics," *Studies in Medieval and Renaissance History*, n.s. VII (1985), 1–67. Bachrach has commented frequently on Anjou and its neighbors in a manner that frequently has not been consistent with the views of Halphen and Guillot. *v*, e. g., "Enforcement of the *Forma Fidelitatis*: The Techniques Used by Fulk Nerra, Count of the Angevins (987–1040)," *Speculum*, 59 (1984), 796–819; "The Angevin Strategy of Castle Building in the Reign of Fulk Nerra, 987–1040," *AHR*, 88 (1983), 533–560; "Fortifications and Military Tactics: Fulk Nerra's Strongholds *circa* 1000," *Technology and Culture*, 20 (1979), 531–549; "Robert of Blois, Abbot of Saint-Florent de Saumur and Saint-Mesmin de Micy (985–1011), a Study in Small Power Politics," *Revue Bénédictine* 88 (1978), 123–146; "A Study of Feudal Politics: Relations Between Fulk Nerra and William the Great, 995–1030," *Viator*, 7 (1978), 111–122; "The Family of Viscount Fulcoius of Angers: Some Methodological Observations at the Nexus of Prosopography and Diplomatics," *Medieval Prosopography*, 4.1 (1983), 1–9; "Fulk Nerra and His Accession as Count of Anjou," *Saints, Scholars, and Heroes: Studies in Medieval Culture in Honour of Charles W. Jones*, eds. M. King and W. Stevens (Collegeville, Minn., 1979), 2, 331–341; "Henry II and the Angevin Tradition of Family Hostility," *Albion*, 16 (1984), 111–130; "King Henry II and Angevin Claims To The Saintonage," *Medieval Prosopography*, 6.1 (1985), 23–45; and "The Cost of Castle Building: The Case of the Tower at Langeais, 992–994," *The Medieval Castle: Romance and Reality*, eds. K. Reyerson and F. Powe (Dubuque, Iowa, 1984), 46–62. The best treatment of the later ninth and early tenth century history of the Angevin counts is K. F. Werner, "Untersuchungen zur Frühzeit des französischen Fürstentums (9.–10. Jahrhundert)," *Die Welt als Geschichte*, 18 (1958), 264–286.

[11] There is no systematic treatment of Angevin taxation covering the period under discussion here. Useful information can be gleaned from the works listed below although these studies provide interpretations of the data that do not form an integrated whole. *v* Louis Halphen, "Prevôts et voyers du XIe siècle: région angevine," *Le Moyen Age*, 15 (1902), 297–325 (reprinted in Louis Halphen, *À Travers*

THE
UNIVERSITY OF WINNIPEG
PORTAGE & BALMORAL
WINNIPEG, MAN.   R3B 2E9
CANADA

BERNARD S. BACHRACH   39

l'histoire du moyen âge (Paris, 1950), 203–225. Hereafter cited as *À Travers*. All of Halphen's reprinted articles hereafter will be cited in the reprint edition.) Halphen, "La justice en France au XIe siècle: région angevin," *Revue historique*, 77 (1901), 279–307; reprt. *À Travers*, pp. 175–202; and Halphen, *Le comté*, pp. 98–111. Guillot, *Le comte*, I, 370–429, builds on Halphen's work. More useful from the point of view of detail are: Jacques Boussard, "La vie en Anjou aux XIe et XIIe sièecles," *Le Moyen Age*, 56 (1950), 29–68; and two series of articles by J. M. Bienvenu, "Recherches sur les péages angevins aux XIe et XIIe sièles, *Le Moyen Age*, 63 (1957), 209–240; 63 (1957), 437–467; and "Pauvreté, misères et charité en Anjou aux XIe et XIIe siècles," *Le Moyen Age*, 72 (1966), 389–424; 73 (1967), 6–34; 73 (1967), 189–216. G. d'Espinay, *Les cartulaires angevins: étude sur le droit de l'Anjou au moyen âge* (Angers, 1864), though well out of date is occasionally of use.

12 F. L. Ganshof, "Les traits généraux du système d'institutions de la monarchie franque," *Settimane di Studio del Centro Italiano di Studi sull'alto medioevo* (hereafter *SSCI*), 9, (Spoleto, 1962) 91–127, and translated into English as "The institutional framework of the Frankish monarchy: a survey of its general characteristics," in *The Carolingians and the Frankish Monarchy*, trans. J. Sondheimer (London, 1971), 86–110, discusses the state of the question (p. 99–all citations to the latter). But cf. F. L. Ganshof, "Charlemagne et les institutions de la monarchie franque," *Karl der Grosse*, ed. H. Beumann (Dusseldorf, 1965) I, 349–393, and translated into English in expanded form as "Charlemagne and the Institutions of the Frankish Monarchy," in *Frankish Institutions under Charlemagne*, trans. B. and M. Lyon (Providence, 1968), 3–55, 102–151, where an even more pessimistic view is taken and what he formally considered almost a direct tax is now considered a "personal" or "real rent" (pp. 42–43, of the English translation). This latter view is quite extreme and largely unjustified. With regard to the matter of continuity, the position on Anjou is summarized by Guillot, *Le comte*, I, 2, where Geoffrey Greymantle is characterized as "un personage encore carolingien." However, the very perceptive observations concerning continuity in the post-Carolingian era by John Le Patourel, *The Norman Empire* (Oxford, 1976), p. 4, n. 1, deserve careful consideration.

13 Ganshof, "The Institutional Framework of the Frankish Monarchy," p. 99.

14 Yvonne Mailfert, "Fondation du monastère bénédictine de Saint-Nicholas d'Angers," *Bibliothèque de l'Ecole des Chartes*, 92 (1931), *p.j.* 4. *v* also *Cartulaire de Saint-Laud d'Angers*, ed. A. Planchenault (Angers, 1903), no. 25, where the *census* is seen to be owed upon a variety of arable, meadow, and vines that were constituted as an alod.

15 Henri Dubled, "Allodium dans les textes latins du moyen âge," *Le Moyen Age*, 57, (1951), 241–246, is hardly comprehensive but neverless it is useful. *N.b.* that the term alod has very different meanings in the south. *v*, e.g., Robert Boutruche, *Une société provinciale en lutte contre le régime féodal. L'alleu en Bordelais et en Bazadais du XIe au XVIIIe siècle* (Paris, 1947). One of the rather infrequent occasions when d'Espinay, *Les cartulaires*, pp. 115–121, provides some useful material concerns "des alleux".

16 The *census* that was levied by the count on the entire *castrum* of Château-Gontier was a new impost since this stronghold was orignally founded in 1007 as a *castellum*. However, the document that records this *census* is filled with problems regarding its authenticity. Halphen, *Le comté*, p. 260, considered it suspect, and Guillot, *Le comte*, II, 283–284, labeled it a forgery. Actually, the document (*Cartulaire de Saint-Aubin*, ed. Bertrand de Broussillon (Angers, 1896), no. 1) is a compilation of at least five

notices. Some of these are based upon extant *cartae* while others are drawn from *cartae* that subsequently have disappeared. Some of the information may also have been drawn from *acta* that were never written down in proper form. *Au fond*, both Halphen and Guillot did not realize that the redactor in drawing up this compilation of notices confounded the witness list of several of the *acta* mentioned above and gave the entire document the date of the final *actum*. This, of course, has caused problems for modern scholars because several of the witness to the earlier *acta* were dead by the time that the final *actum* had been given.

[17] *Cartulaire de La Trinité-de-Vendôme*, ed. Charles Métais (Paris, 1893), I, no. 158. Cf. Guillot, *Le comte*, I, 370–379.

[18] *Cartul. de la Trinité de Vendôme*, nos. 47, 91.

[19] *Cartulaire noir de la Cathédrale d'Angers*, ed. Charles Urseau (Angers, 1908), no. 45. This text, however, may be dealing with an alod since the holder had purchased the land under consideration and exercised testamentary right over it. For a general treatment of the *census* as a rent *v* d'Espinay, *Les cartulaires*, pp. 137–151.

[20] J. F. Niermeyer, *Mediae Latinitatis Lexicon Minus* (Leiden, 1984), pp. 1023–1024, where the first preference in spelling is given to *terraticus*.

[21] Bibliothèque nationale: Collection Touraine-Anjou (Dom Housseau), II. 1, no. 412; *Cartul. de Saint-Aubin*, no. 197; *Cartul. de La Trinité de Vendôme*, nos. 36, 38; and Bibliothèque nationale, n.a. Lat. 1930, fols. 77 r.-v. Niermeyer, *Lexicon Minus*, pp. 1023–1024, provides additional references from Anjou. Like many of the other taxes imposed by the Angevin state we learn of the *terragium* from successful and unsuccessful, legal and illegal efforts to evade it. For both the use of immunities and for assarts *v* below.

[22] Wichkam, "Transition," pp. 9–10, would seem to exaggerate the weight of the direct tax on land levied by the Roman government relative to the vast array of other taxes both direct and indirect collected throughout the empire. In this Wickham follows A. H. M. Jones, *The Later Roman Empire, 284–602* (Norman, Okla., 1964), 2 vols., I, 462–469, whose work on these matters is highly debatable. For example, Wickham, himself, correctly points out (p. 9) that Jones's "statistics are shoddy" when treating the *collatio lustralis* and allied imposts but then goes on to accept his estimates. However, Jones's data on these points (p. 465) can produce percentages more than 100% greater. Such calculations would not, of course, undermine the fact that the direct tax on land was the premier revenue producer for the Roman government but it does call into question its relative weight in the system, and Wickham's characterization of that system.

[23] As will be seen *passim* the term *consuetudines* does not refer only to the taxes levied directly upon the production of the land and on other forms of production but is used ostensibly for all taxes owed to the Angevin state or as the *Cartul. de Saint-Laud*, no. 25, puts it: *"omnes consuetudines terra et flumines*. Sometimes a synonym such as *exactio, costuma*, or *lex* is used for *consuetudo*.

[24] Dom Housseau, II.1, no. 447.

[25] *Cartulaire du Ronceray*, ed. Paul Marchegay (Angers, 1856), no. 5.

[26] *Cartul. noir*, no. 45.

[27] Bib. nat. n.a. Lat., 1930, fols. 28v–29r.

[28] *Cartul. noir*, no. 41.

[29] Dom Housseau, II.1, no. 447.

[30] *Cartul. du Ronceray*, no. 5.

[31] Bib. nat. n.a. Lat. 1930, fols. 98v–99r.

[32] The *vinagium* or *vinaticum* is a term that is frequently applied in an ambiguous manner. For example, it sometimes applies to the indirect tax levied by the government on the purchase and sale of wine (*v* below). In the present context it is also ambiguous. *Cartul. de Saint-Laud*, no. 25, treats the *conseutudo vinearum* which may be thought of as tax on vineyards and perhaps similar to *Cartul. de Saint-Aubin*, no. 216, where we find "vinagium de vineis." However, Bib. nat. n.a. Lat. 1930, fols. 28v–29v, shows us that the *vinagium* is paid in wine and levied on the normal unit of viticulture, the arpent or some fragment of the arpent (Bib. nat. n.a. Lat. 1930, fol. 117v.). Thus we may be looking at a land tax levied on a unit of cultivation, i.e. the arpent, or perhaps a tax on the production of wine or perhaps both. The importance of wine in this region might well account for a form of "double" taxation of the direct sort. These, of course, do not include the taxes on buying and selling that will be discussed below along with the normal transport tolls charged on all cargoes.

[33] *Cartul. de Saint Laud*, no. 25.

[34] Bib. nat. n.a. Lat. 1930, fols. 28v–29r.

[35] Rates of taxation are discussed below, n. 80.

[36] Carlrichard Bruhl, "Das frankische Fodrum," *Zeithschrift der Savigny-Stiftung fur Rechtsgeschichte, Germ. Abt.*, 76 (1959), 53–81; and the same author's *Fodrum, Gistum, Servitium Regis* (Cologne 1965), 2 vols., which provides a broader chronological, geographical, and institutional treatment. F. L. Ganshof, "*La Tractoria*. Contribution à l'étude des origines du droit de gîte," *Tijdschrift voor rechts-geschiedenis*, 8 (1928), 69–91, is also of use. Concerning the great weight of this burden see *Loup de Ferrières, Correspondance*, ed. and trans., Léon Levillain (Paris, 1927, 1935), 2 vols. : nos. 21, 32, 39, 57, 62, 63, 72, who provides an abundance of information concerning both the weight and importance of *fodrum*. From a military perspective see Bernard S. Bachrach, "Animals and Warfare in Early Medieval Europe," *SSCI*, 31 (Spoleto, 1985), 708–716. the Angevin government appears to have collected the *fodrum* on two occassions each year under normal conditions. *v* Bib. nat. n.a. Lat. 1930, fols. 31r.–v., and *Cartul. du Roncerary*, no. 5.

[37] For an overview of *fodrum* in Anjou *v* Guillot, *Le comte*, I, 379–381. For additional details on the burdensomeness and ubiquity of this tax *v*: Dom Housseau, II.1, no. 326; *Cartul. de Saint-Aubin*, no. 178; and Bib. nat. n.a. Lat. 1930, fol. 26v.

[38] *Cartul. noir.*, no. 27.

[39] Archive de Maine-et-Loire, H 1840, no. 7.

[40] *Cartulaire de Notre-Dame de Saintes*, ed. T. Grasilier (Niort, 1871), no. 1; and *Cartul. noir.*, no. 27.

[41] *v*, e.g., Archive de Maine-et-Loire, H 1840, no. 7; Bib. nat. n.a. Lat. 1930, fols. 96v–97r; and Mailfert, "Saint-Nicholas d'Angers," *p.j.* 4.

[42] *Cartul. noir*, no. 45; Bib. nat. n.a. Lat. 1930, fols. 31r.–v.

[43] *Cartul. de Notre-Dame de Saintes*, no. 1.

[44] Ganshof, "La *Tractoria*," p. 88, discusses the use of this institution to provide what was needed by *missi* and more particularly by the *heribannitores* to carry the summons to war issued by the king. In this context the *submonitio* issued by the Angevin count and carried by his *legati* is of importance, and the latter are likely to have been supported in this same manner (*v* below n. 40).

[45] *Cartul. de la Trinité de Vendôme*, no. 158.

[46] Roger Grand, "Une curieuse appelation de certaines corvées au moyen âge. Le 'bain', 'biain', ou 'bien'," *Mélanges dédiés à la mémoire de Félix Grat* (Paris, 1946), 1, 289–300, provides a background sketch of marginal value. Guillot, *Le comte*, I, 382–384, is more useful but tends to blur the distinction between the *bidamnum* which was a regular service taken annually on a local basis and similar service taken in time of war on the frontiers and in enemy territory that was coupled with active military service. For the latter *v* below.

[47] Bib. nat. n.a. Lat. fols. 29v–30r. *v* also Jean Besly, *Histoire des comtes de Poitou et des ducs de Guyenne* (Paris 1647), p. 357, who provides an edition of Arch. mun. de Rheims, Collection Tarbe, carton I, no. 15, where *coloni* are seen performing the *bidamnum*; *Cartul. noir*, no. 45, for *villani*. For the background on *laeti* see Bernard S. Bachrach, *Merovingian Military Organization, 481–751* (Minneapolis, 1972), pp. 70–73; 78–80.

[48] Guillot, *Le comte*, I, p. 383.

[49] Bib. nat. n.a. Lat. fols. 29v–30r, where the abbot of Saint Florent arranged to pay the Angevin count 200 *solidi* per year so that the landholders at the villa of Saint-Georges would not be required to perform the *bidamnum*. For the classification of the *bidamnum* as a *consuetudo v*, e.g., *Cartul. du Ronceray*, no. 5 and Archive de Maine-et-Loire, H 1840, no. 7.

[50] Dom Housseau, II.1, no. 326.

[51] Wickham, "Transition," pp. 31–32, tries to undermine the traditional view of the bi-partite organization of the villa or manor with its *terra indominicata* and tenements in so far as he greatly undervalues the role of labor services provided by the tenents throughout the Western half of what had been the Roman empire. Wickham, however, does recognize (p. 31) the validity of the bipartite model with a substantial measure of labor service in the region between the Loire and the Rhine where the evidence of the polyptchs cannot be explained away.

[52] The background sketch of "Le service militaire" by Guillot, *Le comte*, I, 384–391, is very useful.

[53] Archive de Maine-et-Loire, H 1840, no. 7.

[54] *Cartul. noir*. no. 45; Mailfert, "Saint-Nicholas d'Angers," *p.j.*, 4; *Cartul. de la Trinité de Vendôme*, no. 158; *Cartul. du Ronceray*, no. 5; *Cartul. de Saint-Aubin*, no. 216. Like much of the available information on Angevin institutions during this period these documents frequently illustrate efforts to deviate from the norm and in doing so make clear the nature of the usual practices.

[55] Archive de Maine-et Loire, H 1840, no. 7.

[56] *v*, e.g., Mailfert, "Saint-Nicholas d'Angers," *p.j.*, 4; Bib. nat. n.a. Lat. 1930, fols. 31r.–v.; and *Cartul. noir*, no. 45. Cf. *Cartul. du Ronceray*, no. 5, where one can see how a confusion might take place concerning fortification work in time of war and the *bidamnum*.

[57] Bachrach, "The Strategy of Castle Building," pp. 533–560.

[58] *Cartul. de Saint-Aubin*, no. 220, and the discussion by Bachrach, "The Strategy of Castle Building," p. 545, n. 4. Cf. Jane Martindale, "Aimeri of Thouars and the Poitevin Connection," *Anglo-Norman Studies VII* (Woodbridge, 1985), p. 240, n. 67, who fails to grasp the significance of the word "nisi" which makes clear that the obligation of the *homines* of Méron to guard the stronghold of Montreuil was an *antiqua consuetudo* from the days of Fulk Nerra and pertained to those situations when the *caballarii* of Montreuil "vadunt in hostem cum comite foras suam terra."

Later in the eleventh century the lord of Montreuil (in the days of Fulk Nerra and Geoffrey Martel, Montreuil was under the control of a comital castellan) usurped the ban and focused his activity on Thouars which of course also was beyond the frontiers. As Guillot, *Le comte*, I, 390, makes clear at least some of these *homines* from Méron merit being considered *villani*.

[59] Guillot, *Le comte*, I, 391–394, provides a good account of "La forêt" but does not treat it from the point of view of comital revenues. Thus he does not treat assarts. Concerning these and the licences see Bib. nat. n.a. Lat. 1930, fols. 99r–100v.

[60] *Cartul. de la Trinité de Vendôme*, no. 158, with regard to the licence to fish. Guillot, *Le comte*, I, 391 394, for the rest.

[61] Bienvenu, "Les péages angevins," pp. 209–240, 437–467, provides an excellent collection of material but unfortunately much of it comes from the period after that treated in the present study. For the period prior to that treated here *v* F. L. Ganshof, "A propos du tonlieu a l'éponque carolingienne," *SSCI*, 6 (Spoleto, 1959), 485–525, and more generally Ganshof, "The institutional framework of the Frankish monarchy," p. 100, with regard to indirect taxes. The material covered by Ganshof and Bienvenu (cited above) suggest strong similarities as do the documents cited below that focus more explicitly on the period under discussion here. However, the evidence for direct continuity is far more tenuous. Concerning the tax on ships see *Cartul. de la Trinité de Vendôme*, nos. 88, 157; *Cartul. de Saint Laud*, no. 25; and *Breviculum fundationis et series abbatum Sancti Nicholai Andegavensis*, ed. L. Lepeletier (Angers, 1616), p. 15.

[62] Archive de Maine-et-Loire, H 1840, no. 7, and *Cartul. de la Trinité de Vendôme*, no. 77, are good examples.

[63] Bienvenu, "Les péages angevins," pp. 437–450, treats these practices in a later period but it is clear that earlier methods are being represented rather than revolutionary change. That the later practices are similar to Carolingian practices as shown by Ganshof, "The institutional framework of the Frankish monarchy," p. 100, where he treats the wheel tax, is clear.

[64] Bienvenu, "Les péages angevins," p. 224.

[65] Bib. nat. n.a. Lat. 1930, fols. 12r.–v.

[66] Ibid., fols. 92r.–v.

[67] Ibid., fol. 27v.

[68] *Breviculum fundationis . . . Sancti Nicolai Andegavensis*, p. 14, and Archive de Maine-et-Loire, H 1840, no. 7, provide good examples. See also *Cartul. de la Trinité de Vendôme*, no. 77.

[69] *Cartulaire de Saint-Maur de Glanfeuil*, ed. P. Marchegary (Angers, 1843), no. 63 (in appendix).

[70] F. L. Ganshof, "Charlemagne et l'administration de la justice dans la monarchie franque," *Karl der Grosse*, I, 394–419, and translated "Charlemagne and the Administration of Justice," *Frankish Institutions*, pp. 71–97, 161–183, for the carolingian background, and Ganshof, "The institutional framework of the Frankish monarchy," pp. 97–98, concerning the profits of justice. Halphen, "La justice," 98–111, focusses upon the last third of the eleventh century when the situation is very different in Anjou.

[71] For the reservation of major crimes and the fines therefrom *v Cartul. de Saint– Aubin*, nos. 2, 22, 24, 26; for striving to obtain profits from minor crimes at small jurisdictions see *Cartul. du Ronceray*, no. 5; Archive de Maine–et–Loire, H 1281, no.

4; Mailfert, "Saint Nicholas d'Angers," *p.j.* 4; Bib. nat. n.a. Lat. 1930, fol. 28r.;
31r.–v; and regarding forgeries see the interpolations in *Cartul. de Saint Laud,* no.
25; and Halphen, *Le comté, p.j.* no. 5, with the comments of Guillot, *Le comte,* II,
145–146, and 59–60, respectively.

[72] *v,* above, nn. 51–58.

[73] The background is provided by Guillot, *Le comte,* I, 394–395, for Anjou, and
Ganshof, "The institutional framework of the Frankish monarchy," p. 97, for the
Carolingian background. It is perhaps of some interest that the counts retained a
monopoly over money changing and only gave it up in the city of Angers and its
suburbs in 1093 (*Cartul. noir,.* no. 57).

[74] *Cartul. de la Trinité de Vendôme,* nos. 38; 158; Archive de Maine-et-Loire, H 1840, no.
7; H 1281, no. 4, provide good examples.

[75] Jones, *Later Roman Empire,* I, 411–427, provides a useful account of the *res privata.*
Cf. Wickham, "Transition," p. 10, n. 12.

[76] Bib. nat. n.a. Lat. 1930, fols. 96v–97r; Archive de Maine-et-Loire, H 1840, no. 7;
and *Cartul. de la Trinité de Vendôme,* no. 92.

[77] Cf. Bienvenu, "Pauvreté, misères et charité en Anjou," pp. 389–424; 6–34; 189–
216.

[78] Wichkam, "Transition," p. 23.

[79] Bib. nat., n.a. Lat. 1930.

[80] Wickham, "Transition," p. 10, emphasizes the Roman analogue. However, as suggested above, Wickham seems to exaggerate the relative importance of the direct
tax on land in the Roman empire in the total mix of fiscal revenues while it is likely
that we have underestimated the role played by the direct tax on the land in the mix
of revenues collected by the Angevin state. Concerning Angevin rates *v* Bib. nat.
n.a. Lat. 1930, fols. 28v.–29r, where a tax of one-half of a *modius* is levied on the
wine production of each arpent of vineyard. In this context it is of some importance
that a survey which was made ca. 820 of the productive capacity of nineteen
vineyards located somewhat to the east of the Angevin region indicates an average
production of five *modii* of wine per arpent each year. *v Polyptyque de l'Abbe Irminon* .
. . , ed. B. Guérard (Paris, 1844), 2 vols, I, *villae* 2–10, 14–19, 21, 22, 24, 25. The
returns from the *villa* of Verrières (no. 5) clearly suffers from a recording error by
the copiest where he indicated that 95 arpents produced 1,600 *modii* of wine. This
figure of 16.8 *modii* per arpent or 336 gallons from a little more than one-third of
an acre of vineyard is not possible under early ninth century conditions in this
region. The totals recorded for the *villa* at Le Coudray (no. 18) also evidences an
error but the numbers are too small to be significant.

[81] Wickham, "Transition," pp. 31–32; but he certainly underestimates the importance
of the demesne in the great estates of Merovingian *regna.* The observation (n. 34)
that "No demesnes are visable on estates of St. Martin of Tours in the seventh
century is certainly incorrect, and to base this conclusion on *Documents compatables de
Saint-Martin de Tours à l'époque merovingienne,* ed. P. Gasnault and J. Vezin (Paris,
1975), is tendentious. This collection is based upon fragments of manuscripts that
were rescued from book bindings and the way they were cut up left only those
sections that dealt with the tenements. Even a cursory reading of Gregory of Tours
who wrote during the late sixth century indicates the flourishing of demene-
holdings in the Touraine and other regions with which he was acquainted. One can
hardly believe that the entire agricultural structure of these regions underwent

revolutionary change during the last decade of the sixth century. For example, the stories recorded in *Gregorii episcopi Turonensis, Libri Historiarum*, ed. B. Krusch and W. Levinson, *Monumenta Germania Historica, Scriptores rerum Merovingicarum* (Hannover, 1951), Bk. IV, 47; Bk. V, 48, 49; Bk. VI, 36; Bk. VII, 22, 29; Bk. VIII, 32; Bk. IX, 35, 40, provide a substantial body of evidence for lands held *indominicatum*.

[82] Boussard, "La vie en Anjou," p. 35.

[83] *Polyptyque de l'Abbaye de Saint-Germain des Près rédigé au temps de l'Abbé Irminon*, ed. A. Longnon (Paris, 1885), 2 vols., I, 237, shows that the arable in demesne at the *villae* belonging to Saint Germain was about 30% of the total arable. However, when all of the lands at these *villae* are taken into consideration, and particular attention must be paid to the wooded lands, the demesne was more than 5,000 acres greater in size than the tenements. For a general introduction to this type of evidence *v* Robert Fossier, *Polyptyques et Censiers* (Turnhout, 1978); and even more important Walter Goffart, "Merovingian Polyptychs. Reflections on Two Recent Publications," *Francia*, 9 (1981), 55–77.

[84] The basic work remains Georges Duby, *Rural Economy and Country Life in the Medieval West*, trans. C. Postan (London, 1968), pp. 22–27, 102; by the mid-twelfth century a slight increase seems to have been made possible, and only by ca. 1300 could an average yield of between 3:1 and 4:1 be expected. Some efforts have been made recently to reevaluate these ratios upward. *v*, e.g., Massimo Montanari, "Rese cerealicole e rapporti di produzione, considerazioni sull'Italia padana dal IX al XV secolo," *Quaderni medievali*, 12 (1981), 36–44, who concentrates on Italian data; and especially the study by Vito Fumagalli, "Rapporto fra grano seminato e grano raccolto, nel politico del monastero di S. Tommaso di Reggio," *Rivista di storia dell'agricoltura*, 6 (1966), 360–362, which is based upon a tenth-century inventory, and which provides a range of returns from 1:1.7 on the low side to a rather large 1:3.3. The value of Italian data for conditions between the Loire and the Rhine is of course problematic. More to the point is the critique of Duby's calculations by R. Delatouche, "Regards sur l'agriculture aux temps carolingiens," *Journal des savants* (Apr.–June, 1978), 73–100, who raises some important questions concerning methodology. However, Delatouche's own assumptions are at least as problematic as those used by Duby, and the former are unsupported by data. For a further critque of Delatouche *v* Bachrach, "The Cost of Castle Building," p. 61, n. 48.

[85] Concerning the amount of labor required to farm with various tools and under various conditions *v* the important study with much comparative data by K. D. White, "The Productivity of Labour in Roman Agriculture," *Antiquity*, 39 (1965), 102–107; which fits very well with the data provided by Duby, *Rural Economy*, p. 38.

[86] With regard to seed grain quantities *v* B. H. Slicher Van Bath, *The Agrarian History of Western Europe: A.D. 500–1850*, trans. O. Ordish (London, 1963), p. 137; and Duby, *Rural Economy*, pp. 24, 128. At Saint-Germain-des-Près (*Polyptyque*, ed. Longnon, vol. I) on average 3.5 *modii* (the *modius* is that of Louis the Pious set at 68 litres) were used as seed per *banuarium* of arable for the total demesne arable in the course of a year. However, since only approximately two-thirds of the arable was cultivated each year an average of about 5 *modii* per *banuarium* was used. These data sustain Duby's calculations of a 2:1 average return on seed grain discussed in note 84, above.

[87] Colin Clark and Margaret Haswell, *The Economics of Subsistence Agriculture* (London, 1970), pp. 11–13, 58, provide the basic data with extensive comparative material.

However, nutritional science has since forced some modification of their calculations as shown in the works cited by Donald W. Engels, *Alexander the Great and the Logistics of the Macedonian Army* (Berkeley, 1978), 123–125.

[88] There are a large variety of indices all pointing to substantial population and economic growth. For example, in the reign of Geoffrey Greymantle it was necessary to enlarge the circuit walls of the city of Angers in order to enclose suburbs that required protection. There were also new suburbs at Angers beyond the walls as well as new burgs and towns such as Châteauneuf at Amboise. Some were fortified by Geoffrey (Bachrach, "Geoffrey Greymantle," pp. 41, n. 9, and p. 31). This continued development also is seen in the large increase in the numbers of *burgi* associated with the building of new strongholds by the government and accompanied also by the construction of new churches (Halphen, *Le comté*, pp. 88–96, provides only a small portion of the available evidence). Other indicators of growth can be found in the explosive increase in the number of mills and in assarts. I hope to publish a study of Angevin demographic patterns during this period in the near future.

[89] "*v*' the recent study by J. C. Russell, *Late Ancient and Medieval Population Control* (Phila., 1985), pp. 151–153.

[90] John Evans, "*Plebs Rustica*. The Peasantry of Classical Italy II: The Peasant Economy," *American Journal of Ancient History*, 5 (1980), 134–174, discusses these matters within the context of Roman history with a substantial body of comparative and scientific data.

[91] Of great interest is Dorothy Hartley, *Lost Country Life* (New York, 1979), *passim*, for the Middle Ages; and Evans, "*Plebs Rustica*," pp. 134–174, for the Roman era. *v* also Barbara Hanawalt, *The Ties That Bind: Medieval English Peasant Families* (Oxford, 1985).

[92] Evans, "*Plebs Rustica*," p. 158, Table 4.

[93] *v* Bib. nat. n.a. Lat. 1930, fols. 17r–18r; 37r.–v; 37v.–38r.; *Cartul. de Saint-Aubin*, no. 265.

[94] *v* Bib. nat. n.a. Lat. 1930, fols. 9r.–10r.; 10r.–v.; 37v.; 38r.; 113r.; Archive de Maine-et-Loire, H 2117, no. 1; *Cartul. de Saint-Aubin*, no. 39.

[95] Bib. nat. n.a. Lat. 1930, fols. 36v.–37r.

[96] Concerning complaints *v* below with regard to *malae consuetudines* and the references above at n. 76. With regard to a possible inference concerning rent *v*, e.g., Bib. nat. n.a. Lat. fols. 38v.–39r, which is based upon the fact that the man is forced into poverty but does not mention the tax burden as the cause.

[97] This formula appears frequently in Bib. nat. n.a. Lat. 1930, *v*, e.g., the documents recorded in fols. 10r.–12r.; *v* also *Cartul. de Saint–Aubin*, no. 40, which uses this same formula as well. See above notes 93 and 94.

[98] Bib. nat. n.a. Lat. 1930, fols. 77v. 78r; 78v.–79r.

[99] Ibid., fols. 130v.–131v.; 134r.; but cf. a *coliberta* who was sold "with all of her things" for seven pounds of *denarii*.

[100] Archive de Maine-et-Loire H 3497, no. 3; *Cartul. du Roncerary*, nos. 175; 187; *Cartul. de la Trinité de Vendôme*, no. 276; Bib. nat. n.a. Lat. fols. 68v.; 78v; 130v.–131v; *Cartul. de Saint-Aubin*, no. 269. For background *v* the very valuable studies by Robert-Henri and Anne-Marie Bautier, "Contribution a l'histoire du cheval au moyen âge," *Bulletin philologique et historique*, (1976), 209–249; (1978), 9–75; and esp. pp. 211–212, with regard to prices.

[101] Lynn T. White, Jr., *Medieval Technology and Social Change* (Oxford, 1962), p. 29, for a discussion of Isanhard and the costs of outfitting a fully armed mounted fighting-man.

[102] For eighth-century values *v Lex Ribuaria*, 40, 11, ed. R. Bayerle and R. Buchner (*Monumenta Germania Historica, Leges*, II (Hannover, 1954).

[103] *v*, above, nn. 46–49.

[104] Concerning rates of travel *v* Bachrach, "The Angevin Strategy of Castle Building," p. 542, n. 27, with the focus on men mounted on horseback. *v* also the important study by Majorie Nice Boyer, "A Day's Journey in Medieval France," *Speculum*, 26 (1951), 597–608. The movement of equipment and supplies to sustain the workers raises some important questions with regard to both capacity and speed. John Langdon, "Horse Hauling: A Revolution in Vehicle Transport in Twelfth- and Thirteenth-Century England?" *Past and Present*, 103 (1984), 37–66, has shown that in England oxen dominated as the major power for plowing through the Middle Ages. Wagons were rarely used before the late thirteenth century, and than they were generally pulled by oxen. In the late twelfth century horses were introduced for hauling carts. Before the development in the use of the horse-cart, pack horses dominated for hauling goods in England. The efforts by A. Leighton—"A Technological Consideration of Early Medieval Vehicles," *Fifth International Conference on Economic History: Leningrad, 1970* (The Hague, 1974), 346–348; and "Eleventh Century Developments in Land Transport Technology," *The Eleventh Century; Acta*, i (Binghamton, N. Y., 1974), 20-22—to show that horse-pulled wagon transport of goods became important in the late eleventh century are not soundly based. With regard to the basic capacity of wagons and carts, *v* A. Leighton, *Transport and Communication in Early Medieval Europe, A.D. 500–1000* (Devon, 1972), pp. 77, 161; and Engels, *Logistics*, pp. 14–16. Majorie Nice Boyer, "Medieval Pivoted Axles," *Technology and Culture*, 1 (1960), 135, is probably correct in arguing that the whipple tree—pivoted front axle system was available in the thirteenth century.

[105] *v*, above, n. 49

[106] For the count's military household *v* Bachrach, "*Forma Fidelitatis*," pp. 808–809, n. 63; and above, note 100, for the value of horses.

[107] The focus for operations from the stronghold of Montreuil-Bellay was the region of Thouars about 20 kilometers to the South. For the *caballarii* of M-B to operate in this area required two days of travel if they were to maintain their horses in battle-ready condition (Bachrach, "The Angevin Strategy of Castle Building," p. 542, n. 27). Although the center of the *villa* at Méron was only about four kilometers from the stronghold at M-B, the *villani* at the former had to be mustered in their scattered homesteads for the journey to the fortications. Clearly, any operations beyond Thouars would require correspondingly greater amounts of time and effort. Bachrach, "Animals and Warfare," 716–726.

[108] There is no detailed study at the present time of Angevin military campaigning. Halphen, *Le comté*, pp. 113–153, treats "les conquêtes" but this is hardly complete. *v* also Bernard S. Bachrach, "The Practical Use of Vegetius' *De Re Militari* During the Early Middle Ages," *The Historian*, 47 (1984), 239–255; and the same author's "The Angevin Strategy of Castle Building," pp. 533–560; and "Fortifications and Military Tactics," pp. 531–549.

[109] E. Muller-Mertens, *Karl der grosse, Ludwig der fromme, und die Freien* (Berlin, 1963), but with some exaggeration.

[110] *Cartul. de Saint-Maur,* no. 26.
[111] Boussard, "La vie en Anjou," p. 55, and the works cited in note 103, above, with regard to the use of horses. Concerning the government's breeding of draught animals *v* Mailfert, "Saint-Nicholas d'Angers," *p.j.,* 4.
[112] *v* either the edition by Guérard or Longnon cited above.
[113] Jean Durliat, "Le polyptyque d'Irminon et l'impot pour l'armée," *Bibliotheque de l'Ecole des Chartes,* 140 (1983), 183–201.
[114] *Polyptyque de Irminon,* no II, "Breve de Palatiolo," *passim.*
[115] Ibid.
[116] Archive de Maine-et-Loire, H 1840, no. 7; and Bib. nat. n.a. Lat. 1930, fols. 96v.–97r.
[117] The data are developed by Bienvenu, "Recherches sur les péages," pp. 437–454, with charts. However, much of the data comes from the century following our period and may be tainted by a modicum of inflation. Some of this "late" material is really of an earlier vintage but was only codified at the later date. Also some of the taxing powers identified during this later era had passed from the Angevin government to smaller units of competence as a result of the weakening of the central power in the wake of the civil war of 1067 and subsequent internal conflicts of a more localized nature.
[118] Halphen, *Le comté,* pp., 81–88, highlights the major efforts by both Fulk Nerra and Geoffrey Greymantle. This list is by no means complete.
[119] *Cartul. du Ronceray,* nos. 1, 2, 4, 6, 7, 15, 18, 19, 28, 35, 63, 78, 126, 173, 174, 220, 229, 237, 238, 240, 258, 281; *Cartul. de la Trinité de Vendôme,* nos. 8, 18, 19, 21, 28, 35, 44, 47, 49, 51, 57, 62, 64–67, 71, 79, 82, 85, 88, 90–92, 96, 105, 121, 122, 130, 132, 153, 276; For Saint Nicholas *v Breviculum,* pp. 5, 7, 14, 44–48 (this does not represent a complete list of government donations to Saint Nicholas); and for Beaulieu, Bernard S. Bachrach, "Pope Sergius IV and the Foundation of the Monastery at Beaulieu-lès-Loches," *Revue Bénédictine,* 95 (1985), 240–265.
[120] This accounting is accomplished by comparing the gifts made by the counts as indicated above in note 119 with the gifts made by others as indicated in the same collections. *N.b.* Beaulieu was founded in 1007, St. Nicholas in 1020, Ronceray in 1028, and Trinity of Vendôme in 1032.
[121] For Geoffrey Greymantle *v* Bachrach, "Geoffrey Greymantle," pp. 8–9; with regard to Fulk Nerra see *Historia Sancti Florentii Salmurensis,* pp. 280–281 (*Chroniques des églises d'Anjou,* ed. P. Marchegay and E. Mabille [Paris, 1869]); Bib. nat. n.a. Lat. 1930, fols. 12r.–v., 99r.–100v., 104r., 106r.–v., 111r.–v., 117r.; Archive de Maine-et-Loire, H 1840, nos. 7, 9: H 2117, no. 3; H 3247, no. 1; H 3714, fols. 68r.–v., concerning the monastery of Saint Florent; for other examples of Fulk's use of ecclesiastical resources *v Cartul. de Saint Aubin,* nos. 197, 327, 932; *Cartul. de la Trinité de Vendôme,* nos. 44, 66, 67; Archive de Maine-et-Loire, II, 857 and Bachrach, "Robert of Blois," pp. 123–146. These examples are not exhaustive concerning Fulk nor is the following list concerning Geoffrey Martel: Archive de Maine-et-Loire H 1840, no. 5; *Cartul. de la Trinité de Vendôme,* nos. 66, 67; *Cartul. de Saint Aubin,* no. 677; Ambrose Ledru, *La maison de Maillé,* 3 vols. (Paris, 1905), II, *p.j.* 4.
[122] Of the four bishops of Angers chosen during the period 960–1060, two are clearly simoniacs and the other two were probably simoniacs although the case cannot be proven. On the bishops *v* Richard Hogan, "The *Rainaldi* of Angers: 'New Men' or Descendents of Carolingian Nobiles?" *Medieval Prosopography,* 2.1 (1981), 37;

Stephen Fanning, "Family and Episcopal Election, 900–1050, and the case of Bishop Hubert of Angers (1006–1047)," *Medieval Prosopography*, 7.1 (1986) 39–56 Cf. Guillot, *Le comte*, I, 249–252, concerning Bishop Eusebius and with regard to abbots, pp. 127–197. Guillot tends to see far more reform than there actually was. For example, Bachrach, "Geoffrey Greymantle," pp. 9, 43–44, n. 48, 52, n. 59, shows how the Angevin count both chose the abbots and disposed of the resources of the monasteries as he saw fit. Concerning Beaulieu under Fulk Nerra *v* "Les débuts du monastère de Beaulieu," pp. 143–144 in *Chroniques des comtes d'Anjou et des seigneurs d'Amboise*, eds. L. Halphen and R. Poupardin (Paris, 1913). With regard to Saint Serge, Steven Fanning, "Les origines familiales de Vulgrin Abbé de Saint-Serge d'Angers (1046–1056) et Evêque du Mans (1056–1065) petit-fils du vicomte Fulcrade de Vendôme," *La Province du Maine*, 82 (1980), 243–255.

[123] Guillot, *Le comte*, I, 156–159, 182–183, for Abbot Theoderic and Abbot Sigo, respectively. A careful reexamination of the Saint Aubin "election charters" does not sustain Guillot's observations concerning periodic reforms dating from 966.

[124] Concerning these "client states" *v* Bachrach, "The Angevin Strategy of Castle Building," p. 553, n. 69; Bachrach, "Geoffrey Greymantle," p. 14; and for the appointment of bishops *v* Steven Fanning, "From *Miles* to Episcopus: The Influence of the Family on the Career of Vulgrinus of Vendôme (ca. 1000–1065)," *Medieval Prosopography*, 4.1 (1983), 9–30; and Bachrach, "King Henry II and Angevin Claims to the Saintonge," pp. 23–45, which provide two good examples.

[125] David Braund, *Rome and the Friendly King: The Character of Client Kingship* (New York, 1984), with the review by Bernard S. Bachrach in *History*, 13 (1984), 47.

[126] Halphen, *Le comté*, pp. 104–106.

[127] Bachrach, "The Practical Use of Vegetius' *De Re Militari*," p. 253, n. 76.

[128] Fulbert, *Epist,.* no. 13 (*The Letters and Poems of Fulbert of Chartres*, ed. and trans. Frederick Behrends [Oxford, 1976]), provides a good example of the activities of Abbot Hubert of Saint Aubin in Fulk's service.

[129] Guillot, *Le comte*, I, 468–469, provides a critical edition of this charter. Fulk Nerra's earlier imposition on Saint Aubin of this duty of *custodia* probably dates to the abbacy of Hubert (1001–1027), who became abbot at a time when the count was angry with the monks and deprived them of any jurisdictional rights over their dependents (see *Cartul. de Saint-Aubin*, no. 25). When Primald was made abbot in 1027 there were no complaints by the count and he restored to the monastery rights over low justice (*Cartul. de Saint-Aubin*, no. 26).

[130] Steven Fanning, "La lutte entre Hubert de Vendôme, Evêque d'Angers, et l'Archevêque de Tours en 1016: une épisode dans l'histoire de l'église des principautés territoriales," *Bulletin de la Société archéologique, scientifique et littéraire du Vendômois* 82 (1980), 31–33 (in quarto), where the dating of Fulbert, *Epist.*, no. 71, is revised.

[131] Bachrach, "The Angevin Strategy of Castle Building," pp. 533–560.

[132] Bachrach, "The Cost of Castle Building," pp. 46–62.

[133] *v*, above, concerning the *bidamnum*.

[134] Bachrach, "Fortifications and Military Tactics," pp. 531–549.

[135] Bernard S. Bachrach, "*Caballus et Caballarius* in Medieval Warfare," *The Teaching of Chivalry*, ed. H. Chickering (Kalamazoo) forthcoming; Bernard S. Bachrach, "Some Observations on the Military Administration of the Norman Conquest," *Anglo-Norman Studies*, 8 (1986), p. 12; and Bachrach, "Animals and Warfare," pp. 716–720.

[136] Bachrach, "The Cost of Castle Building," p. 53.

[137] Bachrach, "Military Administration," p. 12, n. 22.

[138] Guillot, *Le comte*, I, 282–296, 456–468, provides the most complete list of strongholds now available. However, Guillot's observations concerning when the government lost control of the so-called "seigneuries châtelaines" are open to question as shown by Bachrach, "The Angevin Strategy of Castle Building," pp. 533–560, and Bachrach, *"Forma Fidelitatis,"* pp. 796–819.

[139] *v*, above, notes 36, 37.

[140] Leighton, *Transport and Communications*, pp. 77, 161.

[141] Engels, *Logistics*, pp. 14–16, concerning speed, and above n. 108.

[142] The earliest mention of the Angevin government hiring mercenaries comes from the campaign of 992 when Fulk attacked Nantes. However, it is likely that the Angevin government had used mercenaries at an earlier date. For a discussion of this *v* Bachrach, *"Forma Fidelitatis,"* pp. 808–809, n. 63, and for the general background Jacques Boussard, "Services féodaux, milices, et mercenaires dans les armées en France aux Xe et XIe siècles," *SSCI*, 16 (Spoleto, 1970), 131–228.

[143] *Cartul. noir*, no. 45.

[144] The importance of this state of affairs as indicative of an "ancient" economy is underscored by Wickham, "Transition," p. 24.

[145] Wickham, "Transition," p. 23.

[146] Ibid., p. 24.

[147] Concerning the problem of aristocracy and nobility *v* the review essay by Bernard S. Bachrach, "Some Observations on the *Medieval Nobility*," *Medieval Prosopography*, 1.2 (1980), 15–33.

[148] A detailed study of the entire Angevin aristocracy in this period is an important *desideratum*. Concerning the castellans in the reign of Fulk Nerra see Bachrach, *"Forma Fidelitatis,"* pp. 796–819; and Halphen, "Prevôts et voyers," pp. 203–225, who treats the *vicarii* and *praepositi* but with a far too small sample. His observations that the *prevôts* came from families that were more important than those of the *vicarii* is questionable. Olivier Guillot, "Administration et Gouvernement dans les états du comte d'Anjou au milieu du XIe siècle," *Histoire comparée de l'administration (IVe–XVIIIe siècles)*, ed. W. Paravicini and K. F. Werner (Munich, 1980), does not focus upon office holders.

[149] Wickham, "Transition," p. 8.

[150] The body of evidence to demonstrate this is immense and a small sample is developed by Bachrach, "Geoffrey Greymantle," pp. 4–9.

[151] Archive de Maine-et-Loire, II 857.

[152] *Gesta Ambaziensium Dominorum*, pp. 89–90, in *Chroniques des comtes d'Anjou et des seigneurs d'Amboise*, ed. L. Halphen, and R. Poupardin (Paris, 1913).

[153] *Cartul. de Saint-Aubin*, nos. 1, 677. Concerning the authenticity of the former document see, above, note 16.

[154] Archive de Maine-et-Loire, H 2107, no. 1; and a better copy with full subscriptions in Bib. nat. n. a. Lat. 1930, fols. 17r.–v.

[155] *Gesta Ambaziensium Dominorum*, pp. 79, 84; and *Chronica de Gestis Consulum Andegavorum*, pp. 48, 54, in *Chroniques des comtes d'Anjou et des seigneurs d'Amboise*, ed. L. Halphen and R. Poupardin (Paris, 1913). Lisoius was recruited after Herbert had already become count of Maine ca. 1014–1015 but when the new count was still "pernimium juvenis." However, by 6 July 1016 when Herbert led the reserve in support of Fulk at the battle of Pontlevoy he had obviously already reached his majority. Thus, Lisoius would seem to have been established sometime before 6

July 1016 but not earlier than 1014. Concerning Herbert's accession see Robert Latouche, *Histoire du comté du Maine pendant le Xe et le XIe siècle* (Paris, 1910), p. 22. With regard to the age of majority see Bachrach, *"Forma Fidelitatis,"* p. 805, n. 48, with the literature cited there.

156 *v*, above, n. 34, for the *servientes* and for foresters *v Cartul. du Ronceray*, no. 7. The lesser officials of the Angevin government are badly in need of study. Guillot, "Administration et Gouvernement," pp. 311–332, does not cover these functionaries. Concerning the administration of justice and the higher office holders *v* Halphen, "La justice," pp. 175–202; and "Prevôts et voyers," pp. 203–225. Also of interest here is Jacques Boussard, "Le droit de *vicaria*, à la lumière de quelques documents angevins et tourangeaux," *Mélanges E.-R. Labande: Etudes de Civilisation Médiévale: IXe–XIIe siècles* (Poitiers, 1974), 39–54. For comparative purposes *v* K. F. Werner, "Königtum und Fürstentum des französischen 12. Jahrhunderts," in *Probleme des 12. Jahrhunderts* (Sigmaringen, 1968), 177–225. The history of these administrators and the administrative cadres in Anjou remains to be written.

157 Halphen, "La justice," pp. 175–202; and "Prevôts et voyers," pp. 203–225, provides evidence for this process but his categories of analysis are seriously flawed. *v* also n. 117, above, where indirect taxes are the focus.

158 Boussard, "La vie en Anjou," p. 53, on the extent of land development from forests and swamps in general. *v* the texts cited in nn. 20, 21, and 76 above.

159 *v*, above, note 88 and more particularly the example in *Cartul. du Ronceray*, no. 5.

160 For the history of Durtal *v* Bachrach, "The Angevin Stategy of Castle Building," p. 555, n. 78; For Angevin dominance at Le Mans during this period *v* the discussion by Guillot, *Le comte*, I, 94, and for the Jews at Durtal *v* I. A. Agus, *Urban Civilization in Pre-Crusade Europe* (New York, 1968), I, 160–168, and 341–342, for easy access to the Hebrew materials in English translation. At present I am working on an article dealing with Jews who settled in the Angevin state along the Loir frontier.

161 Guillot, *Le comte*, I, 370–375, presents a view of both the *consuetudines* and the *malae consuetudines* that is not accepted here. His contention that these taxes first appear in the reign of Fulk Nerra connot be sustained. For example, Bib. nat. Coll. Baluze, vol. 76, fol. 256, makes clear that Geoffrey Greymantle had imposed *malae consuetudines* on land belonging to Saint Martin of Tours which Fulk Nerra agreed to give up: "dimissasque in perpetuum esse volo omnes malae consuetudines quas ego et genitor meus Gauzfridus hactenus injuste teneuimus in beati martini potestatibus." The document then goes on in the next sentence to indicate that those (legitimate) *consuetudines* that were taken in the days of Fulk Nerra's grandfather, Fulk the Good, were not abolished: "Illas autem quas tenuit aevus meus Fulco ad praesens non dimitto . . . " Guillot, (p., 372, n. 91) cannot explain away this text and his efforts to explain away (p. 372) the existence of the *consuetudines* that were taken in the reign of Geoffrey Graymantle as found in *Cartul. noir*, no. 22, is unconvincing. There Fulk Nerra agrees to give up the *malae consuetudines* that did not exist in the time of his father. However, during the father's reign the *theloneum* was collected by the count's *ministri* from those who crossed the bridge that spanned the river Maine at Angers. This *theloneum* was clearly a (legitimate) *consuetudo*. In addition, it should be of some small importance that in the *prooemium* of this document the count subscribed to the idea that for the public good(s) "de rei publicae utilitatibus" the act was written down so that 'in curte lex antiqua decrevit quod per caracteres scripta. . . . " Geoffrey Martel's reference (*Cartul. noir*, no. 45) to

the "damnosarum exactionum consuetudines . . . pater meus Fulco sive an-
tecessores ejus violenter impreserant" is clearly intended to include Geoffrey
Greymantle and perhaps Fulk the Good as well.

162 v, e.g., *Cartul. de Saint-Aubin*, nos. 26, 45, 161, 178, 179; Bib. nat. n.a. Lat., 1930,
fols. 12r.v., 26v., 28r.v., 57r.–58r., 96r.v., 99r.v., 129r.v., 130v–131r; *Cartul. noir*,
no. 22; Jean Besly, *Histoire des comtes*, p. 357; *Cartulaire de Saint-Vincent du Mans*, ed.
R. Charles and S. Menjot d'Elbenne (Mamers, 1886) no. 610; Mailfert, "Saint-
Nicholas d'Angers," *p.j.* 4; *Cartul. du Ronceray*, nos. 7, 35, 64, 100; Bib. nat. ms. lat.
12878, fol. 108r.; Dom Housseau, I. no. 326, II.1, no. 525, II.2, no. 658, XII, nos.
6686, 6687; *Breviculum fundationis . . . Sancti Nicolai Andegavensis*, pp. 14, 15; *Cartul.
de la Trinité de Vendôme*, nos. 13, 22, 92, 157, 158, 162; *Chartes de Saint-Julien-de-
Tours*, ed. L.-J. Denis (Le Mans, 1912), no. 25; *Cartul. de Saint-Maur*, no. 17; and
Archive de Maine-et-Loire, H 2107, no. 1. This list is in no sense intended to be
exhaustive.

163 An interesting example of both the officiousness of the Angevin administrators and
perhaps also an indication of the fact that these petty office-holders earned their
livelihood from a portion of the tolls that they collected is to be found in Dom
Housseau, II.1, no. 470, where count Geoffrey Martel granted a ship from the
monastery of Marmoutier an immunity from tolls along the Loire from Champ-
toceaux all the way to Tours but found it necessary to send one of his household
retainers, Aimo Daurellus, on board for the journey so that this vessel that was
carrying salt would not be troubled by the toll collectors. Another act, this one from
Cartul. de Saint-Maur, no. 18, dealing with weights and measures is also instructive in
this context as to administrative concern with detail.

164 In the *Miracula Martini Abbatis Vertavensis*, ed. Bruno Krusch, *Monumenta Germania
Historica: Scriptores Rerum Merovingicarum*, III (Hannover, 1896), which were composed ca. 1000 at the monastery of Saint Jouin-de-Marnes under the influence of
the Renaud-clan, sometime adversaries of the Angevin counts, a story is told (ch. 7)
about King Dagobert I's (d. 639) efforts to have the holy places of the *regnum
Francorum* inventoried so that half of these resources might be taken over by the
royal fisc. That Dagobert I undertook such a massive inventory is unlikely since no
other source speaks of it. By contrast, Geoffrey Greymantle and Fulk Nerra who
controlled the monastery of Saint Jouin and exploited its resources used terminology in their documents very similar to that used by the author of the *Miracula*. Since
the political circumstances, i.e. the Renaud-clan's hostility to the Angevin count at
this time and Angevin comital control of the monastery, would have made it very
uncomfortable for a direct criticism of either Geoffrey Greymantle or Fulk Nerra to
be made, the author's use of King Dagobert and his "very tricky" advisor who came
to no good as a result of their exploitation of Saint Jouin's resources may be seen as
a "lesson" intended to foreshadow the fate of the Angevin counts should they
continue the exploitation of the monastery's resources. Concerning the Renaud-
clan and its relation with the Angevin comital family *v* Richard M. Hogan, "The
Rainaldi of Angers: 'New Men' or Descendants of Carolingian *Nobiles?*" *Medieval
Prosopography*, 2.1 (1981), 35–62; Bachrach, "The Family of Viscount Fulcoius," pp.
1–9. With regard to Angevin domination of the Monastery of Saint Jouin des
Marnes *v* Bachrach, "The Angevin Strategy of Castle Building," p. 550; and with
regard to Angevin exploitation of the resources of Saint Jouin see *Cartul. de
Saint-Aubin*, no. 821; and *Cartul. de Saint-Jouin de Marnes*, p. 19 (as dated by
Bachrach, "Forma Fidelitatis," pp. 805–806, notes 48, 49, and pp. 20–21, where Fulk

Nerra is mistakingly identified as Fulk le Réchin's *magnus avunculus* rather than as his grandfather by analogy with the correct identification of Geoffrey Martel as his *avunculus*. Concerning the stylistic similarities *v*, e.g., *Cartul. de Saint-Aubin*, no. 2. Compare my treatment of this text in Bernard S. Bachrach, "Charles Martel, Mounted Shock Combat, the Stirrup and Feudalism," *Studies in Medieval and Renaissance History*, 7 (1970), 70, n. 70.

> Whether we conclude that Dagobert I ordered and saw at least partially carried out the inventory of ecclesiastical wealth discussed in *Miracula*, ch. 7, or whether either Geoffrey Greymantle or perhaps Fulk Nerra did it, or whether both the Frankish king and an Angevin count both did so, is certainly problematic. What is not at issue, however, is that the author of the *Miracula* surely believed that his audience would not regard the type of massive administrative undertaking he describes as so foreign to their understanding that the story would be without significant meaning for them.

[165] Bachrach, "Geoffrey Greymantle," p. 8.

[166] *Cartul. de la Trinité de Vendôme*, no. 2, which mentions Fulk Nerra imposing these taxes on the Vendômois. Fulk could not have taken possession of the *comté* until after the death of his brother-in-law, Bishop Renaud of Paris, who last appears in an act dated 22 April 1016 and certainly was dead by 9 June 1017 when he failed to appear at the coronation of young Hugh (for a discussion of this act see Guillot, *Le comte*, II, 38–39). After Renaud's death his grandnephew Bouchard, who was also Fulk Nerra's grandson, received the honor. Bouchard, however, was a minor, and the Angevin count took the Vendômois under his own control (*Cartul. de la Trinité de Vendôme*, no. 6). Certainly by no later than 29 December 1022, and perhaps no later than 25 December 1021, Fulk Nerra is seen personally ruling the Vendômois (*Livre de Serfs de Marmoutier*, ed. A. Salmon [Paris, 1845], no. 52). Fulk Nerra returned the Vendômois to Bouchard no later than 16 August 1025 when Viscount Hubert of Vendôme is already dead (*Cartul. noir*, no. 29). The Viscount, of course, was still living when the *consuetudines* recorded in *Cartul. de la Trinité de Vendôme*, no. 2, were laid out.

[167] Ganshof, "Apropos du Tonlieu," 485–508, generally, and also Ganshof, "The Institutional Framework of the Frankish Monarchy," p. 100.

[168] *Cartul. de la Trinité de Vendôme*, no. 2.

[169] *v*, e.g., Bib. nat. n.a. Lat. 1930, fols. 28r.v; 28v.–29r.; Dom Housseau, II.1, no. 326.

[170] *v*, e.g., *Cartul. de la Trinité de Vendôme*, no. 92.

[171] *v* above, nn. 20 and 21.

[172] *Gesta Consulum*, pp. 36–37. Despite the fact that Halphen and Poupardin (*Chroniques des comtes d'Anjou*, vii-xlvi, *passim*) question the value of this chronicle for the early history of the Angevin counts, Sir Richard Southern, *The Making of the Middle Ages* (New Haven, 1953), p. 83, relies on this text but does not justify his use of it. In addition, Southern consistent with his argument that we are unable to discern "design" to any great extent in the activities of the Angevin counts, omits mention of Fulk's alleged "kind generosity" in bringing migrants to Anjou. As will be seen below, the activities of Geoffrey Greymantle, Fulk the Good's son and successor, strongly suggest that the reign of the former saw both an important increase in population and significant economic development. Thomas of Loches was correct.

[173] It may be suggested, in addition, that it is highly likely that the count took even more active steps to encourage immigrants through the use of *locatores* which is what his later contemporaries in Flanders found to be necessary. In short, com-

munications in tenth-century Europe were such that vigorous efforts had to
be undertaken in order to let would-be immigrants from "foreign" if not from
"surrounding regions" know where generous opportunities and fertile lands
were to be found. Concerning the Flemish analogue *v* Bryce D. Lyon, "Medieval
Real Estate Developments and Freedom," *American Historical Review*, 63 (1957),
47–61.

174 Bachrach, "Geoffrey Greymantle," p. 53, no. 68.

175 Boussard, "La vie en Anjou," p. 53.

176 *v* above, n. 88.

177 Halphen, *Le comté*, pp. 89–97.

178 *v* above, n. 119.

179 Bachrach, "The Angevin Strategy of Castle Building," pp. 533–560.

180 Bienvenu, "Pauvreté, misères et charité en Anjou," pp. 389–424, 6–34, 189–216. It
is instructive to compare the reports from before 1060 to the later eleventh and
early twelfth centuries.

181 *Gesta Consulum*, p. 36.

182 *v* above, nn. 20 and 21.

183 Archive de Maine-et-Loire, H 1840, no. 7; and Bib. nat. n.a. Lat. 1930, fols.
96v.–97r.

184 Bib. nat. n.a. Lat. 1930, fols. 99r.–100r.

185 For a variety of licenses *v Receuil des actes de Philippe Ie*, ed. M. Prou (Paris, 1908), no.
157; Bib. nat. n.a. Lat. 1930, fols. 96v.–97r., 99r.–100v.; *Cartul. de la Trinité de
Vendôme*, no. 158; *Cartul. de Saint-Aubin*, no. 34; *Cartul. de Saint-Laud*, no. 25; *Cartul.
du Ronceray*, nos. 64, 241; *Cartulaire de Saint-Jouin de Marnes*, ed. Ch. de Grandmaison (Niort, 1854), p. 22; "Fragments de chartes du Xe siècle provenant de
Saint-Julien-de-Tours," ed. Ch. de Grandmaison, no. 23, in *Bibliothèque de l'Ecole des
Chartes*, 46 (1885).

186 *v* above, n. 162.

187 Bachrach, *"Forma Fidelitatis,"* pp. 976–819.

188 For the purpose of simplifying the citation of the plethora of evidence that supports
the impression of the ubiquity of the public roads in the region it can be noted that
from a sample of thirty-two documents in the Livre noir de Saint-Florent de
Saumur a full 25 percent mention a *via publica*. *v* Bib. nat. n.a. Lat. 1930, fols.
9r.–20v. the mention of a *via publica* occur in fols. 9r.–10r.; 10r.–v.; 14r.–v.;
16v.–17r.; 17r.; 17r.–v.; 18r.; and 20r.–v.

189 Concerning the "public war," *v* Guillot, *Le comte*, I, 384; and for other types of wars
v Bachrach, "The Angevin Tradition of Family Hostility," pp. 118–125. *v* also
Cartul. de Saint-Laud, no. 25; and Bib. nat. ms. Lat. 12878, fol 174.

190 Besly, *Histoire des comtes*, p. 357.

191 *Cartul. noir*, no. 22.

192 *v* the references to the army of officials in n. 162, above.

193 Pierre d'Herbecourt, *Anjou Roman*, for the basic material. In addition, support for
this observation is to be found in *Touraine Romane*, by O. Aymard, **et al.;** and *Val de
Loire Roman*, 2nd ed. by O. Aymard, **et al.** All are Zodiaque editions published at La
Pierre-qui-Vire, 1957, 1957, 1965, respectively. J. Mallet, *L'art roman de l'ancien
Anjou* (Paris, 1984). N. b. There is considerable subjectivity in these judgments.

194 *v* above, n. 171.

195 *v*, e.g., *Cartul. du Ronceray*, nos. 129, 238, for Geoffrey Martel; and *Cartul. noir*, no.
218, for Eusebius.

196 Bachrach, "The Practical Use of Vegetius' *De Re Militari*," pp. 239–255.

[197] Romanesque style in fortifications *v* André Chatelain, *Donjons Romans des pays d'Ouest* (Paris, 1973); and for some nuances on dating *v* Bachrach, "Fortifications and Military Tactics," pp. 531–549.

[198] For the *laeti v* above, n. 47; and for the *exactores v Breviculum fundationis . . . Sancti Nicolai Andegavensis*, p. 15.

[199] Bachrach, *Merovingian Military Organization*, pp. 70–73, 78–80; for the *laeti* and for the *exacti v* R. W. Davies, "The Daily Life of the Roman Soldier Under the Principate," *Aufstieg und Niedergang der römischen Welt*, 2.1 (Berlin, 1974), 312–313.

[200] *v* above, n. 162.

[201] Bachrach, "The Practical Use of Vegetius' *De Re Militari*," pp. 254–255, as a gloss on Alexander Murray, *Reason and Society in the Middle Ages* (Oxford, 1978), pp. 110–137. Concerning the Normans *v* the discussion by Bachrach, "The Military Administration of the Norman Conquest" pp. 5; 7.

[202] Bernard S. Bachrach, "The Pilgrimages of Fulk Nerra," in *Studies in Early Medieval History Dedicated to Richard Sullivan*, eds. T.F.X. Noble and John Contreni (Kalamazoo, MI, 1987), 205–217, which provides a good introduction to the range of Fulk Nerra's travel. Concerning Geoffrey Greymantle's visit to Rome *v* Bachrach, "Geoffrey Greymantle," pp. 37–38; and for Geoffrey Martel's travels to Apulia *v* Halphen, *Le comté*, p. 128.

[203] Concerning Norman contacts with the Byzantines *v* Krijnie Ciggaar, "England and Byzantium on the Eve of the Norman Conquest (The Reign of Edward the Confessor)," *Anglo-Norman Studies*, 5 (1985), 83–84; and Bernard S. Bachrach, "On the Origins of William the Conqueror's Horse Transports," *Technology and Culture*, 26 (1985), 514–517, and p. 529, n. 64, for a discussion of the likelihood that William used skeleton construction of Mediterranean design for his horse transports.

[204] There are a large variety of interesting biblical texts illustrating aspects of governmental behavior in the area of administration and tax collecting. *v*, e.g., 1 Kings, 4:1–19; 9:10 ff.; 2 Kings, 23:33; Josh., 16:10; Ezra, 4:14, 20, 21; 6:8; Romans, 13:6, 7; Luke, 2:1–5; 3:12–13; 7:29, 34; 15:1; 19:2; 23:2; and for the ever-present tax collectors Matthew, 5:47; 9:10, 11; 10:3; 18:17; 21:31. This list obviously is not intended to be exhaustive.

[205] J. M. Wallace-Hadrill, *The Barbarian West, A.D. 400–1000* (2nd revised ed., New York, 1962), p. 146, where he observes, "early medieval men could live like barbarians; but they could think that they were Romans."

[206] At present I am preparing a study, "Huns and Goths: 337–425," for volume XIII of the second edition of the *Cambridge Ancient History*. My researches, however, suggest that some parts of the western provinces in the Roman empire did not look much like Wickham's model of an "ancient" social formation. Concerning the Ravannate see Wickham, "Transition," p. 11; Walter Goffart, "Old and New in Merovingian Taxation," *Past and Present*, 96 (1982), 3–21, concerning the Franks and the same author's *Barbarians and Romans, A.D. 418–584* (Princeton, 1980).

[207] *The Making of the Middle Ages*, p. 86.

[208] R. Allen Brown, *The Origins of English Feudalism* (London, 1973), provides a most lucid definition of "military feudalism" along with a cogent defense of its value.

[209] Concerning Count Paul see Gregory, *Hist.*, Bk. II, ch. 20.

[210] Easy access to the controversy over the Pirenne thesis is to be found in *The Pirenne Thesis*, ed. Alfred Havinghurst (3rd ed., Boston, 1976). For a fully rounded appreciation of Pirenne's work and life *v* Bryce D. Lyon, *Henri Pirenne: A Biographical and Intellectual Study* (Ghent, 1974).

CHIVALRIC ROMANCES IN THE ITALIAN RENAISSANCE

Paul F. Grendler
University of Toronto.

CHIVALRIC ROMANCES IN THE ITALIAN RENAISSANCE

Renaissance Italians living in the most urban, commercial society of Europe loved feudal chivalric romances.[1] Townspeople who earned their living by trade and manufacturing doted on knights who did not work but spent their time fighting and loving. Having won their independence from imperial authority, Italians thrilled to knights who served Charlemagne. Deaf to papal calls for crusades to redeem the Holy Land, Italians loved to read about warriors who fought Saracens for Christ. Despite the enormous contradictions between their own lives and values, and those of fictitious knights and ladies, fifteenth- and sixteenth-century Italians read, listened to, and composed chivalric romances as enthusiastically as any other European people. The mythical knights and ladies of chivalry played a major role in Italian Renaissance culture.

Yet, except for the acclaimed poems of Pulci, Boiardo, and Ariosto, Italian chivalric romances have been little studied because they are seen as derivative and lacking great literary worth.[2] The romances are guilty as charged. Authors of the vast majority of Italian chivalric romances translated or refashioned tales previously told in other languages. And no scholar claims that Andrea da Barberino's *I Reali di Francia* merits comparison with Dante's *Commedia*. But neither should chivalric romances be dismissed as uninteresting in content or worthless as literature. They deserve attention because they probably comprised the largest measurable corpus of secular vernacular literature to be found in the Renaissance. They rivalled saints' lives in popularity, insofar as such things can be determined.[3] Nor were all romances devoid of literary quality. And as a body of popular literature the romances offer insights into Italian Renaissance life and culture.

"Popular" means in simplest terms a work that exerts a very broad, nearly universal appeal. Popularity has three components. First, it indicates widespread enjoyment by all or nearly all elements of society. Chivalric romances provided literary entertainment for all;

it is very difficult to suggest that chivalric romances appealed only or mostly to one group, such as the nobility. In similar fashion, it is misleading to attempt to apply terms as "high culture," "middle culture," or "low culture" to the phenomenon. The literate read them; all might listen to minstrels declaiming the exploits of knights. Second, popular literature responds to beliefs, ideals, perhaps inchoate feelings in the audience. The readers empathize with the literary characters. A strong audience bond must be forged for a work of literature to become popular. If through lack of proximity, or unfamiliarity with the subject matter, such a bond is not immediately apparent, an author can adapt his material in order to achieve the audience bond. Italian narrators of romances reworked French material to do this, just as nineteenth-century travelling companies shaped Shakespeare's tragedies to the tastes of American frontier audiences.[4] Third, the content of popular literature need not necessarily be banal, nor its intellectual level so low as to appeal to men and women of limited intelligence and narrow outlook. It only seems that way in the late twentieth century. In other words, the notion that "popular" must denote a work of minimal aesthetic quality was no more true in the Renaissance than in any other epoch. Again the comparison with the popularity of Shakespeare in nineteenth-century America is instructive. Some chivalric romances were well-written, appealing, dramatically challenging, and thoughtful. Others were not.

This paper offers a brief survey of Italian chivalric romances during the Italian Renaissance. It will review the different narrative cycles of the romances and analyze some examples. Next, it will suggest ways in which the romances evolved as they entered the Renaissance and authors adapted them to their audiences. Finally, the paper will note evidence of their integration into Renaissance culture and society. The approach is that of an historian surveying a field in an effort to understand the place of the romances in Italian culture. The modest goal is to introduce historians and others to a relatively neglected but important area of popular literature.[5]

I

Almost all the stories and themes of Italian chivalric romances originated elsewhere, but practically nothing is known of their introduction into Italy. Merchants following traditional trade routes from France into Italy, and French pilgrims travelling through Italy in order to embark for the Holy Land from southern Italian ports, may have brought the tales with them. For example, several Italian romances included the story of how Milone and Berta fled Paris for Italy where Berta gave birth to Orlando (Roland) at Sutri in central Italy.[6] Their fictitious journey may have followed the route of French pilgrims.

Three kinds of evidence document the presence of chivalric romances and minstrels in twelfth-century Italy, especially in the area of Padua and Verona in the north and Campania and Puglia in the south. Italian variants of chivalric names, such as "Artusius," "Tristano," and "Rolandus," and references to the Round Table, began to appear in non-chivalric sources.[7] Second, chivalric matter was literally carved in stone between c. 1120 and c. 1140: bas-reliefs over the north door of the cathedral of Modena portray with pictures and names Arthurian knights storming a castle while a lady looks on. Similar bas-reliefs of c. 1140 featuring Carolingian heroes are found over the portals of churches in Verona and elsewhere.[8] Such evidence presupposes that the romances arrived in Italy sometime before being written into documents and being carved above cathedral portals. Finally, a Veronese source of 1168 mentioned an Italian minstrel, called an *ioculator*, possibly the earliest documented notice of one.[9]

Chivalric romances were very well established in Italy in the thirteenth century. Manuscripts copied at the end of the thirteenth or beginning of the fourteenth century and now resting in the Biblioteca Marciana in Venice document the point. They were sometimes written in *Franco-veneta,* a linguistic mix of French and Italian in which an Italian suffix might be appended to a French stem. Lovato Lovati (c.1237–1309), the Paduan judge and pre-humanist, described a minstrel in Treviso who declaimed to an audience by altering the ends of French words.[10] Indeed, Lovati tried his hand at writing a romance in Latin on Tristano and Isotta.[11]

By the second half of the thirteenth century, Italian minstrels sang of the exploits of chivalric heroes in the piazzas of northern and north-central cities. They made scheduled appearances in designated places, such as the arcade of the communal place in Bologna and the piazzetta next to the church of San Martino del Vescovo (at Via Dante Alighieri and Via S. Margherita) in Florence. Occasionally these regular performances raised protests. The singing of minstrels next to a female monastery in Viterbo led the Commune to pass a statute in 1251 ordering them to move further away so that the nuns would not have to hear these "vanities." The Commune of Osimo in 1371 ordered minstrels not to sing on Sunday mornings or on holydays lest they divert the good citizens from their religious obligations.[12]

More often civic leaders approved the minstrels and sometimes paid them for their efforts. The Commune of Siena paid a minstrel one hundred *soldi* for a ballad celebrating a Sienese military victory of 1255. Governments also rewarded troubadours who sang of peaceful events: in 1321 the Sienese Commune paid a minstrel for composing and singing a ballad celebrating the translation of scholars from Bologna to Siena. Troubadours performed at the dinners of the priors of Perugia in the late fourteenth century. In the following century and a half they descended to the piazza below the Palazzo dei Priori to entertain the people. The Commune supported financially these regularly scheduled recitations from 1461 onward.[13] *Cantatori* continued to perform through the middle of the sixteenth century.[14]

Some minstrels sang or declaimed their tales to the accompaniment of early lutes, viols, fifes, and some form of a bagpipe. One can imagine a single minstrel strumming a lute, or a musician or two playing while he recited. Italian minstrels apparently did not memorize romances or invent the story as they went along, but relied on a text.[15] The minstrel in Treviso described by Lovati probably had a French text before him which he "italianized." A minstrel might need several days to complete a romance. Indeed, the division of romances into chapters if prose, and cantos if poetry, facilitated serial performance over several days. The minstrel could break off his tale at a critical point and resolve the crisis the next day.

Romances in *ottava rima*, i.e., stanzas of eight lines with an ABABABCC rhyme scheme, appeared in the mid-Trecento, possibly because *ottava rima* lent itself to musical accompaniment. Giovanni Battista Giraldi Cinthio (1504–73) in his discussion of romances held this view. The first composers of romances sang or pretended to sing their compositions before princes, Giraldi Cinthio began. Both speaker and listeners needed to pause regularly. But because *terza rima* did not give minstrel and audience an adequate rest, romancers chose *ottava rima*. It could tell more of the story in eight lines, and its harmonious conclusion pleased the ear. Moreover, the ear quickly learned to anticipate the concluding rhyme and the pause, which gave minstrel and audience time to draw breath without interrupting the continuity of the work, Giraldi Cinthio concluded.[16] Whether or not he accurately described the much disputed origins of *ottava rima*, Giraldi Cinthio summarized some of its advantages. In any case, prose and poetic romances coexisted; often the same romance circulated in both versions.

II

Three distinct bodies of material provided the sources for Italian romances. The Arthurian or Bretonic cycle balanced amours and battles. Its major stories focussed on a trio of lovers: Tristano, Isotta, and King Marco, to give them their Italian names, or King Artù, Queen Ginevara, and Sir Lancilotto. Major romances deployed all six plus subsidiary characters. The Bretonic romances devoted considerable attention to the analysis and commentary on the emotions of the chief characters. Tristano, et al., loved, sighed, and fought mostly in the restricted geographical area of Cornwall and Ireland.

The earliest surviving Arthurian romance found in Italy is the so-called *Tristano Riccardiano,* i.e., Manuscript 2543 of the Biblioteca Riccardiana of Florence, written in Tuscan-Umbrian dialect perhaps by an author from Cortona at the end of the thirteenth or first years of the fourteenth century. [17] This prose version, which may not be the earliest Italian redaction, follows the main lines of the story of Tristano and Isotta and adds new material that may have been original. The tale begins with the birth of Tristano. A queen searching for her husband (who is busily committing adultery elsewhere) gives birth to a son in the forest. She names him Tristano, so that he might remember her sorrow *(tristezza),* and dies. Two knights wish to kill the baby, but the queens's gentlewoman rescues him and returns him to his father. [18]

Tristano is no exception to the rule that chivalric heroes must survive threatening childhoods. Before long Tristano's erring father is ambushed and killed. The stepmother makes several attempts on Tristano's life, such as preparing for him a poisoned meal of beans and roast chicken. [19] Like most chivalric heroes, Tristano becomes a runaway; he leaves the paternal home to begin his adventures at the advanced age of eleven. He goes to a court in Gaul where a king's daughter falls passionately in love with him. When Tristano informs her that he will accept only a "leale amore" such as that between faithful spouses, the girl falsely denounces him for forcing his attention on her. [20] Eventually Tristano is exonerated and leaves the court, while the king's daughter kills herself, a suicide reminiscent of that of the passionate Dido when Aeneas abandons her (*Aeneid*, IV, 670–705).

The story goes on. Tristano fights in tournaments and individual combats, but only a limited amount of blood is shed, usually
that of a very deserving villain. Arthurian knights seldom joined
battle in large forces or embarked on crusades against Muslims, but
preferred individual duels. A series of love relationships pursued
through complex patterns of trust and betrayal, honor and deception,
provided the central theme pursued with the usual technique of
interlacing, i.e., the alternation and interweaving of episodes and
themes in order to keep more than one story present in the reader's
mind.[21] Eventually Tristano journeys to Ireland to bring back Isotta
as a bride for King Marco, and the two drink the love potion. *Tristano
Riccardiano* wends its way to the conclusion in which both lovers die.
The work is fairly laconic, displays few flourishes, and leaves some
loose ends.

A later prose version of the same material indicates how
Italians began to adapt received chivalric material to their own tastes.
La tavola ritonda, probably written by a Tuscan in the second quarter
of the fourteenth century, survives in at least eight fourteenth- and
fifteenth-century manuscripts.[22] It presents the same central material
on Tristano and Isotta as *Tristano Riccardiano* but introduces more
characters and adventures. The author developed this full romance
in several ways: he translated both literally and freely from an original
non-Italian source, he interpolated additional episodes drawn from
other sources, and he added new material perhaps of his own invention.

La tavola ritonda begins with accounts of other knights and
the history of the houses of the kings of Cornwall and Liones, and
then shifts to Lancilotto's birth, battles, and love for Queen Ginevara.
Tristano is finally born in chapter twelve. Additional knights, ladies,
and adventures are interpolated into the long central story of Tristano. After Tristano and Isotta die in chapter 129, another sixteen
chapters complete the romance by narrating "the destruction of all
chivalry."[23] King Artù and his knights seek revenge on Marco for
Tristano's death, a quest which culminates in a battle of the knights of
Cornwall against those of Ireland. They capture King Marco and
imprison him in an iron cage on top of a tower 880 feet high built in
front of Tristano's sepulchre. They do not mistreat Marco, but feed
him so well that he dies "of fatness" after thirty-two months, an
ignominious end for the thwarted groom and treacherous king.[24]
King Artù and Sir Lancilotto return to Camelot and the Round Table

which has disintegrated through sloth, pleasure, and luxury. Lancilotto and Ginevara make love and run away together, which leads to
more fighting. Eventually King Artù and Queen Ginevara die, while
Lancilotto goes into the wilderness to do penance. He becomes a
priest and dies after fifteen months. With this the brotherhood of the
Round Table falls; Camelot is abandoned, and the remaining knights
go their separate ways.

 This rendering of the Arthurian matter showed a development from *Tristano Riccardiano*. To be sure, courtly love and its consequences dominate the work. But the author of *La tavola ritonda* has
shaped his material with more authority and coherence than *Tristano
Riccardiano* manifests. He more often poses questions and/or discusses
the moral consequences of episodes. Most interestingly, in an effort to
give the romance more coherence, he slightly orients his material
toward the form of an historical chronicle by introducing a limited
amount of precise information such as dates. He informs us that
Tristano and Isotta were born in 333 and 337 respectively, and died
in 368.[25] (Hence, they were mature adults, not infatuated teenagers
as were most Carolingian romantic couples.) The author sometimes
gives the order of battle, the number of opposing knights and
footsoldiers, and casualty figures.[26] In other words, the Italian commercial world, in which exact dates and precise quantities mattered a
great deal, has begun to intrude on the chivalric romance of northern
Europe.

 The last section of the romance self-consciously inserted
historical space between a distant past and the present. The dates tell
the reader that the golden age of gallant knights and ladies ended
almost a thousand years ago. The nostalgic tone in combination with
the dates helped to emphasize the author's own era and institutions.
By stating that the brotherhood of the Round Table and Camelot
disappeared almost a millenium earlier in 399, the author also
affirmed that Italian feudalism has ended.[27] The new society, the
urban, profit-driven world of the Trecento, is far removed and considerably different from the Italian feudal past. All that remains of
chivalry is a story.

III

Carolingian matter provided the source for the second group of
Italian chivalric romances.[28] On 15 August 778, Basque marauders

wiped out a rearguard of French barons in the mountains of northern Spain. The fallen knights of Roncesvalle became the subject of an heroic epic and numerous chivalric stories later. The tales contered on Roland and other knights who served Charlemagne, but not the battle of Roncesvalle itself, which disappeared from the stories. Carolingian matter emphasized battles much more than amours. Its knights roamed throughout Europe, the Near East, and even North Africa in order to battle villains and Saracens. A brave warrior knight who loyally served his king and faithfully loved one woman dominated the Carolingian stories. Italians wrote more romances based on the Carolingian tradition and seemed to have preferred the chansons de geste of Charlemagne's knights to the other chivalric matters. The straightforward action and unambiguous relationships of the Carolingian cycle may have attracted Italians more than the illicit passions and doomed lovers of the Arthurian romances. Or possibly the Carolingian romances arrived first.

Italian romances reached a high point of development in the late fourteenth and first half of the fifteenth century. Now integrated into Italian culture, they absorbed and reflected some of the concrete details, ideals, intellectual habits, and even the ambiguities of Renaissance urban life. The Carolingian matter in the hands of Andrea da Barberino illustrated the Italian prose chivalric romance at its zenith.

Unlike almost all earlier authors of romances, Andrea da Barberino left some traces. Born c. 1370 as Andrea Magiabotti or Mangiabotti, a family that came from Barberino Val d'Elsa, about thirty kilometers south of Florence, Andrea lived in Florence. He listed his profession as *cantatore*, although he wrote prose romances to be read. His *catasto* declarations of 1427 and 1431 show that he owned the house on Via della Pergola where he lived plus some farmland. On 14 August 1431 he made his will in favor of his *nipote* who declared the goods inherited from Andrea on 31 May 1433. Hence, Andrea died sometime between the two dates.[29] He left a brief personal statement for posterity. In the preface to *Guerrin Meschino*, he expressed pleasure at the thought of writing "historie nuove," and that "new authors" pleased all. He had not received a great amount of God's bounty, but others had been given less. He then briefly affirmed his belief in man's reason and free will: we can choose virtue or vice; in the end we must blame ourselves, not fortune, for what befalls us. He concluded with a musical analogy: everyone has the wit to learn to play an instrument, but one must be careful to avoid "false chords."[30]

Andrea certainly wrote six substantial romances and may have written others in his very productive career. He had the felicitous idea of organizing some of his romances into a chronological whole, called *I Reali di Francia,* his most famous work. Adenet li Rois, a thirteenth-century French author of romances, and unknown collaborators composed most of the stories that later became *I Reali di Francia.*[31] Many of these characters and episodes then appeared in *Franco-veneta* versions of the end of the thirteenth or early fourteenth century, and are found in the famous Codex Francese XIII of the Biblioteca Marciana in Venice. But only Andrea da Barberino combined the material into a comprehensive epic. *I Reali di Francia* purported to tell in six books of varying length the story of a royal line of knights descending from the Roman Emperor Constantine the Great (d. 337) and culminating in King Pepin and Emperor Charlemagne of the eighth century. Indeed, Book 6 narrated a fictional life of Charlemagne from a highly romantic birth through his coronation at Rome.[32] In other words, Andrea da Barberino cast *I Reali di Francia* in the form of a medieval dynastic chronicle. Four other independent romances are set in Charlemagne's reign: *Aiolfo del Barbicone,*[33] *Aspramonte,*[34] *Guerrin Meschino,*[35] and *I Nerbonesi.*[36] Andrea set a sixth romance, *Ugone d'Alvernia,* after Charlemagne's death in the reign of Charles Martel whom Andrea either by mistake or design anachronistically made into Charlemagne's grandson.[37] Andrea probably did not compose his romances in chronological order; indeed, assigning composition dates has proven to be well-nigh impossible. In all his works Andrea freely rewrote earlier Carolingian sources and added original material.

Building on the chronicle approach, Andrea da Barberino transformed the chivalric romance into pseudo-history. Above all, he recognized and made use of the development of historical consciousness, which was a key element of the Italian Renaissance.[38]

The broad meaning of "history" and the example of the medieval Italian chronicle encouraged Andrea da Barberino to cast his romances as histories. Like its Latin predecessor, the Renaissance Italian word *historia* or *istoria* meant a narrative of past events. But the events narrated might vary considerably. For the humanist historian Leonardo Bruni, *historia* meant a critical, interpretive, and sometimes patriotic account of past events in the life of a political unit, such as the city of Florence.[39] But *historia* could narrate legendary or imaginary events as well.[40] Indeed, the chronicle in the Middle Ages and Renaissance did not necessarily distinguish between legend and fact, and humanist historiography did not completely exorcise fabulous, imaginary, and/or supernatural events.[41]

Chivalric romances which mixed together historic figures and fictitious knights, natural events and magical occurrences could also be considered histories, and were natural fellow travelers of the medieval chronicle and humanist history. Giraldi Cinthio in his treatise on romances wrote "that the composition of the poet should be legendary, yet with material drawn from history. . . ."[42] Tommaso Garzoni (1549–89), the encyclopaedist, called chivalric romances "histories" long after Renaissance historians and theorists had discussed at length the nature of history. In his discourse on historians in *La piazza universale* (first ed. 1585), Garzoni named and commented briefly on a long list of historians and theoreticians of history from the ancient world (Polybius, Lucian, etc.), medieval times (Paulus Diaconus, etc.), and his own times (Flavio Biondo, Francesco Robortello, etc.). Toward the end of his discourse Garzoni noted the chivalric histories: "Others write merely fictitious histories, as those of the Reali di Francia, Morgana, Falerina, Margolana, Melusina, Amadis (di Gaula), Florando (i.e., Florindo), Tirante (lo Blanc), Florisello, Conamoro, Arturo, Lancilotto, and other similar ones."[43] Even if Garzoni had his tongue partly in his cheek, he numbered chivalric romances among Clio's brood. Indeed, numerous printings of chivalric romances were entitled "Historia:" *La historia di Florindo e Chiarastella, La historia del nascimento di Orlando,* etc.[44]

Andrea gave his works the appearance of history by introducing historical personages at appropriate dates. *I Reali di Francia* begins with the appearance of two significant historical actors, Emperor Constantine the Great and Pope Sylvester (314–335).[45] In the introduction of Book 3, Andrea informs the readers that this was the year 438 when Theodosius and Valentinian were Roman emperors and Felix the pope.[46] Indeed, Theodosius II ruled the eastern empire between 408 and 450, and Valentinian III ruled the west from 425 to 455, but the pope was St. Leo I (440–461), not St. Felix III (483–492). But chroniclers and humanist historians also made mistakes. Andrea tried to position his knights in history, rather than allowing them to drift in a vague mythical past.

Andrea da Barberino was also a man of the fifteenth century who absorbed some of the techniques of early Renaissance humanistic historiography. Following the example of ancient historical works, humanist historians employed set speeches in order to clarify the psychological motivations of historical actors. They regularly inserted such orations into the narrative just prior to a battle: the captain addressed his troops in order to explain the reasons for fighting and to urge them to victory. [47] Such speeches were not to be found in documentary sources and were, hence, fictional, but they clarified motivation and lent excitement to the narrative. Andrea da Barberino borrowed the technique, perhaps for the same reasons.

Midway through Book 1 of *I Reali di Francia,* the Christian forces are engaged in a desperate battle against the Saracens. On the morning of the fourth day of the battle, Fiovo, leader of the Christian army, delivers a long oration to his assembled troops. Most noble kings, princes, dukes, *signori,* fathers and brothers, he began. There are the things of this world and heavenly things; but certainly the most important in this life is good reputation *(buona fama).* He who does not love good fame does not love God. Although we are born naked and return naked to earth, our deeds remain. When the soul leaves the body, good reputation remains. Now we have been fighting for three days and many have fallen. We are certain that they are among the martyrs before God; and in this world they will always live in perpetual fame in the minds of those who will hear of their virtue. We must be ferocious in battle in order to win riches and glory. If you die, you will be rich, for what treasure is worth more than the glory of God upon falling in battle? And if you conquer and live, the captured treasure will be large. You are certain of two kinds of glory, that of God and worldly glory through perpetual fame. So, fight for your *patria.* Consider also, who will defend our sons, our women, and our aging fathers if we lose? We will be sold as slaves and tortured like beasts. Do not despair; God will give us victory. But you will not attain either the kingdom of heaven nor fame in this world without great effort. [48]

In this oration worthy of inclusion in a humanist history, fighting for eternal reward in heaven and for worldly aims receive equal emphasis. Indeed, the oration sees worldly glory as winning perpetual fame among men, a concept to be found in the writings of some Quattrocento humanists. [49] The speech also hints at the humanist ideal of action: one must perform deeds, such as defending the *patria* and defeating the Saracens, in order to win worldly fame and eternal rewards. Given his date of birth, it is not likely that Andrea da Barberino received a humanistic education, because Latin humanities schools did not become common until the 1430s and later. [50] The more plausible explanation is that he absorbed some of the humanistic approach through his Florentine environment. Mixing a bit of humanistic historiographical technique into a vernacular work of a different genre was not unique with him. Giovanni Cavalcanti (1381– c. 1451), a Florentine contemporary, injected some humanistic historiographical methodology into an essentially medieval vernacular treatise on virtues and vices which uncritically accepted medieval legends.[51]

Andrea da Barberino further manifested his assimilation of a humanistic mentality by his habit of inserting into his narrative *sententiae* (pithy aphoristic bits of universal wisdom) on fortune's role in determining the rise and fall of men and states. After setting the scene in the introductory chapter of *Aspramonte*, Andrea wrote ". . . many times it happens that a small spark ignites a great fire, and fortune through a small movement upsets the states of this world and pulls *signori* from great heights into the profound abyss."[52] Elsewhere he wrote: "Fortune, mover of states, works her course in many ways . . .; she germinates new travail for one who lives in the past."[53] And "Fortune in this world is a force that cannot be opposed."[54] Such *sententiae* on fortune would not have been out of place in the *ricordanze* of a Florentine merchant-statesman or in the missives of a humanist chancellor. Of course, Andrea da Barberino described the rise and fall of fictitious leaders and states.

Andrea's romances manifested a lay, secular tone much like Renaissance historiography and the Italian Renaissance generally. The fact that his heroes were good Christians, and that some Saracens embraced Christianity in his works, did not alter the dominant lay tone. Clergymen, except for fourth-century popes, played no role in his romances, which did not propagate any spiritual or ecclesiastical message. On the contrary, Andrea condemned the temporal power of the papacy. Writing in *I Reali di Francia*, Andrea noted that Emperor Constantine gave land to the church, possibly an allusion to the alleged Donation of Constantine. But, he continued, the emperor did not realize that the church's pastors would acquire temporal goods for their use and become "spiritual tyrants."[55] The statement reflected Florentine suspicion of the papacy's temporal power, and would be echoed by other Renaissance figures.

In similar fashion, Andrea's tales never tried to manifest the working out of God's plan on earth. Naturally, virtuous knights triumphed, while villains received their just deserts. But his romances displayed moral balance rather than supernatural design. Valor and skill at arms, rather than divine intervention, secured victory. Strange creatures, such as Pulicane, the half-dog, half-human, faithful companion and protector of Drusiana in *Buovo d'Antona*, appeared, but no miracles or divine signs.[56] Through these omissions Andrea's romances exhibited a more secular world view than some medieval chronicles. For example, challenging God and/or the church led to retribution in Giovanni Villani's chronicle; a cycle of historical events that included sinful deeds, omens, and portents restored God's rule.[57] God's punishment confirmed the spiritual significance of history for Villani, but not for Andrea da Barberino. Like all Italian chivalric romances, his works offered formal deference toward organized religion but lacked piety. Italian chivalric romances were secular works.

Andrea da Barberino gave the Carolingian romances a chronicle format and injected a little of the techniques of humanist historiography. The new habits of mind fostered by the *studia humanitatis* touched chivalric romances. But Andrea did not go further, e. g., to develop political themes. Chivalric romances were still tales of adventure in which battles, villanies, vengeances, escapes, journeys, chance encounters, duels, tournaments, loves, births, and deaths carried the story.

IV

An action-filled narrative involving attractive chief characters remained the center of chivalric romances. Concreteness of expression with domestic detail drawn from contemporary life further enhanced the popularity of Andrea da Barberino's romances. *Buovo d'Antona*, Book 4 of *I Reali di Francia*, but frequently copied or printed separately, was the best known and loved of his romances and, perhaps, of all the Italian romances before the *Orlando furioso*.[58] It is based on an original French version and found in a *Franco-veneta* version in Ms. Francese XIII of the Biblioteca Marciana. The story also appeared in other languages, becoming, for example, *Bevis of Hampton* in England.[59]

The story begins with the birth in Antona (i.e., Southampton, England) of Buovo, the son of Duke Guido (over sixty years of age) and Brandoria (about fourteen).[60] A faithful friend raises the infant Buovo in a village "with better air" about three miles distant

from Antona. Three wetnurses continuously available suckle him for
seven years. At the age of ten he returns to his pleased father who
hires a master to teach him to read.[61]

But all is not well in the household of Duke Guido. His
young wife is very unhappy because the aged Guido "has little love for
women," and seems reluctant to beget another son. Brandoria, vow-
ing not to lose any more time, sends a message to the son of a baron
whom Guido had killed. Through her scheming Guido is killed.
Brandoria marries his thirty-five-year-old murderer who takes
Guido's duchy. She then gives birth to a son, Gailone of Maganza, a
name taken from the line of archvillains who populate all the romances based on Carolingian matter. Brandoria tries to poison
Buovo, now eleven, but he escapes.

Although chivalric tradition dictated the hero's childhood
history, Buovo's early life reflected some of the circumstances and
fears of Renaissance society. Italian noble and middle-class families
often removed a child from the parental household and gave him
over to a wetnurse for two years and more. Buovo's father guarded
against the perpetual anxiety of Renaissance parents that the wetnurse would lose her milk and the baby go hungry by hiring three of
them.[62] A large age gap between elderly husband and very young
wife characterized many upperclass Florentine marriages in the fifteenth century. The majority of wealthy males did not marry until
their mid-thirties, some waited longer. Upper-class girls, on the other
hand, often became brides at fifteen and sometimes before.[63] Because
of this age difference, many Renaissance families were dissolved by
the death of the much older husband, although presumably not as a
result of murder instigated by his spouse. If, as in the case of Buovo,
the father died and the mother remarried and produced a new heir,
Italians worried that a child of the initial union would suffer. Brandoria's hostility to Buovo reflected the contemporary belief that a
remarried widow would abuse or steal the patrimony of the children
of the first marriage.[64] Andrea obviously exaggerated domestic details and fears for artistic effect; nevertheless, such grounding in
reality promoted audience identification with his imaginary characters.

Having escaped his homicidal mother, Buovo disguised and
denying his noble birth, is picked up by merchants. They take him to
Asia Minor where he is sold to the King of Armenia who makes him
into a servant. After five years of servitude, Buovo meets Drusiana,
the beautiful and vivacious daughter of the king, and the two fall in

love. That the daughter of the court should become enamoured with
the young hero from afar is a staple of chivalric romances that
authors handled in different ways. Andrea da Barberino turns it into
a charming story.

    After the stark drama of uxoricide and a mother who tries to
kill her own son, Andrea lightens the mood with the story of the two
lively teenagers, who are sixteen and fourteen, in one of the happiest
and artistically most successful interludes in the entire romance. Drusiana is spirited, bold, and very likeable, a delightful character. Buovo
is handsome and brave, but very shy. So she pursues him. She
arranges a dinner and dance, and orders Buovo (known as Agostino)
to serve. When the music begins, she takes him by the hand and leads
him to the dance. After two whirls, she asks him his story, and he tells
her a sad, fictitious tale that he is the son of a miller and a washer-
woman from far away. She cries, and he cries. But then they revert to
being playful teenagers: water is brought for washing before dinner,
and Drusiana throws a handful in Buovo's face! He reddens, but does
not retaliate. She taunts him: surely you are the son of a miller,
because when a girl throws water in your face, you don't throw back
the whole basinful.[65]

    Then follows a scene often noted by scholars. The members
of the party are seated at the table, with Buovo one of the attending
servants. Drusiana wants to kiss Buovo.

> "She let fall her knife, and then leaned over and showed that she
> could not reach it. She said, 'Agostino, get me that knife.'
> Buovo bent over, and when he was under the table, she said, 'Here
> it is!'
> And she grabbed him by the hair and the chin, and kissed him. She
> picked up the knife and stood up. Buovo emerged from under the
> table completely changed in color for shame, and Drusiana burning
> with love. . . ."[66]

    But they cannot marry yet. Drusiana's father, the king, and
his knights are taken in battle by Saracens. Buovo, armed by Drusiana, leads the rescue force. Before going into battle, Buovo reveals
his identity including the news that he is descended of Constantine,
and they plight their troth. Naturally, Buovo and his forces defeat a
giant and win the battle. He frees Drusiana's father who consents to
the marriage.

Further perils menace the pair. The defeated suitor for Drusiana plots against them. Through a ruse, he sends Buovo away to the area that is now Yugoslavia and Hungary where Buovo is captured and sentenced to be hanged. But he again attracts the eye of a princess, the daughter of Buovo's putative executioner. She begs her father to consign him into her hands so that she may torture him. Instead she confines him in a tower and offers Buovo his freedom if he will marry her. He remains faithful to Drusiana and accepts his fate, which is death by starvation. But every night the girl sends him food attached to the collar of a dog. He remains a prisoner for three years and four months.

Back in Armenia, the king after waiting two years for Buovo, promises Drusiana, now practically an old maid at sixteen, in marriage to another. She reluctantly consents, but only if the suitor will wait another year for consummation. As the day nears when she must be delivered to the marriage bed, Buovo escapes the tower and rushes to the rescue. Disguised as a pilgrim, he arrives and begs her to flee with him. But Drusiana fails to recognize him. (Protagonists of chivalric romances frequently fail to recognize each other after lengthy absences, as improbable as it seems.) Then he uncovers the birthmark on his right shoulder borne by all members of the French royal line, shows her his sword, and the ring given him by Drusiana. She is overjoyed; together they drug the man to whom she is promised and make their escape.

In the course of their escape, Buovo fights and kills various soldiers and guards, the secondary thugs whose bodies litter adventure stories of all centuries. Buovo and Drusiana consummate their marriage and the story plunges forward. The love interest recedes for many chapters while Buovo fights battles and either he or Drusiana escape dire perils. Andrea continues to insert homely domestic details to promote audience identification. Buovo and Drusiana escape by horseback through the forest—forests seem endless in chivalric romances—even though poor Drusiana is eight months and fifteen days pregnant. The author interrupts to speak directly to his audience: oh think how miserable the poor girl was!"[67] Before long she gives birth to masculine twins. (The frequency of masculine twins in chivalric romances defies statistical probability.) Eventually Buovo returns to claim his duchy and succeeds in a great battle against overwhelming odds. He kills his stepfather in battle. Buovo will not kill his mother, but does insist that King Pepin condemn her to death.

She accepts her guilt, repents, and urges her second son, Gailone, to be a loyal subject to Buovo. She is then quartered, possibly after being first executed by other means, although the text is not specific.[68] Chivalric romances did not spare women cruel punishment for heinous crimes.

After many additional perils are surmounted, Buovo, Drusiana, and their two sons are united in Antona, only this time it is Buovo who is rescued from a second marriage in the nick of time and initially does not recognize his wife and sons. For the reunion Andrea constructs a light-hearted scene full of embarassment and laughter.[69] After this interlude, many more adventures follow. Buovo sails up and down the Mediterranean, coming to the rescue of old comrades in arms with his special sword. His super horse Rondello carries him to victory, even when over twenty-five years old. Between adventures, Drusiana gives birth to eleven children. Buovo and Drusiana become grandparents and grow old gracefully.

The author prepares for the end of his saga. Gailone, Buovo's half brother, is taunted by evildoers for failing to avenge the death of his father. He plots to kill Buovo by sneaking up on him while Buovo kneels in prayer in a small country chapel. Andrea describes the foul deed in precise, pedantic detail: Gailone plunges his very sharp knife into the nape of the neck and through the throat in such a way that Buovo cannot cry out. "And so died Buovo d'Antona, flower of the knights of the world in his time."[70] Gailone escapes to the Sultan of Babylonia where he denies God and tramples on the cross. Drusiana comes upon the body of Buovo and expires of grief. With this ends the story of Buovo d'Antona, Book 4 of *I Reali di Francia*—but not before the stage is set for the next saga.

Overall, Andrea da Barberino wrote a quickly-paced action narrative. Like a good historian, he excluded extraneous details. He did not pause to describe the scenery in new lands or to develop minor characters. When he did pause to expand the narrative, e. g., for the charming and innocent interludes of love or reunion inserted periodically to relieve the tension of battles, he drew his readers in. The author telegraphed the approach of these scenes in order to prepare the audience and to create a bond of complicity between author and audience. Contemporary details and concreteness of expression, a noted Renaissance characteristic, permeated the romance.[71] They seemed to reflect the merchant's realistic perception of the world. Indeed, Andrea portayed merchants constantly sailing up and down the Mediterranean, an accurate picture of some of them.

Buovo d'Antona and the other Italian romances based on Carolingian material generally manifested a different attitude toward love and fidelity than those based on Arthurian material. Love relationships were as important as battles and duels in the latter. Illicit love created great tension and served as catalyst for action; Tristano and Lancilotto simultaneously cuckolded and served Kings Marco and Artù. In similar fashion, Marco is torn between hatred and admiration for Tristano. The conflict between honor and love provided much of the interlacing and gave the author room for comments on the effects of passion. But Buovo d'Antona and the Carolingian romances pursued different paths. The adventures and combats of a knight struggling to regain his patrimony, pursuing a villain, or fighting Saracens dominated; the love interest took second place. In Andrea da Barberino's Guerrin Meschino, a somewhat extreme case, the love interest scarcely mattered. Carolingian romances were "books of battles," not books of amours.

Even more important, Andrea da Barberino's characters, and Carolingian heroes and heroines generally, remained faithful lovers who honored their marriage vows. They lived up to the ideals that the Renaissance bourgeoisie proclaimed for themselves: loyalty to family, patria, and religion.[72] Virtue prevailed—after a little audience titillation. The story of Berta the Big Foot ("Berta del gran piede," whose right foot was larger than the left) illustrates the point.[73] Promised in marriage to King Pepin the Short (714?–768), she was displaced by a double on her wedding night, taken to the forest, and left to die. A kindly hunter rescued her and took her into his home. She, in turn, taught the hunter's daughters to embroider so well that the family became rich through the sales of their handiwork within five years.[74] Surely the middle-class audience applauded a noble lady with such a useful, financially rewarding skill. Then as kings were wont to do in romances, King Pepin came to the hunter's cottage. Smitten by Berta's beauty, but failing to recognize her, Pepin invites her to spend the night with him. To the horror and disgust of the good hunter and his wife, she accepts the royal offer. The hunter and his wife call her a common prostitute; their objections underscored the honorable sexual code of the Carolingian romances that Berta seemed about to violate. The author built up the erotic anticipation through a conversation between Pepin and Berta, and a description of the luxurious bed prepared for them on the bank of a

stream. The audience knew that she was a "good girl," but could savor
the titillation. When evening comes, Berta goes to Pepin and reveals
her identity. He looks at her large foot (how could he have failed to
notice the oversized extremity before?) and believes her. He asks if
she is a virgin (she is), and then "according to human nature used
matrimony. And that night she conceived a son," Charlemagne.[75]
Virtue triumphed, as the audience hoped it would, after some teas-
ing. But Pepin's behavior, on which the author did not comment,
seemed to confirm the existence of a double standard as well. However, he was a king, not a princess or a merchant. He had been deceived
on his wedding night and was now united with his lawful bride.
Trickery in the conjugal bed was a staple of some literary genres,
especially in *novelle;* authors form Boccaccio onward handled it with a
wink and a leer.[76] Here the episode manifested an innocent air.

However, a great deal of killing countered the light-hearted
scenes in *I Reali di Francia.* The romances featured so many battles
that the public called them "books of battles."[77] Further, the descriptive titles of many printings mentioned battles.[78] Heroic combats did
not oppress, but set pulses to racing. But the assassinations, the quick
and savage quarrels, and the casual slaying of servants, added an
ominous air. Nevertheless, the violence and vendettas found in all
chivalric romances mirrored and accentuated Italian reality. Communal governments had attempted to curtail noble violence by various draconian legal means, such as the famous Ordinances of Justice
in Florence at the end of the thirteenth century, but the vendetta lived
on.[79] Violence lurked jut beneath the surface and sometimes
erupted.[80] Since Renaissance Italy had not fully shed its belief in
vendetta nor the habit of violence, they lived on in the chivalric
romance.

The stern judicial punishments meted out to evildoers produced a more oppressive air than the fighting. The romances implicitly argued that mercy was an ill-conceived policy yielding bitter
fruit; stern justice was preferable. The guilty invariably paid a cruel
price; male and female villains were decapitated, burnt, or quartered
alive. Even innocent children were threatened with horrible ex-
ecutions.[81] Those with the power of life and death over others, such
as the hero who has vanquished the traitor, habitually argued for the
death penalty, especially if the melefactor was a near relative. When
the hero granted mercy, the spared villain usually repaid leniency
with vengeance. Fictitious chivalric societies mirrored the stern
penalties written into Renaissance judicial codes; murder, treason,

robbery, and sodomy earned death through hanging, decapitation, or burning, according to the laws of Italian city-states.[82] In reality, however, Italian Renaissance courts often, perhaps in the majority of cases, tempered justice with mercy and imposed lighter penalties. Not so in the chivalric romances. Andrea da Barberino and other chivalric authors imposed the full cruelty of the law on evildoers.[83]

V

Antiquity provided the third source for Italian chivalric romances. The tales of antiquity probably never completely disappeared in Italy after the disintegration of Roman authority. Various towns, especially in northeastern Italy, boasted civic legends claiming that survivors of Troy had founded them. Classical and early medieval sources, especially Ovid's *The Metamorphoses*, spread classical mythological lore which unknown authors reworked into romances. Chivalric romances based on antiquity came third numerically and in importance to Italians.

The stories and heros of Troy were the best-known and most numerous of the classical romances. The Sicilian poet Guido delle Colonne of Messina (flourished 1242–87) wrote the *Istorietta Troiana*, the most important medieval vehicle of this tradition. Based on earlier Latin and French versions of "the matter of Troy," it carried the Troy romance into the Renaissance.[84] Domenico da Montechiello, about whom nothing is known, retold the story, and added material from other Troy versions, in his *Libro di Troiana* in the fifteenth century.[85] First printed in Florence, 1491, and reprinted several times in the sixteenth and seventeenth centuries, the *Libro del Troiana* was written in mediocre *ottava rima* and mixed in material from other romances.[86]

The *Libro del Troiano* begins with the story of Jason and Medea, but soon goes further.[87] Jason and Achilles are the sons of kings. Just before his death, Jason's father commends him to his brother king, but the latter, hoping for his demise, sends Jason in quest of the golden fleece. In the course of his search Jason meets and falls in love with Medea. She agrees to help him, they consummate their love, and Jason promises to marry her. He obtains the golden fleece, but marries another. She takes her revenge by murdering her children by Jason. But the sprawling romance also includes tales of Hector, Paris, Helen, Achilles and his loves, the siege of Troy, and other Greek legends. Even more important, these figures from classi

cal mythology take on the coloration of, and behave like, the knights
and ladies of the Arthurian and Carolingian romances. Indeed, the
Greek heroes become *baroni* in the *Libro del Troiano*.

Other romances based on classical material included the
Storie d'Enea which adds new material to Vergil's epic, *Li fatti di Cesare*
which took advantage of the medieval fascination with Julius Caesar,
Lucrezia Romana which retold the story found in Livy and Ovid of the
Roman matron who kills herself after having been violated, the
Babylonian lovers *Piramo e Tisbe* (which had numerous printings), and
others.[88] In contrast to the sprawling Carolingian and Arthurian
romances, several of the classical romances narrated only one story.
These relatively short romances tended to focus on an episode in
which a protagonist suppressed natural human emotions for the sake
of a cruelly appropriate revenge. When described against a very
distant and mythological background of Greek gods and goddesses,
such savagery might seem unreal. But when set within a more familiar
setting, the episodes are horrific. And as in the Arthurian and Carolingian romances, the settings and chief characters of the classical
romances were domesticated, with the help of some anachronism.
Piramo and Tisbe behaved much like Italian youths of the Tre- and
Quattrocento, and Hector received "the Holy Sacrament" before going into battle.[89] While important, the classically-based romances
were less numerous and enjoyed less popularity than the Arthurian
and Carolingian romances.

VI

The High Renaissance (c. 1450–1600) produced three significant changes for chivalric romances. First, various poets, most of
them anonymous, reworked the prose romances into lengthy *ottava
rima* poems. Buovo d'Antona and other traditional heroes now fought
and loved in heroic stanzas of eight lines with an ABABABCC rhyme
scheme. Since the invention of printing followed shortly, the majority
of surviving printings of Italian chivalric romances are *ottava rima*
rather than prose versions. However, they retained their original
character and spirit.

Next, learned poets from north Italian courts seized on the
chivalric genre to create self-conscious literary versions of a different
mood. Luigi Pulci (1432–84), from a Florentine noble family fallen on
hard times, wrote *Morgante* (definitive edition 1483). On one hand
Pulci retold the heroic deeds of Orlando and other knights loyal to

Charlemagne. But he also introduced two comic figures of his own invention, Morgante the giant and Margutte the half-giant, who burlesqued chivalric ideals through their boasts and deeds. Pulci skilfully combined high tragedy and low comedy.[90] Then Count Matteo Maria Boiardo (1441–94), a noble administrator for the Este princes, wrote *Orlando innamorato*, left unfinished at his death. In the poem Angelica exerted a magical attraction on Charlemagne's knights who all pursued her. Boiardo used the Carolingian material plus his own inventiveness in order to tell an elaborate adventure story full of impossible loves, great battles, enchantments, and stories within a story. In a long, complex poem full of variety, Boiardo entertained while genuinely celebrating aristocratic ideals.

Ludovico Ariosto (1474–1533), nobleman and faithful courtier of the Este family of Ferrara, followed with *Orlando furioso* (1516, revised edition 1532). Picking up the story where Boiardo left it, Ariosto introduced Orlando who lost his senses through love. The poem pursued the courtship of Ruggiero and Bradamante, the madness of Orlando, the war between Charlemagne and the infidel Agramante, as well as lesser stories. *Orlando furioso* functioned on two levels. Like its traditional predecessors, it narrated an action story of combats and loves, warriors and ladies, and conflict between good and evil. Readers could enjoy the work on this level. But ambiguity and chance clouded the message: chivalric ideals collided with the less courteous reality, and irony permeated the work. Things were not what they seemed, as Ariosto frequently upended the tradition with amusing or disturbing results.[91] Ariosto also consciously invoked the classical epic, especially that of Vergil. *Orlando furioso* functioned as a traditional romance, a "book of battles" for a popular audience, while simultaneously betraying the genre.

Orlando furioso achieved an enormous popular and critical success, possibly greater than that of any other Italian poetic work of the late Middle Ages and Renaissance. Contemporary observers stressed that all classes and occupations read the work.[92] It may have been the most often printed work of secular vernacular literature in sixteenth-century Italy. From the first edition of 1516 through mid-century, about seventy printings appeared; by the end of the century, over 150, perhaps as many as 183 printings appeared.[93] Neither Dante's *Commedia* nor Petrarch's *Canzoniere* attained a similar level of quantitative success in the Renaissance.

The enormous popular success of *Orlando furioso* stimulated a critical appraisal of chivalric poetry by the learned. Beginning in

1549 and continuing through the rest of the century and beyond, numerous Italian literary theorists subjected Ariosto's great poem and the genre of the verse romance more generally, to the tests of Aristotelian poetical theory. Critics objected that Ariosto violated Aristotle's canon that a work should have a single plot; indeed, all romances had diverse stories and many characters. Moreover, Ariosto's improbable and marvelous events failed the Aristotelian test of verisimilitude. In reply, Ariosto's defenders broadened or reinterpreted Aristotelian dicta and developed new canons in order to permit *Orlando furioso* to sneak into the pantheon of great poems.[94]

Other writers honored Ariosto by hastening to write new romances that tried to imitate *Orlando furioso* and, to a lesser extent, Boiardo's poem. A series of ottava rima romances with "Orlando," "Rinaldo," "innamorato," or "innamoramento" in their titles appeared in the first three decades of the sixteenth century.[95] The process continued, but only a few titles can be mentioned here. Bernardo Tasso published *L'Amadigi* in 1560, while Ludovico Dolce (1508–68) wrote four romances: *Sacripante* (1535–36) which continued *Orlando furioso*, *Palmerino* (1561) and *Primaleone, figliuolo di Palmerino* (1562), both reworkings of Spanish romances, and the more original *Le prime imprese del Conte Orlando* (published 1572) whose story attempted to provide the antecedents to both Boiardo's *Orlando innamorato* and Ariosto's work.[96] The vernacular presses of Venice brought them all to the public in inexpensive editions. But only the works of Torquato Tasso (1544–95) offered a serious challenge to the critical acclaim of *Orlando furioso* and the popularity of the older romances.

Third, Spanish romances, like Spanish soldiers and viceroys, invaded Italy. Italian translations and continuations of the Spanish *Amadis de Gaula* rivalled the popular, but not the critical, success of *Orlando furioso*. Garci Rodriguez de Montalvo, about whom little is known, published in Saragossa, 1508, the first surviving edition of *Amadis de Gaula,* an expanded and rewritten version of material circulating in Spain since the fourteenth century. The first three books clearly derived from earlier French Arthurian matter. Amadis (which means "ill-timed") was the issue of a secret union between the King of Gaul and Princess Elisena.[97] She concealed the birth of her son and launched him on a stream and out to sea. Rescued, the baby Amadis was taken to the British Isles where he grew up and met the Princess Oriana to whom he vowed eternal love. After many adventures, Amadis and Oriana were united in another clandestine mar-

riage and produced a son, Esplandian, whose birth was concealed. He
became the hero of the sequel to *Amadis de Gaula.* And so on and so
forth. The work met with such successs that many continuations and
offshoots followed. Spanish printings of the original appeared in Italy
in 1519 if not earlier.[98] Italian translations began to appear in the
1540s. Mambrino Roseo da Fabriano (c. 1500–c. 1584), the major
Italian translator, and others soon created original Italian sequels.[99]
Amadis de Gaula enjoyed enormous success in Italy: 184 printings of
twenty-four different Italian *Amadis* romances (translations and original sequels) appeared between 1544 and 1630.[100]

　　　　Amadis de Gaula differed in a number of ways from the older
Italian romances of Andrea da Barberino and other *cantastorie.* The
former had more loves, many more enchantments and acts of magic,
but fewer battles than Italian Carolingian romances. Indeed, additional women appeared in the Amadis romances, while men and
women talked to each other about love more often. Although the
Amadis romances avoided the adulterous loves of Tristano and Isotta,
Lancilotto and Ginevara, the heroes and heroines were less chaste and
faithful than those found in *I Reali di Francia.* Most revealing of the
new times of the sixteenth century was the elevation of monarchy and
religion to new heights of importance. The *Amadis* romances un-
questionably celebrated kingship and aristocratic values, whereas
Charlemagne's monarchy existed mostly as background in Italian
Carolingian romances.[101] Numerous references to God's will, the
Virgin Mary, churchmen, sacraments, and hearing mass emphasized
the renewed, orthodox piety characteristic of sixteenth-century Spain
and Italy.[102] The Italian *Amadis de Gaula* romances offered readers
perfumed magic and an atmosphere somewhat different than that
found in the traditional Italian romances.

　　　　Neither Ariosto's masterpiece nor Spanish invaders drove
traditional Italian chivalric romances, whether good or bad, from the
field. *Altobello*, which lacked an orderly plot, developed characters,
genealogical order, and geographical precision, typified the mediocre
romances. It first appeared in fourteenth-century Tuscany, but little
more is known. The titlepage of a 1547 printing in *ottava rima* proclaimed it to be a book of battles featuring the barons of France and
the "daring and stalwart young Altobello."[103] Altobello can be translated as "Tall and Handsome;" the chief object of his affection was,
naturally, Aldabella. The basic story is that of the brothers Altobello
and Re Troiano, two Muslim princes who come to France to attack

Charlemagne. But the romance alternates between the adventures of Altobello, who becomes a Christian, and Charlemagne's knights, Orlando and Rinaldo, in no easily discernible order. A bewildering succession of battles enable the work to live up to its titlepage promises. The love interludes offered an analogous series of copulations also lacking coherence. Valerano, a Saracen king lusted for the beautiful fifteen-year-old Queen Fiordispina, who chose to sleep with Rinaldo and later married Troiano. Aldabella, although married to Altobello, spent the night with Orlando. And so on; the major figures behaved much like the characters in a late-twentieth-century soap opera. Meanwhile, the battles continued. The story need not be, perhaps cannot be, summarized. Although a twentieth-century observer can find little coherence or literary quality in the work, Renaissance publishers issued the work and readers presumably read it. Six incunabular editions plus at least six sixteenth-century printings are known.[104] As always, the known surviving printings may be only part of those issued.

VII

Chivalric romances resonated throughout Italian society. Contemporary references to them invariably demonstrated their deep penetration into the fabric of life, not least through the numerous chivalric titles mentioned.

Because chivalric romances portrayed a feudal society led by heroes and heroines of noble blood, it might be assumed that members of the upper classes were the primary intended audience in the Renaissance. Occasionally a scholar concludes that this is the case, or that a resurgence of interest in aristocratic ways made the romances popular.[105] It is much more likely that the reading and listening audience transcended class boundaries and exhibited a variety of reading tastes of which the romance was one. That is, Renaissance readers of vernacular literature included the men, and to a much smaller extent the women, of the professions, nobility, wealthy merchant class, shopkeepers and artisans, and the poor working classes, probably in that order. For its non-learned vernacular reading, the public had several different sacred and secular choices: saints' lives and legends, *novelle*, popular history, sermons and meditational literature, classics in translation, and chivalric romances. The last clearly enjoyed a privileged position in this literary cafeteria.

Anton Francesco Doni (1513–74), a popular author and
one-time publisher, made this point in a free-wheeling dialogue on
good and bad books in his *I Marmi* (1552–53) set in Florence. Borgo,
the first speaker, says that he is one of those who prefers to buy and
read *Buovo d'Antona* rather than Aristotle's *Poetics*, Seneca's *Epistles*, or
a treatise on the art of dying well, all in the vernacular. My profession
is fighting, not that of watchman for a company like you. You have
the *Prediche sopra Amos* (of Savonarola) in your hand, because you
prattle on about the love of God. I prefer the *Furioso* because I go
jousting on the first of May to entertain the people.[106]

Chivalric romances also appealed to women, or so a female
author argued. Tullia d'Aragona (1508–56), daughter of a famous
Roman courtesan and an unknown father, perhaps Cardinal Luigi
d'Aragona of the Neapolitan royal house, followed her mother's
profession. She became the friend and/or lover of several important
literary figures and also wrote poetry and a dialogue on love.[107] She
prepared an *ottava rima* version of Andrea da Barberino's *Guerrin
Meschino* which was published posthumously in 1560. In her preface,
Tullia d'Aragona praised reading for its own sake. In contrast to
other Renaissance discussions endorsing reading as a means of building character, she approved reading for pleasure: nothing is so delightful and honest as reading something light and pleasing. All other
pastimes—walking about, games, and amours—involve difficulties.
But we can arrange our reading completely to our satisfaction without
expense or travail. Books are the perfect solace for every man and
especially for every woman.[108]

But books such as Boccaccio's *Decameron* and Pietro Aretino's
I ragionamenti are morally unsuitable for both women and men. Readers prefer poetry but even here difficulties exist. Chivalric poems
such as *Il Morgante* (of Pulci), *Ancroia*, "Innamorati d'Orlando" (possibly Boiardo's *Orlando innamorato*), *Buovo d'Antona*, *Leandra*, *Mambriano*, and even Ariosto's work contain lewd, dishonest, and un-
worthy things making them inappropriate for nuns, maidens,
widows, wives, and "public women," ("donne publiche"), possibly an
oblique reference to her own status. Having searched for a good
romance, she has found this one. It is completely chaste, pure, and
Christian in its examples and words. It can be read by every honorable man and every married woman, virgin, widow, or nun. Its author
has written with grace and sweetness, pleasure and delight. But be-

cause it lacks the perfection of poetry, she has rendered it into verse, not into learned poetry but the "middle way" of facility and grace found in Pulci, Boiardo, and the *Mambriano*. Rather than following the language of one province, she will employ the Italian spoken by judicious persons throughout the peninsula.[109]

She concluded with a brief promotional description of the work's contents (here paraphrased). *Guerrin Meschino* presents a circuit of almost the whole world. It is full of pious charity, long exiles, incomparable acts of chivalry, extraordinary tests of combat, glorious virtues, inviolate love, and highest faith. Guerrin visits the heights of the sun and descends into the cave of the sibyl where he sees the torments of hell and the glory of paradise. Many other notable things in the book give delight and pleasure.[110] It was not a bad description of the contents.

Tullia d'Aragona made several points that explained the popularity of chivalric romances. To begin, both sexes read them.[111] Second, her argument that reading was one of the supreme pleasures of life, plus her search to find a delightful but chaste romance, made the obvious point that Italians read romances for pleasure and escape. She implied that readers paid little attention to the characters' morals, but concentrated on their travels to faraway lands, the exciting battles, and the love stories. She noted that readers preferred to follow the adventures of knights and ladies in ottava rima rather than in prose. Possibly the great turn from prose to poetry in the second half of the fifteenth century occurred simply as a result of reader preference. Finally, she suggested that readers liked all chivalric romances indiscriminately. She did not distinguish between the high artistry of *Orlando furioso* and the mediocrity of some of the others. Like her times, she saw them as a genre.

Chivalric romances frequently appeared in the inventories of private libraries. A census of Florentine private libraries of the fifteenth and sixteenth centuries uncovered numerous chivalric romances. Most often inventories listed chivalric romances in generic terms: "il libro di chantari" or "dicie de' fatti d'un chavaliere.[112] But sometimes the inventories listed specific titles, notably the works of Andrea da Barberino and, later, *Orlando furioso*.[113]

With the advent of printing, the publishing format securely identified chivalric romances as part of Renaissance popular culture. Literary genres and titles inherited from the late Middle Ages and

intended for popular consumption assumed a distinctive physical
appearance in print. Such books as saints' lives and chivalric romances
were often published in small formats, either 15 x 10 cm. (16° according to descriptive bibliography standards) or about 20 x 15 cm. (12°).
Such texts were printed in double columns in a semi-gothic or roman
type through the middle of the sixteenth century, long after the vast
majority of vernacular texts, especially new works, and many Latin
books appeared in italic type in Italy.[114] The addition of small wood-
cuts and numerous typographical errors further identified chivalric
romances as works of popular diffusion, because printers set type
quickly and carelessly when sales were assured. Certain publishers
specialized in works of popular vernacular culture, including chivalric
romances, especially the firm of Francesco Bindoni and Maffeo Pasini
in Venice (active 1524 through 1551) and the Meda family of printers
(I fratelli da Meda, Valerio da Meda, or Valerio e fratelli) in Milan
(active c. 1550 through c. 1580.

　　By the middle of the sixteenth century, Italians had a very
large selection of romances from which to choose. Anton Francesco
Doni in his *La libraria* (1550), the first bibliography of Italian vernacular authors and works, listed fifty-three of them: *Ancroia
Regina*[115], *Altobello, Antifor di Barosia*[116], *Buovo d'Antona, Falconetto*[117],
etc. He included the well-known *Orlando furioso,* Boiardo's *Orlando
innamorato,* Pulci's *Morgante,* and some romances now forgotten and
difficult to identify.[118] Elsewhere Doni listed eight Italian translations
or imitations of Spanish romances.[119]

　　A famous parody of chivalric romances hinted at another
reason for their popularity: schoolboys read romances instead of
assigned schooltexts. The restless macaronic poet Teofilo Folengo
(1491–1544) wrote two mock romances, *Orlandino* in Italian (written
before *Baldus,* not published until 1526) and his masterpiece *Baldus*
(first edition 1517). Folengo wrote *Baldus* in macaronic Latin, a free,
comic Latin incorporating newly coined onomatopoeic words and
Italian stems with Latin suffixes. In an early scene, little Baldus went
off to school and made excellent progress. In three years' time he
could read any book and recite Vergil by heart. Chivalric romances
inspired this description of Baldus' rapid academic progress, for the
heroic knights invariably learned quickly and well. For example,
Ajolfo del Barbicone learned fencing and a good deal of Latin in less
than six months.[120] Meschino learned Greek, Latin, Turkish, and
"many languages useful for trade and navigation."[121] But then little

Baldus began to read chivalric romances: *Ancroia, Trabisonda,*[122] *Danese Ugieri,*[123]*Buovo d'Antona, Antifor di Barosia, I Reali di Francia, L'Innamoramento di Carlo Magno,*[124] *Aspramonte, La Spagna,*[125] *Altobello,* Pulci's *Morgante, Guerrin Meschino, Valentino et Orsone,*[126] *Leandra* (attributed to Pietro Durante da Gualdo),[127] *Orlando innamorato,* and *Orlando furioso.*[128] Orlando and Rinaldo so intoxicated Baldus that he pummelled his teachers, wrecked the schoolroom, and ran away to become a knight. In the rest of the book, as in his *Orlandino,* Folengo parodied chivalric romances and voiced social criticism of his own times through Baldus' gross adventures.[129]

Later in the sixteenth century, the censorious encyclopaedist Tommaso Garzoni described schoolboys reading Ariosto instead of assigned texts. In a discourse on teachers and schools, Garzoni noted that schoolboys recited Ariosto rather than the *Epistles* of Ovid. Then they ran out of school like devils unleashed, Garzoni concluded.[130]

Folengo and Garzoni, churchmen who probably attended Latin schools, may not have realized that *Orlando furioso* and other chivalric romances were an important part of the syllabus in vernacular schools that trained boys for the world of work. At least thirteen Venetian teachers operating schools with a vernacular literature and abbaco (commercial mathematics) curriculum stated in 1587 and 1588 that they taught chivalric romances: *Buovo d'Antona, Orlando furioso,* "a book of the wars of Troy," and, most frequently, "books of battles" ("libri di batagia").[131] One teacher explained that he taught these books to satisfy the parents. The pupils "bring to school books of battles, the *Orlando furioso,* and similar books." "I teach to the satisfaction of the fathers," he concluded.[132] In other words, chivalric romances were such an entrenched part of cultural life that if teachers omitted them, parents sent their boys off to school with the books demanding that they be taught.

Much other evidence documents the deep penetration of chivalric romances into ordinary life. Italian maiolica portrayed heroes and scenes from chivalric tales.[133] And parents named their children for mythical knights and ladies. One ironical example will have to suffice for many. Lancellotto Politi (1484–1553), a Sienese nobleman, took a law degree at Siena in 1502 and taught at the university there under his given chivalric name. He then underwent a religious experience which caused him to join the Dominican Order in 1517 and to change his name to Ambrogio Catarino. Under the latter name he wrote a series of anti-Protestant polemical works.[134]

As might be expected, a few churchmen took a dim view of
chivalric romances. St. Antoninus (Antonio Pierozzi, 1389–1459),
archbishop of Florence from 1446, made a slighting remark about
them in the preface to his instructional book for priests. It would not
hurt laymen also to read our little book, he wrote. It would be more
beneficial for their salvation than reading Dante, the *Decameron* or
Corbaccio of Boccaccio, or "poems about paladins."[135]

St. Antoninus did not condemn chivalric romances, but some
Counter Reformation churchmen did. Antonio Possevino (1533–
1611), famed Jesuit diplomat, scholar, and controversalist, charged
that the *Amadis de Gaula* "and other such books" diminished piety, and
opened the door to magic, the occult, and even to heresy. They were
Satan's stratagems to tempt men: they appealed to the lower passions
of anger, covetousness, "foolhardy strength," and libidinous desire.
He denounced by name *Lancellotto del lago, Parsaforesto, Tristano,
Girone il Cortese, Primaleone,* and "Ariosto's poem."[136] Gian Pietro
Giussani (1540–1615), priest, scholar, and the first biographer of
Carlo Borromeo, wrote a broad educational treatise telling fathers
how they might oversee the spiritual welfare of their families. Sons
over fourteen or fifteen were a special concern. Parents should provide them with good spiritual literature and forbid "those books full
of dreams, such as the *Amadis de Gaula, Palmerino,* and similar books
written by ministers of the devil in order to waste time and induce a
thousand dishonest thoughts and sins into unhappy youths."[137] Both
Possevino and Giussano condemned Arthurian and/or Amadigian
romances but not the more popular and morally less objectionable
Italian Carolingian romances.

Yet, St. Antoninus, Possevino, and Giussani were exceptions.
The vast majority of Renaissance and Counter Reformation preachers and moralists seem to have ignored chivalric romances.[138] They
did not condemn the romances even though some heroes and
heroines fornicated and committed acts of adultery, murder, and
cruel violence. St. Antoninus and Possevino grouped romances with
Boccaccio's *Decameron* and *Corbaccio,* his scurrilous, misogynistic por-
trait of an unfaithful woman who read French romances instead of
praying. Most moralists and even the papal *Indices librorum pro-
hibitorum* distinguished between other fiction considered morally
objectionable and chivalric romances. Various papal *Indices* banned or
ordered expurgated the *Decameron* and much of the *novelle* literature,
but ignored chivalric romances. The vast majority of churchmen

probably considered them innocuous or such an integral part of Italian life that condemning them would provoke intense opposition from all sides.

VIII

Although chivalric romances came from abroad, Italians embraced them as enthusiastically as any other Europeans. Of the three sources of chivalric tales, Italians preferred Carolingian romances by a wide margin. Readers living in the urban commercial society of the Italian city-states vicariously enjoyed the adventures of Buovo and Drusiana who lived and loved in a distant feudal world. At the same time, Italian *cantastorie* showed considerable skill in adapting the stories. While retaining plots, characters, and most of the conventions of medieval French chivalric romances, Italian authors made them conform to their own world through modifications in attitude and detail. The best of the Italian romances exhibited freshness of spirit and concreteness of expression, and borrowed homely details from contemporary life. Above all, Italian *cantastorie* treated romances as works of history. That is, authors described chivalric heroes and heroines as historical personages who lived, acted, and died on precise dates, within a chronological framework, and in actual geographical places. The broad and multiple definitions of history current in the Italian Renaissance encouraged this tendency. While definitely a product of medieval vernacular culture, the chivalric romances also absorbed a little of the techniques of Latin humanistic historiography. The romances were lay and secular in tone: divine events and ecclesiastical persons played little role.

Numerous references document that romances appealed to a broad range of the literate and illiterate public. The sophisticated courtier read them, the *popolo* gathered around the minstrel in the piazza. The habit of reading aloud practiced by both high and low enabled listeners in the home, shop, or court to follow the adventures and amours of chivalric heroes. With the advent of printing, romances may have become even more popular. Fifty or more Italian romances (some of them partial versions of larger works), plus translations, variations, and continuations of Spanish romances, circulated in printed form in the sixteenth century. Romances were even read as part of the curriculum of vernacular schools. Learned poets as Pulci, Boiardo, and especially Ariosto, created literary classics out of

chivalric material. Nevertheless, Renaissance Italians did not read
Orlando furioso as a canonical work of literature, but as one title in a
popular genre. Despite the fact that the heroes and heroines of
chivalric romances sometimes violated Christian sexual and marital
ethics, few churchmen tried to ban or discourage the reading of
chivalric romances. Men and women of all classes read and enjoyed
chivalric romances because they provided such excellent entertainment.

NOTES

[1] I wish to thank David Quint and an anonymous reader for their helpful suggestions. The Guggenheim Foundation and the Social Sciences and Humanities Research Council of Canada provided financial support for the research and writing
of this paper done inter alia over several years. Appointment as Visiting Associate at
the Center for Advanced Study of the University of Illinois at Urbana-Champaign
made it easier to use that institution's splendid library during the academic year
1979–80.

[2] Led by Pio Rajna, scholars of the late nineteenth and early twentieth century
pioneered the study of Italian chivalric romances. But then romances languished,
as literary scholars turned to *i maggiori*, major authors of greater literary merit.
Scholars won attention and academic posts by publishing studies on two or three
major figures drawn from different centuries, not by focussing on a genre. Fortu-
nately, a modest revival of interest has occurred in recent years, producing some
excellent studies and anthologies, many of which will be noted in this article. But
much remains to be done; critical editions and bibliographies of manuscripts and
printed editions are especially needed. In addition to the studies and editions listed
in the following pages, I would like to mention here a handful of other works that
have been useful. Giulio Ferrario, *Storia ed analisi degli antichi romanzi di cavalleria e
dei poemi romanzeschi d'Italia*. 4 vols. (Milan, 1828–1829). Francesco Foffano, "Il
l'Amadigi di Gaula' di Bernardo Tasso," *Giornale storico della letteratura italiana*, 25
(1895), 249–310; and *Il poema cavalleresco* (Milan, 1904). Luigi Russo, "La letteratura
cavalleresca dal 'Tristano' ai 'Reali di Francia,'" *Belfagor*, 6 (1951), 40–59. Carlo
Dionisotti, "Appunti su antichi testi," *Italia medioevale e umanistica*, 7 (1964), 77–131.
Domenico De Robertis, "Cantari antichi," *Studi di filologia italiana*, 28 (1970), 67–
175. Daniela Delcorno Branca, *L'Orlando furioso e il romanzo cavalleresco medievale*
(Florence, 1973). *I cantari. Struttura e tradizione. Atti del Convegno Internazionale di
Montreal: 19–20 marzo, 1981*, eds. M. Picone and M. Bendinelli Predelli (Florence,
1984).

[3] Saints' lives and devotional literature (here seen as separate but related genres) may
gave been comparable to chivalric romances in the number of works written and
quantity of printed editions.

[4] Lawrence W. Levine, "William Shakespeare and the American People: A Study in
Cultural Transformation," *AHR* 89/1 (1984), 34–66. Although the above definition
of popular is my own and not found in Levine's study, the latter has influenced my
thinking.

[5] This study is similar in some ways to Paul F. Grendler, "Francesco Sansovino and Italian Popular History 1560–1600," *Studies in the Renaissance*, 16 (1969), 139–180.

[6] "La storia di Milone e Berta e del nascimento d'Orlando," found in several versions. *v Cantari cavallereschi dei secoli XV e XCI*, ed. Giorgio Barini. Collezione di opere inedite o rare dei primi tre secoli della lingua pubblicata per cura della R. Commissione pe' testi di lingua nelle Provincie dell'Emilia (hereafter abbreviated as Collezione followed by the number), 89. (Bologna, 1905), pp. 51–53, 227–228; also Andrea da Barberino, *I Reali di Francia*, eds. Giuseppe Vandelli and Giovanni Gambarin (Bari, 1947), Bk. 6, ch. 53, p. 539.

[7] Edmund G. Gardner, *The Arthurian Legend in Italian Literature* (London and New York, 1930), p. 11; Daniela Delcorno Branca, *Il romanzo cavalleresco medievale* (Florence, 1974), pp. 3–6.

[8] Gardner, *Arthurian Legend*, pp. 4–6; Delcorno Branca, *Il romanzo cavalleresco*, pp. 3–4; Lorenzo Renzi, "Il francese come lingua letteraria e il franco-lombardo. L'epica carolingia nel Veneto," in *Storia della cultura veneta. I: Dalle origini al Trecento* (Vicenza, 1976), pp. 566–567. The entire article, pp. 563–589, is a good discussion of the introduction of French chivalric material into northern Italy.

[9] Francesco A. Ugolini, *I cantari d'argomento classico con un'appendice di testi inediti* (Geneva and Florence, 1933), pp. 11–12.

[10] Delcorno Branca, *Il romanzo cavalleresco*, pp. 14–15.

[11] J. K. Hyde, *Padua in the Age of Dante. A Social History of an Italian City State* (Manchester and New York, 1966), p. 292.

[12] Ugolini, *I cantari d'argomento classico*, pp. 12–13.

[13] Ezio Levi, *I cantari leggendari del popolo italiano nei secoli XIV e XV* (Turin, 1914), pp. 6, 12, 14, 16; Ugolini, *I cantari d'argomento classico*, p. 11.

[14] " . . . that through the piazzas and public places these compositions might be sung among the benches in the manner of those nowadays who with lyre on arm sing their idle nonsense to earn their bread. . . . " From Giovanni Battista Giraldi Cinthio's *Discorso intorno al comporre dei romanzi* (completed 1549, published 1554); I quote from the English translation: *Giraldi Cinthio on Romances. Being a translation of the 'Discorso intorno al comporre dei romanzi'*, with introduction and notes by Henry L. Snuggs. (Lexington, KY, 1968), p. 7.

[15] Levi, *I cantari leggendari*, pp. 20–22.

[16] *Giraldi Cinthio on Romances*, pp. 83–84.

[17] *Il Tristano Riccardiano*, ed. E. G. Parodi. Collezione, 74 (Bologna, 1896). I cite the more accessible, very substantial partial text in *Prose di romanzi. Il romanzo cortese in Italia nei secoli XIII e XIV*. ed. Felice Arese (Turin, 1962), pp. 33–260. This anthology contains parts of three other Italian Arthurian romances as well. Major secondary sources on Arthurian romances are Gardner, *Arthurian Legend;* and Daniela Branca, *I romanzi italiani di Tristano e la Tavola Ritonda* (Florence, 1968).

[18] *Prose di romanzi*, ch. 2, pp. 38–40.

[19] Ibid., ch. 5, p. 48.

[20] Ibid., chs. 7–8, pp. 51–52.

[21] Eugène Vinaver, *The Rise of Romance* (New York and Oxford, 1971), pp. 71–98.

[22] *La tavola ritonda o l'istoria di Tristano testo di lingua citato dagli Accademici della Crusca ed ora per la prima volta pubblicato secondo il codice della Mediceo-Laurenziana*, ed. Filippo-Luigi Polidori, 2 vols. (Bologna, 1864–65). I cite the English translation: *Tristan and*

the Round Table. A Translation of La Tavola Ritonda, trans. Anne Shaver. Editorial
assistance by Annette Cash. Illustrations by Catherine M. Hiller (Binghamton, New
York, 1983).

²³ *Tristan and the Round Table,* ch. 138, p. 335.

²⁴ Ibid., ch. 137, p. 333.

²⁵ Ibid., ch. 130, p. 323.

²⁶ Ibid., ch. 136, p. 330; ch. 137, p. 333, and elsewhere.

²⁷ Ibid., ch. 145, p. 346.

²⁸ In addition to the secondary sources cited in n. 2 and the scholarship on Andrea da
Barberino's romances cited below, *v* Delcorno Branca, *Il romanzo cavalleresco
medievale,* pp. 14–21, 26–34. The introductions to critical editions and anthologies
are usually informative. However, the following comparative remarks are based on
my own reading.

²⁹ The facts of Andrea da Barberino's life are summarized by Giorgio Varanini,
"Andrea da Barberino," *Dizionario critico della letteratura italiana* (Turin, 1974), I, pp.
65–67; and Andrea da Barberino, *L'Aspramonte,* ed. Luigi Cavalli (Naples, 1972), p.
29.

³⁰ "Naturalmente, piacciono à ciascuno gli Autori novelli. . . . Per questo me son
delettato di cercar molte Historie nuove, & ho havuto gran piacere di molle: tra le
quali, questa molto me piacque. Onde io non voglio esser ingrato del beneficio
ricevuto da Dio, e da la humana natura. Benchè da la sua bontà ricevi più, che non
merito, però che la conditione mia è bassa; ma io mi conforto, che io veggio molti di
maggior natione far peggio di me; o che sia per loro peccati, overo de loro parenti,
questo non lo giudico, io solo lo lascio giudicare à Dio . . . Niuna cosa ne scusa per il
libero arbitrio, che noi habbiamo . . . però non li tolse il libero arbitrio di far come a
lui piacea, e cosi non lo tolse mai à niuno, e però siamo chiamati animali rationali,
cioè che la ragion è data a noi . . . che noi siamo diversi istrumenti del mondo, e però
ogniun se ingegni d'imparar à suonar buon instrumento, e la fortuna gli lo intonerà
perfettamente; ma guardi, che le corde non siano false." Andrea da Barberino,
*Guerino detto il Meschino. Nel quale si tratta come trovò suo Padre, & sua Madre, in la Città
di Durazzo in prigione. Et diverse vittorie havute contra Turchi.* In Venetia, 1635.
Appresso Ghirardo Imberti, pp. 2^{r-v}.

³¹ Antonio Viscardi, *Le letterature d'Oc e d'Oil,* rev. ed. (Florence and Milan, 1967), pp.
330–331.

³² A substantial part of the *Franco-veneta* version of *Karleto* from Codex Francese XIII,
on which Book 6 is based, is reprinted in *Le origini. Testi latini, italiani, provenzali e
franco-italiani,* ed. Antonio Viscardi et al. (Milan and Naples, 1956), pp. 1115–1135.

³³ The critical edition is *Storia di Ajolfo del Barbicone e di altri valorosi cavalieri compilata
da Andrea di Jacopo di Barberino di Valdelsa,* ed. Leone del Prete, 2 vols. Collezione 2
and 3. (Bologna, 1863–64).

³⁴ The critical edition is Andrea da Barberino, *L'Aspramonte, romanzo cavalleresco in-
edito,* ed. Marco Boni. Collezione, nuova serie (Bologna, 1951). *v* also Andrea da
Barberino, *L'Aspramonte,* ed. Luigi Cavalli (Naples, 1972).

³⁵ I do not know of a critical edition; hence, I have used the Venice, 1635, edition
noted above. Giacomo Osella, *Il Guerrin Meschino* (Turin, 1932), is a secondary
study.

³⁶ *Le storie nerbonesi romanzo cavalleresco del secolo XIV,* ed. I. G. Isola, 3 vols. Collezione
47–49. (Bologna, 1877–80).

[37] Charles Martel (688?–ruled 715–died 741) was, in reality, the father of Pepin the Short (714?–768) and an ancestor of Charlemagne. I have not seen *Storia di Ugone d'Alvernia volgarizzata nel sec. XIV da Andrea da Barberino, non mai fin qui stampata*, eds. F. Zambrini and A. Bacchi Della Lega (Bologna, 1882), but rely on the selection based on several manuscripts in *Romanzi dei Reali di Francia*, ed. Adelaide Mattaini (Milan, 1957), pp. 1183–1236. This is a good anthology whose notes to the various works on pp. 25–32 list the most important bibliography.

[38] *v* the well-known studies of Hans Baron, Eugenio Garin, and Felix Gilbert.

[39] Donald J. Wilcox, *The Development of Florentine Humanist Historiography in the Fifteenth Century* (Cambridge, MA, 1969), chs. 2–4.

[40] *v* definitions 6 and 8 of *istoria* in *Grande dizionario della lingua italiana*, VIII: *Ini-libb* (Turin, 1973), p. 612.

[41] *v* Louis Green, *Chronicle into History. An Essay on the Interpretation of History in Florentine Fourteenth-Century Chronicles* (Cambridge, 1972), *passim*.

[42] *Giraldi Cinthio on Romances*, p. 14.

[43] "altri scrivono historie meramente favolose come quelle di Reali di Francia, di Morgana, Falerina, Margalona, Melusina, Amadis, Florando, Tirante, Florisello, Conamoro, Arturo, Lancilloto, Tristano, & altre simili." Tommaso Garzoni, *La piazza universale di tutte le professioni del mondo. Nuovamente ristampata. . . .* (In Venetia, Appresso Roberto Meietti, 1601), p. 368. It was printed at least twelve times in Italy between 1585 and 1665.

[44] These two examples are no. 86 and 46 in Carlo Angelieri, *Bibliografia delle stampe popolari a carattere profane dei secoli XVI e XVII conservate nella Biblioteca Nazionale di Firenze* (Florence, 1953), but there are many more.

[45] Andrea da Barberino, *I Reali di Francia*, eds. Giuseppe Vandelli and Giovanni Gambarin (Bari, 1947), I, chs. 1–3, pp. 3–7. All textual references will be to this edition. *v* also Andrea da Barberino, *I Reali di Francia. Ricerche intorno ai Reali di Francia per Pio Rajna seguite dal libro delle storie di Fioravante e dal cantare di Bovo d'Antona*, I (Bologna, 1872). Rajna's researches, which occupy the first 330 pp., are the indispensable starting point for study of the work. *I Reali di Francia di Andrea da Barberino*, ed. Giuseppe Vandelli, II, Collezione 71 (Bologna, 1892); and *Romanzi dei Reali di Francia*, ed. Mattaini, pp. 147–402, can also be read.

[46] "Ed era in quel tempo imperadore di Roma Teodosio e Valenziano, ed era papa Filice, che fu romano, negli anni domini quattrocento trentotto." *I Reali di Francia*, III ch. 1, p. 246. Rajna, *I Reali di Francia*, 1872 ed., p. 294, first noted the error.

[47] Felix Gilbert, *Machiavelli and Guicciardini. Politics and History in Sixteenth-Century Florence* (Princeton, NJ, 1965), p. 211.

[48] "Nobilissimi regi, prenzi, duchi e signori e padri, e voi altri a me fratelli, le cose di questo mondo e i beni terrestri sono più tosto da sprezzare che d'apprezzare, e le cose celestiali e divine sono quelle che si debbono magnificare e apprezzare e amare e tenere, e solo una cosa è quella che si dee amare in questa vita presente, a questa si è d'avere buona fama; e chi non ama buona fama, non ama Iddio. Imperò che noi nasciamo tutti nudi, e nudi ritorniamo nel corpo della prima nostra madre, e ogni cosa lasciamo in questo modo che noi ci troviamo, e di noi non ci rimane niente, se non l'operazione che noi abbiamo fatte . . . E pertanto ognuno dì doverrebbe ingegnare d'essere vivo, poi che l'anima sarà partita dal corpo, in questa forma d'ingegnarsi, che di lui rimanga buona fama . . . Almeno e' nostri sono medicati e sono aiutati, e quelli che sono morti siamo certi che sono tra gli altri martiri dinanzi

da Dio: in questo mondo aranno sempre buona e perpetua fama, e sempre saranno vivi nelle menti di coloro che sentiranno la loro virtù essere stata si pronta a morire a difensione della fede di Gesù Cristo . . . Per due cose dobbiamo essere feroci nella battaglia: l'una si è che morendo siete ricchi, e vincendo ancora siete ricchi, imperò che, se voi vincete, quanto fia il tesoro che s'acquisterà? E se voi morite, quale tesoro vale più che la gloria di Dio? E siete certi di due glorie: la prima quella di Dio; seconda quella del mondo, che sarà in perpetua fama; e però ognuno s'affatichi nel bene adoperare, e pensi ognuno di difendere la patria sua. E, pensate, se noi perdessimo, chi difenderebbe e' nostri figliuoli e le nostre donne e i nostri padri vecchi? E noi saremo venduti per servi e straziati come bestie . . . Ma non si puote sanza fatica acquistare il regno del cielo nè la fama del mondo. E 'l santo padre papa Salvestro perdona pena e colpa a chi viene a questa battaglia e muoia; e però siate robusti e fieri e presti delle mani, uccidendo e' saraini nel nome di Dio e di buona ventura." *I Reali di Francia*, I, ch. 37, pp. 60–62.

[49] Alberto Tenenti, *Il senso della morte e l'amore della vita nel Rinascimento (Francia e Italia)* (Turin, 1957; rpt. 1977), ch. 1, esp. pp. 19–23.

[50] See my forthcoming book on Italian Renaissance schooling (The Johns Hopkins University Press), ch. 5, sections 5 and 6.

[51] Marcella T. Grendler, *The 'Trattato Politico-Morale' of Giovanni Cavalcanti (1381–c. 1451). A Critical Edition and Interpretation* (Geneva, 1973), pp. 45–52.

[52] " . . . come assai volte interviene che d'una piccola favilla ingenera gran fuoco e per piccolo movimento la fortuna turba gli stati di questo mondo e manda e' singnori (sic) di grande altura in profonda bassezza." *Aspramonte*, ed. Boni (1951), Bk. 1, ch. 1, p. 4, lines 15–18.

[53] "La fortuna, movitrice degli stati, per molte vie aopera suo corso, come fece in questa parte, che da lungi seminò nuovo travaglio a chi iposava per lo tempo passato." *I Reali di Francia*, Bk. 3, ch. 26, p. 288.

[54] "La fortuna di questo mondo non è alcuna forza che la possa contradiare." *Storia di Ajolfo del Barbicone*, 1863–64 ed., I, ch. 33, pp. 61–62. *v* also his discussion of fortune, reason, and personal responsibility in the preface to readers of *Guerino detto il Meschino*, 1635 ed., pp. 2^{r-v}.

[55] "E fece battezzare tutta Roma, e dotò la chiesa di Dio per la buona fede e per la sua conversione, non pensando che e' pastori della chiesa per lo bene proprio dovessino tutto il mondo quastare per appropiarsi e farsi di spirituali tiranni." *I Reali di Francia*, I, ch. 3, p. 6.

[56] For Pulicane, *v I Reali di Francia*, VI, ch. 27, pp. 340–341; ch. 29, pp. 343–344.

[57] Green, *Chronicle into History*, pp. 17–40.

[58] *v*, e.g., *La morte di Buovo d'Antona. Con la vendetta di Sinibaldo, et Guidone suoi figliuoli, fatta per lui*. No place, printer, or date, but second half of the sixteenth century. This is an ottava rima version. Biblioteca Nazionale, Florence, Palatina E. 6. 5. 3. II. 27. Also see *Libro chiamato Buovo d'Antona: Nel quale se contiene tutti gli suoi fatti mirabilmente che lui fece, con la sua morte*. . . . (In Milano, Per Valerio & Hieronimo fratelli da Meda). Lacking a date, but probably 1550–1580. Written in *ottava rima*. Biblioteca Mai, Bergamo, 4, 1431. A total of twenty-four fifteenth- and sixteenth-century printings of *Buovo d'Antona* alone, plus thirteen more printings of the complete *I Reali di Francia*, are known. While a count of printed editions of chivalric romances based on library holdings remains to be done, two works are fundamental for bibliographical research. Alessandro Cutolo, *I romanzi cavallereschi in prosa e in rima*

del Fondo Castiglioni presso la Biblioteca Braidense di Milano (Milan, 1944), gives full descriptions of 156 editions. *v* nos. 29–34 for *Buovo d'Antona*. Marina Beer, *Romanzi di cavalleria. Il 'Furioso' e il romanzo italiano del primo Cinquecento* (Rome, 1987), pp. 327–392, provides a combined listing in short-title form of the romances listed in incunable catalogues and earlier partial surveys. Moreover, she lists the editions in both alphabetical and chronological order. Unless otherwise indicated, my counts of the fifteenth- and sixteenth-century printed editions of particular romances are based on Cutolo and Beer. Of course, additional printings remain to be found in Italian libraries.

59 *v A Short-Title Catalogue of Books Printed in England, Scotland, & Ireland and of English Books Printed Abroad, 1475–1640*. Compiled by A. W. Pollard & G. R. Redgrave. 2nd ed., W. A. Jackson, F. S. Ferguson, and Katharine F. Pantzer, II, (London, 1926 and 1976), items 1987–1996, for ten printings between 1500 and 1639.

60 Giovanni Villani, by contrast, wrote that Buovo d'Antona came from Volterra and may have been the founder of the town. It is a striking example of the merging of chronicle and romance. "La città di Volterra prima fu chiamata Antonia, e fu molto antica, fatta per li descendenti d'Italo, e però secondo che si legge in romanzi, quindi fu il buono Buovo d'Antona." *Istorie fiorentine di Giovanni Villani* (Milan, 1834), I, ch. 55, p. 20.

61 *I Reali di Francia*, IV, ch. 1, pp. 291–292. However, waiting until the age of ten was unusual. Most Italian boys began school at the ages of six or seven in the Renaissance.

62 James Bruce Ross, "The Middle-Class Child in Urban Italy, Fourteenth to Early Sixteenth Century," in Lloyd deMause, ed., *The History of Childhood* (New York, 1974), pp. 184–195.

63 David Herlihy, "Some Psychological and Social Roots of Violence in the Tuscan Cities," in Lauro Martines, ed., *Violence and Civil Disorder in Italian Cities, 1200–1500* (Berkeley, Los Angeles, and London, 1972), pp. 145–148.

64 Ross, "The Middle-Class Child," p. 201.

65 *I Reali di Francia*, IV, ch. 10, pp. 306–308.

66 "Ella si lasciò cadere il coltellino, e poi si chinava, e fece vista di non lo potere aggiugnere, e disse: 'Agostino, ricoglimi quello coltellino.' Buovo si chinò; e come fu sotto la tavola, ed ella disse: 'Vello qui!' e preselo pe' capelli e per lo mento, e baciollo, e prese il coltellino, e rizzossi. E Buovo uscì di sotto la tavola tutto cambiato di colore per vergogna; e Drusiana, tutta accesa d'amore. . . . " *I Reali di Francia*, IV, ch. 11, p. 308.

67 "Ora pensi ognuno come poteva fare la misera Drusiana ch'era gravida!" *I Reali di Francia*, IV, ch. 35, p. 350.

68 Ibid, IV, ch. 52, pp. 376–377.

69 Ibid, IV, ch. 61, pp. 392–393.

70 "Allora Gailone, vedendo bene affisato Buovo a orare, cavò fuori una coltella bene tagliente e appuntata, e di drieto per lo nodo del collo gliele ficcò, insino dinanzi per la gola, per modo che gli non poté fare motto. E così morì Buovo d'Antona, fiore de' cavalieri del mondo al suo tempo", Ibid, IV, ch. 79, p. 424.

71 Paul Oskar Kristeller, *Renaissance Thought: The Classic, Scholastic, and Humanistic Strains* (New York, Evanston, and London, 1961), p. 20.

72 Gene A. Brucker, *Florentine Politics and Society 1343–1378* (Princeton, N. J., 1962), pp. 38–39.

73 "Egli aveva una figliuola che avea nome Berta del gran piede, perché ella aveva uno
    pie' uno poco maggiore che l'altro, e quello era il pie' destro; ed era per altro una
    bella criatura, ed era la più forte cavalcatora di tutte le donne del mondo." *I Reali di
    Francia*, VI, ch. 1, p. 444.
74 Ibid, VI, ch. 8, pp. 453–455.
75 " . . . e secondo l'umana natura usò il matrimonio, e trovolla vergine. E in quella
    notte ella ingravidò in uno fanciullo maschio." Ibid. VI, chs. 12–14, pp. 460–464,
    quotation on p. 463. Andrea's language, and that found in the Carolingian ro-
    mances generally, for the sexual act tends to be chaste and discreet. By contrast, the
    language and the behavior of the protagonists in the *Amadis de Gaula* romances is a
    little more explicit and erotic.
76 *v*, e.g., Boccaccio, *Decameron*, Day III, tales 2, 6, and 9; VII, 8; IX, 6.
77 *Cinquecento* Venetian schoolmasters called them that; *v* nn. 131 and 132.
78 *v*, e.g., *Libro volgare intitulato la Spagna: Nel quale se tratta gli gran fatti: & le mirabil
    battaglie qual fece il magnanimo Re Carlomano nel la provincia della Spagna* (Vinegia per
    Alovise de Tortis, 1534 a di 9 Decembrio). Biblioteca Apostolica Vaticana Rossiana
    4365. A subsequent printing of Venetia, Appresso Agostin Zoppini, & Nepoti,
    1595, in the Biblioteca Nazionale, Firenze, 21.6.92, has the same title. *v* also *Libro
    chiamato Antifor di Barosia, il qual tratta delle gran battaglie d'Orlando, & di Rinaldo, e
    come Orlando prese Rè Carlo, e tutti li paladini* (Vinegia, & in Padova, per il Sardi), no
    date, but first half of the seventeenth century. *v* also the title of *Altobello* cited in note
    103. Many other examples could be added; *v* Cutolo, *I romanzi cavallereschi*, items 1,
    2, 5, 6, 16, 20, 21, 30, 34, 35, 36, etc.
79 Brucker, *Florentine Politics*, p. 35.
80 Guido Ruggiero, *Violence in Early Renaissance Venice* (New Brunswick, NJ, 1980), ch.
    5 *et passim*.
81 Buovo's mother is quartered with Buovo's approval. *I Reali di Francia*, IV, ch. 52, p.
    377. Gailone, Buovo's murderer, is pulled apart by four horses and the parts
    distributed through the town. Ibid., V, ch. 9, p. 441. The lady who by trickery
    replaced Berta in King Pepin's marriage bed is burnt, and her two sons by the false
    union only spared burning through the cries of the crowd. Ibid., VI, ch. 15, p. 465.
    Charlemagne cuts off the head of his murderous stepbrother after delivering a
    vituperative oration. Ibid., VI, ch. 47, pp. 529–530.
82 For Florence *v* Gene Brucker, ed., *The Society of Renaissance Florence. A Documentary
    Study* (New York et al., 1971), pp. 139–178, with examples from the years 1397 to
    1444. For Venice, *v* Ruggiero, *Violence in Early Renaissance Venice*, esp. pp. 1–2,
    47–49, 180–182, with evidence from the period 1324 to 1406.
83 Brucker, *Society of Renaissance Florence*, p. 140; Paul F. Grendler, *The Roman Inquisi-
    tion and the Venetian Press 1540–1605* (Princeton, N.J., 1977), p. 60.
84 Egidio Gorra ed., *Testi inediti di Storia Trojana preceduti da uno studio sulla leggenda
    Trojana in Italia* (Turin, 1887), 101–166. For the romances of Troy, *v* also H. Morf,
    "Notes pour servir à l'histoire de la légende de Troie en Italie," *Romania*, 21 (1892),
    18–39; 24 (1895), 174–96.
85 Gorra, ed., *Storia Trojana*, 291–333.
86 Hain *15644. *v* Cutolo, *I romanzi cavallereschi*, nos. 152–154, for other printings. I
    have also examined editions of Venice: Manfrino [Bono] de Monte Ferato da
    Strevo, 20 March 1509, and Venice: Francesco di Alessandro Bindoni and Mapheo
    Pasini, 1536, not listed by Cutolo.
87 I use the following edition: *Libro di Troiano composto in lingua Fiorentina nel quale con*

grande ingenio lo auctore have reducte quasi tutte fabule poetica. Colophon: Milan: Leonardo de Vegii, 20 November 1509. Milan, Biblioteca Braidense, Fondo Castiglioni 26/152.

[88] The excellent study of Francesco A. Ugolini, *I cantari d'argomento classico con un' appendice di testi inediti* (Genève and Florence, 1933), provides analysis and some texts.

[89] Ugolini, *I Cantari,* pp. 180–182.

[90] For a new reading of the poem, *v* Constance Jordan, *Pulci's 'Morgante.' Poetry and History in Fifteenth-Century Florence* (Washington, D. C., 1986).

[91] Critical analysis began in the sixteenth century and has continued unabated, but only two studies will be noted here: the pioneer work of Pio Rajna, *Le fonti dell' 'Orlando furioso'.* 2nd rev. ed. (Florence, 1900); and the very recent stimulating and comprehensive reading of Albert R. Ascoli, *Ariosto's Bitter Harmony. Crisis and Evasion in the Italian Renaissance* (Princeton, N. J., 1987). For a survey of recent literature, *v* Robert Rodini and Salvatore Di Maria, *Ludovico Ariosto: An Annotated Bibliography of Criticism, 1956–1980* (Columbia, MO, 1984).

[92] " . . . che se voi pratticate per le Corti, se andate per le strade, se passeggiate per le piazze, se vi trovate ne' ridotti, se penetrate ne' Musei, mai non sentite altro, che ò leggere, ò recitar l'Ariosto. Anzi, che dico Corti, che dico Musei? Se nelle case private, nelle ville, ne' Trugurij stessi, & nelle capanne ancora si trova, & si canta continuamente il Furioso." Giuseppe Malatesta, *Della nuova poesia overo delle difese del Furioso* (In Verona, Per Sebastiano dalle Donne, 1589), pp. 137–138. Giuseppina Fumagalli, *La fortuna dell'Orlando Furioso in Italia nel secolo XVI* (no pl. or date, but Ferrara, 1912), p. 399, quotes this passage and presents additional evidence of the work's popularity in its own century. *v* also Beer, *Romanzi di cavalleria, passim.*

[93] *v* Salvatore Bongi, *Annali di Gabriel Giolito de' Ferrari da Trino di Monferrato stampatore in Venezia.* 2 vols. (Rome, 1890–1897; rpt. Rome, no date), I, p. xxix, n. 1; Walter Binni, *Storia della critica ariostesca* (Lucca, 1951), p. 19; Fumagalli, *La fortuna dell'Orlando Furioso,* p. 182. *v* also the comment of Giuseppe Malatesta: " . . . nel Furioso, il qual quanto più viene stampato ogni giorno. . . . " *Delle difese del Furioso,* p. 142.

[94] The discussion can be followed in Bernard Weinberg, *A History of Literary Criticism in the Italian Renaissance.* 2 vols. (Chicago, 1961), chs. 19 and 20, pp. 954–1073, *et passim.*

[95] Beer, *Romanzi di cavalleria,* pp. 141–206, 230–235.

[96] Ronnie H. Terpening, "Between Ariosto and Tasso: Lodovico Dolce and the Chivalric Romance," *Italian Quarterly,* 27 no. 106, (1986), 21–36. For other continuations, imitations, and parodies, *v* Fumagalli, *La fortuna dell'Orlando Furioso,* pp. 259–310 and ch. 4, pp. 396ff.

[97] I use an English translation of books 1 and 2: *Amadis of Gaul Books I and II. A Novel of Chivalry of the 14th Century Presumably First Written in Spanish,* trans. Edwin B. Place and Herbert C. Behm (Lexington, KY, 1974). Incidentally, Elisena also appears as the fourteen-year-old daughter of the emperor and Guerrino's beloved in Andrea da Barberino's *Guerrin Meschino. v Guerino detto il Meschino,* 1635 ed., I, ch. 6, p. 8, *et passim.*

[98] *v Short-Title Catalogue of Books Printed in Italy and of Italian Books Printed in Other Countries from 1465 to 1600 now in the British Museum* (London, 1958), p. 22.

[99] For Roseo, *v* Romualdo Canavari, "Sulle opere di Mambrino Roseo da Fabriano," in *L'assedio di Firenze di Mambrino Roseo di Fabriano*, ed. Ant. Dom. Pierrugues (Florence, 1894), pp. xi–xlix; and Francesco Ant. Soria, *Memorie storico-critiche degli storici napolitani* (Naples, 1781–1782), pp. 531–533. One wonders if his given name came from the character "Mambrino" in the poetic chivalric romance *Mambriano* written in the 1490s by Francesco Bello (Il Cieco di Ferrara). When Mambrino is murdered, his nephew Mambriano, the hero of the romance, sets off on a path of vengeance which leads to much of the action in the wide-ranging romance. *v* Vittorio Rossi, *Il Quattrocento*. 4th ed. revised. (Milan, 1949), pp. 463–464; and Cutolo, *I romanzi cavallereschi*, no. 75.

[100] Michele Tramezzino of Venice was the major Italian publisher of Italian translations and continuations of Amadis de Gaula in the sixteenth century. *v* Alberto Tinto, *Annali tipografici dei Tramezzino* (Venice and Rome, 1968), nos. 51, 58, 60, 65, 79, 96, 97, 98, 99, 101, etc. *v* also *Short-Title Catalogue . . . Italy*, pp. 22–23; and especially the huge bibliographical survey of Hugues Vaganay, "Les Romans de chevalerie italiens d'inspiration espagnole. Essai de bibliographie," *La bibliofilia*, 9 (1907–08), pp. 121–131; 10 (1908–09), 121–134, 161–167; 11 (1909–10), 171–182; 12 (1910–11), 112–125, 205–211, 280–300, 390–399; 13 (1911–12), 124–133, 200–215, 278–292, 394–411; 14 (1912–13), 87–94, 157–168, 426–429; 15 (1913–14), 413–422; 16 (1914–15), 59–63, 114–122, 382–390, 446–451; 17 (1915–16), 106–111. For the Italian reception of Spanish romances, *v* Henry Thomas, *Spanish and Portuguese Romances of Chivalry. The Revival of the Romance of Chivalry in the Spanish Peninsula, and its Extension and Influence Abroad* (Cambridge, 1920; rpt. New York, 1969), pp. 180–199); Benedetto Croce, *La Spagna nella vita italiana durante la rinascenza*. 4th ed., enlarged (Bari, 1949), pp. 168–180; and *Poeti e Scrittori del pieno e del tardo Rinascimento*, I (Bari, 1958), pp. 310–325; and Augustus Pallotta, "Venetian Printers and the Diffusion of Spanish Literature in Sixteenth-Century Italy," § 4, forthcoming in *Comparative Literature*. Pallotta counts 147 Italian imprints of Spanish romances, 1546 through 1600.

[101] The above impressionistic remarks are based on my reading and Frank Pierce, *Amadis de Gaula* (Boston, 1976), pp. 89–90.

[102] Peirce, *Amadis de Gaula*, pp. 106–110.

[103] *Libro di battaglia delli Baroni di Francia sotto el nome dello ardito & gagliardo giovine Altobello: Nel qual molte battaglie & degne cose se puo vedere*. Colophon: Stampato in Venetia per Augustino Bindoni, 1547. Biblioteca Nazionale, Florence, Palat. E.6.5.69; and Nencini 1.6.1.40.

[104] *v* GW 1582–1587 for incunabular editions of 1476, 1480, 1481, 1487, 1491, and 1499; five of the six are printed in gothic type. Also *v* *Short-Title Catalogue . . . Italy*, p. 21; and Cutolo, *I romanzi cavallereschi*, pp. 8–10, for six sixteenth-century printings and limited bibliography.

[105] John J. O'Connor, *Amadis de Gaule and its Influence on Elizabethan Literature* (New Brunswick, NJ, 1970), pp. 4, 9, 18.

[106] "Borgo: Il sono un di quegli che compro e leggo più volentieri *Buovo d'Antona* che la *Poetica* d'Aristotile, le *Pistole* di Seneca o il *Trattato del ben morire*, perché la mia professione è armeggiare e non esser guardiano di compagnie come voi. A voi sta vene le *Prediche sopra Amos* in mano e a me il *Furioso*, perché voi fate le dicerie per amor di Dio e io armeggio il primo dì di maggio per piacere agli uomini." Anton Francesco Doni, *I Marmi*, ed. Ezio Chiorboli. 2 vols. (Bari, 1928), I, p. 25. On Doni, *v*

Paul F. Grendler, *Critics of the Italian World 1530–1560. Anton Francesco Doni, Nicolò Franco & Ortensio Lando* (Madison, Milwaukee, and London, 1969).

[107] For her biography, *v* Bongi, *Annali di Giolito*, I, pp. 150–198.

[108] *Il Meschino, altramente detto il Guerrino, fatto in ottava rima dalla Signora Tullia d'Aragona. Opera, nella quale si veggono & intendono le parti principali di tutto il mondo, & molte altre dilettevolissime cose, da esser sommamente care ad ogni sorte di persona di bello ingegno* (In Venetia, Appresso Gio. Battista, et Melchior Sessa, Fratelli, 1560), sigs. *3^{r-v}.

[109] *Il Meschino dalla Tullia d'Aragona*, Sigs. *3^v-4^r.

[110] Ibid., p. 1^r.

[111] That is, if women could read. All research to date concludes that the literacy rate for women fell considerably short of that of men in these centuries. Only girls and women of the upper classes had a reasonable chance to acquire literacy.

[112] Christian Bec, *Les livres des Florentins (1413–1608)* (Florence, 1984), pp. 150, 151, 152, 153, 156, 157, 159, etc. See p. 153 (inventory of 1421) and p. 156 (1423) for the quoted entries. No doubt these libraries contained additional chivalric romances, because inventories often listed books only generically, e. g., as "qualche libro."

[113] "j Reale di Francia" (p. 207, inventory of 1497), and "Storie d'Aspromonte" (p. 208, inventory of 1502), in Bec, *Les livres des Florentins*.

[114] For example, twenty-three of the one hundred three sixteenth-century printings of chivalric romances, including imprints of the 1570s and 1580s, listed in Cutolo, *I romanzi cavallereschi*, appeared in semi-gothic type. Fumagalli, *La fortuna dell' Orlando furioso*, pp. 181–182, also notes that a substantial minority of sixteenth-century printings of Ariosto's romance also appeared in semi-gothic type. My bibliographical research confirms this pattern.

[115] This is a Carolingian romance, perhaps from the *Quattrocento*, that includes Rinaldo, Orlando, Danese, the Maganza line of villains, and other Carolingian characters. Four incunabular editions are known: GW 1634–1637. In addition, I have seen editions of Milan, Leonardo di Vegio, 12 August 1510 (Biblioteca Nazionale, Florence, Palat. 25.2.6.15); Venice, Giovanni Andrea Vavassore detto Guadagnino, 1546 (Milan, Braidense, Castiglioni 26/13); and Venice, Fabio & Agostin Zoppini fratelli, 1589 (Biblioteca Nazionale, Florence, Palat. 19.6.149).

[116] This is another undistinguished romance, possibly from the late *Quattrocento*, involving Orlando, Rinaldo, and Charlemagne. I have seen a printing of Venice and Padua, no date but first half of the seventeenth century. *v* n. 78 for the title. *v* Cutolo, *I romanzi cavallereschi*, nos. 14 and 16 for other printings.

[117] Falconetto was a Saracen prince who fought Orlando. *Libro chiamato Falconetto nel quale si contiene le grandissime produzze fatte contra li Paladini di Francia. E del successo della sua morte, cosa molto dilettevole da leggere* (In Trevigi et in Pistoia, no printer or date, but c. 1600 to 1620). Biblioteca Nazionale, Florence, Palat. 12.9.1.2.3. *v* also Cutolo, *I romanzi cavallereschi*, nos. 51–53.

[118] It is worth reproducing Doni's list (without corrections) in order to learn which romances circulated: "Ancroia, Altobello, Antifor di Barosia, Anteo Gigante, Astolfo Borioso, Aspramonte, Aiolfo di Barbicone, Buovo d'Antona, Bellisardo, Ciriffo Calvaneo, Carlo Martello, Continuation d'Orlando, Carlo Inamorato, Dama Rovenza, Delfin di Francia, Danese, Drusiano, Fioretti di Morgante, Falconetto, Fioretti de' Paladini, Filogine, Girone il cortese, Galvano, Gigante Morante, Giusto paladino, Innamoramento d'Orlando, Leandra, Mambriano, Morte di Ruggiero, Morgante, Marphisa Pizzarra, Marphisa Disperata, Morte del Danese, Notte d'Africa,

Orlando furioso, Orlandino, Oronte Gigante, Persiano figliuol d'Altobello, Passamonte, Rinaldo, Reali di Francia, Ruggino, Sacripante, Sfortunato, Spagna, Trabisonda, Troiano, Vendetta di Falconetto, Del (Giovanni Battista) Pigna, Del (Francesco Bello) Cieco Ferrarese, Amori di Marfisa, Innamoramento di Ruggiero, Morte di Ruggeretto." *La libraria del Doni fiorentino* (In Vinegia, Presso Altobello Salicato, 1580), pp. 60 $^{r-v}$. (Note the chivalric given name of the publisher.) Carolingian romances dominate the list, while Arthurian and classical romances are absent. A few other romances can be found elsewhere in Doni's work, e. g., "Guerrin Meschino" on p. 71^v.

[119] They are "Amadis di Gaula," "Cavalier dalla Croce," "Flotir," "Primaleone, Palmerin d'Oliva, Platir Cavalier, Splandiano, Tirante il Bianco." *La libraria del Doni*, 1580 ed., p. 62^v.

[120] "Egli 'mparò in meno di sei mesi a schermire, e parte in grammatica." Andrea da Barberino, *Ajolfo del Barbicone*, 1863–64 ed., I, ch. 14, p. 25.

[121] "il Meschino imparava meglio che Enidonio, imparò Greco, & Latino, & molti linguaggi per l'utilità de la mercanti, e per navigare; imparò Turchesco. . . . " Andrea da Barberino, *Guerino detto il Meschino*, 1635 ed., I, ch. 5, p. 7^v.

[122] Trabisonda is a Italian version of a Spanish romance in which Rinaldo ascends the imperial throne of Trebizond. It first appeared in the 1480s. *v* Cutolo, *I romanzi cavalereschi*, nos. 147–150.

[123] Uggieri is a pagan converted to Christianity and dear to Charlemagne. However, when the emperor's son kills Uggieri's son, he embarks on vengeance. This version had at least eight printings between 1498 and 1599. In the early Cinquecento Cassio da Narni rewrote the work in ottava rima and published it as *La morte del Danese* in 1522 with a reprint in 1534. *v* Beer, *Romanzi di cavalleria*, pp. 149–160.

[124] Charlemagne falls in love with a pagan princess. The work is attributed to Francesco Lodovici (or Ludovici) and first published in 1481. *v* Cutolo, *I romanzi cavallereschi*, nos. 35–37; and Beer, *Romanzi di cavalleria*, ab indice.

[125] This well-known romance on which Ariosto drew is an account of Charlemagne's Spanish campaign that concluded with Roncesvalle. It was probably written in the first half of the Quattrocento, according to Dionisotti. I have seen editions of Venice, Alovise de Tortis, 9 December 1534; and Venice, Agostin Zoppini & Nepoti, 1595; as indicated in note 78. The critical edition is *La Spagna. Poema cavalleresco del secolo XIV*, ed., Michele Catalano. 3 vols. (Bologna, 1939–40). *v* also Carlo Dionisotti, "Entrée d'Espagne, Spagna, Rotta di Roncisvalle," in *Studi in onore di Angelo Monteverdi* (Modena, 1959), I, pp. 207–241.

[126] This is a Carolingian romance featuring two sons of the emperor of Constantinople: *v* Cutolo, *I romanzi cavallereschi*, no. 156.

[127] This is a Carolingian romance in which Leandra throws herself from a tower for love of Rinaldo. Eleven printings, 1508 through 1579, are known.

[128] "Orlando tantum gradant, et gesta Rinaldi,/namque animum guerris faciebat talibus altum./Legerat Ancroiam, Tribisondam, facta Danesi,/Antonnaeque Bovum, Antiforra, Realia Franzae,/innamoramentum Carlonis, et Asperamontem,/Spagnam, Altobellum, Morgantis bella gigantis,/Meschinique provas, et qui Cavalierus Orsae/dicitur, et nulla cecinit que laude Leandram./Vidit ut Angelicam sapiens Orlandus amavit,/utque caminavit nudo cum corpore mattus,/utque retro mortam tirabat ubique cavallam,/utque asinum legnis caricatum calce ferivit,/illeque per coelum veluti cornacchia valavit." "Merlin Cocai" (pseudonym), *Baldus*. Ed. and

trans. Giuseppe Tonna. 2 vols. (Milan, 1958), I, bk. 3, lines 102–114, p. 90: *v* also p. 92.

[129] In *Orlandino*, Buovo d'Antona and other chivalric heroes enter and exit throughout the work. *v* Folengo's *Opere italiane*, ed. Umberto Renda, I, (Bari, 1911). The restless, paradoxical Folengo was also a Benedictine monk who left, then re-entered the monastic life, and was caught up in Benedictine theological renewal. For this aspect of his career and additional bibliography, *v* Barry Collett, *Italian Benedictine Scholars and The Reformation. The Congregation of Santa Giustina of Padua* (Oxford, 1985), pp. 81–85 et passim.

[130] " . . . recitar fra la frotta de' scolari l'Ariosto in cambio dell'epistole d'Ovidio, uscir di scuola come diavoli scathenati. . . . " *La piazza universale*, 1601 ed., p. 726. *v* also the comment of Giuseppe Malatesta: "che non sia scuola, nè studio, nè Academia, dove non faccia conserva di questo mirabil poema." *Delle difese del Furioso*, 1589 ed., p. 138.

[131] The teachers' statements are found in Archivio della Curia Patriarcale di Venezia, "Professioni di Fede richiesta agli insegnati, 1587." Before making their professions of faith (a papal requirement of teachers since 1564, but not always enforced and seldom documented), the teachers answered questions about themselves and their schools. The teachers' statements are found of ff. 21^r, 42^r, 60^v: "Buovo d'Antona ò altri libri de batagia;" 63^r, 106^v: "et qualche libro de batagia che porta i putti;" 136^v: "libri de batagia che portano i puti a schola, el Furioso;" 149^r, 157^r: "altri libri de batagia et de guere;" 173^v: "et de questi Orlandi Furiosi che ghe da i padri et le madri che debbano imparar;" 185^r, 292^r: "et qualche libro dele guere de Trogia." For further information on the curriculum of vernacular schools, *v* ch. 10 of my forthcoming book on Italian Renaissance schools to be published by The Johns Hopkins University Press.

[132] "Per contentar i humori dei padri ghe ne sono anche che portano a schola libri de batagia, el Furioso et simil libri: io ghe insegno a satisfazion dei padri." Archivio della Curia Patriarcale di Venezia, "Professioni di Fede," f. 209^v.

[133] *v* Giuseppe Liverani, *Five Centuries of Italian Majolica* (New York, Toronto, and London, 1960), pl. 43; Wendy M. Watson, *Italian Renaissance Maiolica from the William A. Clark Collection* (London, 1986), pls. 4, 54, and 65, plus p. 138.

[134] For his law degree, *v* Giovanni Minnucci, *Le lauree dello Studio Senese all'inizio del secolo XVI (1501–1506)* (Milan, 1984), p. 31. For a brief biography, *v* Benedetto da Mantova, *Il Beneficio di Cristo con le versioni del secolo XVI. Documenti e testimonianze*, ed. Salvatore Caponetto (Florence, DeKalb, IL, and Chicago, 1972), p. 529 n. 1.

[135] "Alli secolari anchora non nocerà leggere nostra operetta, & sarà loro molto piu salutifera, che leggere Dante, ò cento Novelle, ò Corbaccio di Giovanni Boccaccio, Sonetti, ò canti di Paladini. . . . " *Opera di Santo Antonino . . . utilissima, et necessari alla instruttione de Sacerdoti . . . et il modo di confessarsi bene. . . .* (In Venetia, Appresso Gio. Griffio, 1561), p. 4.

[136] "Inde igitur quò non intrarunt Lancelotus à Lacu, Perseforestus, Tristanus, Gino Cortesius, Amadisius, Primaleo, Boccacciiq. Decamero, & Ariosti poema? ne hic enumerem aliorum ignobiliorum poetarum carmina male texta, & carè vendita." *Bibliotheca selecta qua agitur de ratione studiorum. . . .* (Romae Ex Typographia Apostolica Vaticana, 1593), bk. 1, ch. 25, p. 113. At least six Cinquecento printings of *Lancellotto del lago* are known. *Parsaforesto* was a Cinquecento version of a French work which mixed together Alexander the Great and Arthurian heroes. *v* Cutolo, *I*

romanzi cavallereschi, no. 104. Luigi Alamanni (1495–1556) published in 1548 his verse version of *Girone il Cortese*, an older Italian Arthurian romance. Cutolo, no. 64. *Primaleone* was one of the continuations of Amadis de Gaula rendered into Italian by Mambrino Roseo.

137 " . . . sopra il tutto gli proibirà quei libri che contengono cose oscene e inoneste, e certe narrative di lascivie e amori, come sono certa sorte di poeti, e latini, e volgari, e anche quei libri pieni di sogni, come l'Amadis di Gaula, il Palmerino, a simili libri, scritti dai ministri del Diavolo per fare perdere il tempo, e indurre i miseri giovani a mille pensieri e peccati disonesti." *Instruttioni e documenti a' padri per saper bene governare le loro famiglie* (written c. 1603, published posthumously), quoted from *Il pensiero pedagogico della Controriforma*, ed. Luigi Volpicelli (Florence, 1960), p. 198.

138 This is an impressionistic statement because I have examined only a limited number of such works in a vast literature. Nevertheless, I have not found condemnations of romances in the few volumes sampled of the vernacular sermons of San Bernardino of Siena (1380–1444), Cornelio Musso (1511–74), and Francesco Panigarola (1548–94), three famous preachers.

Postscript. The following excellent study appeared too late to be used: Maria Cristina Cabani, *Le forme del cantare epico-cavalleresco* (Lucca: Maria Pacini Fazzi Editore, 1988). Chapter 3 discusses the *topoi* used to give the romances the appearance of history.

A TALE OF TWO PRINCES: POLITICS, TEXT, AND IDEOLOGY IN A CAROLINGIAN ANNAL

Janet L. Nelson
King's College University of London

A TALE OF TWO PRINCES: POLITICS, TEXT AND IDEOLOGY IN A CAROLINGIAN ANNAL[1]

In chapters 24 through 26 of Book V of the *City of God,* Augustine sketched a picture of the happy Christian emperors who ruled justly. These chapters have been condemned as shoddy, but reprieved as unrepresentative.[2] Elsewhere in the same work, Augustine's mature reflection on the *saeculum* seemed to convince him that justice could be attained in no kingdom save God's. In 873, in a *Mirror of Princes* written for the Carolingian king Charles the Bald, Archbishop Hincmar of Rheims wrote: "Nothing is happier for human affairs than when those men rule who have the science of ruling . . ."; and he then quoted from chapter 24 of Book V of the *City of God:* "We call Christian kings happy if they rule justly".[3] Hincmar did not go on to spurn such ideas: he and other Carolingian churchmen encouraged their kings to provide peace and justice for the Christian people in the Frankish realm.

Modern scholars have tended to conclude that the sheer difficulty of Augustine's political thought defeated his early medieval *epigoni.* It is often implied that from the sixth century, after Gelasius' advocacy of an unworkable dualism between priestly authority and royal power, until the eleventh century, when, one day in March 1081, Gregory VII rediscovered a genuinely Augustinian objectivity, churchmen evaded the problem of secular power in a Christian world. They deluded themselves that the City of God could be built on earth. Either they cultivated an enthusiastic collaboration with divinely-appointed rulers, who could seem latter-day incarnations of Augustine's happy Christian emperors; or, in a travesty of Augustine that has been labelled *l'Augustinisme politique,* they proposed the absorption of the state by the church.[4] Carolingian writers are portrayed as veering between these positions, or confusing them: either way, fundamentally misunderstanding Augustine's conception of the

two cities. The genre to have received most attention from modern
commentators is that of the *Mirrors of Princes*, works by their very
nature one-sided, even sycophantic. Carolingian political thought,
where it has been written of at all, has thus tended to be written off.
Inconsistency, muddle, and naivety are damning traits.

But a reprieve can be sought, for not all the relevant evidence has yet been taken into account. The so-called *Annals of St.
Bertin*, in fact a continuation of the *Royal Frankish Annals* and the
major Carolingian annalistic text of the ninth century, have been
almost completely ignored in standard works on medieval political
ideas. From 861 to 882, the author of these annals was Hincmar of
Rheims.[5] Though he has been accused of the intellectual vices listed
above, little appreciation has been shown for the subtlety of his
thought, least of all as displayed in his historical writing. In what
follows, a truer assessment will be sought through an examination of
just one of Hincmar's annals, that for 873. First of all, its opening two
sections will be quoted in full. They concern two princes, both rebels
against their respective fathers: Carloman against the West Frankish
king Charles the Bald, Charles the Fat against the East Frankish king
Louis the German.

*   *   *   *   *

"There were many in Charles's realm who expected that Carloman
would wreak still further evils in the Holy Church of God and in the
other realms in which Charles discharged the office of a king.
Therefore, with the advice of his faithful men and according to the
custom of his predecessors and of his ancestors, Charles pro-
mulgated laws relevant to the peace of the Church and the internal
strengthening of the realm, and he decreed that everyone was to
obey them. He also gave orders that the bishops of his realm were
to assemble at Senlis where Carloman still was, so that they might
carry out their episcopal responsibility concerning him, in accor-
dance with the sacred canons from which, as Pope Leo says, they
are not permitted to depart through any negligence or presump-
tion. The bishops did what had to be done: they deposed Carloman
from all ecclesiastical rank, according to the sacred rules, and left
him only the communion of a layman. When this had been done,
the ancient cunning Enemy incited Carloman and his accomplices
to exploit another argument, namely, that because he no longer

held any ecclesiastical orders, he could be all the more free to assume the title and power of a king, and that because, by the bishops' judgement, he had lost his clerical rank, he could all the more readily abandon his clerical tonsure. So it came about that, following his deposition, his former accomplices began to rally to him again, more enthusiastically than ever, and to seduce as many others as they could into joining him: their plan was that, as soon as they got the chance, they would snatch him out of the prison where he was being held, and set him up as their king. It was therefore necessary to bring out again into the open all those charges on which he had not been judged by the bishops, and according to what was laid down in the sacred laws, he was condemned to death for his crimes. But so that he might have time and opportunity for doing penance, yet not have the power to commit the still worse offences he was planning, the death sentence was commuted, by the public assent of all present, to a sentence of blinding, in order that the pernicious hope in him on the part of those men who hated peace, might be deceived, and the Church of God and the Christian religion in Charles's realm might not be thrown into disorder by deadly sedition in addition to the attacks of the pagans.

Louis, king of Germany, came before Christmas to the palace of Frankfurt, where he celebrated Christmas and gave notice that his assembly would be held there at the beginning of February. He gave orders that his sons Louis and Charles [the Fat], with his other faithful men, were to attend this meeting, and also the men of the late Lothar's kingdom who had commended themselves to him. While Louis waited there, the Devil in the guise of an Angel of Light came to his son Charles and told him that his father, who was trying to ruin him for the sake of his brother Karlmann, had offended God and would soon lose his kingdom, and that God had arranged that that kingdom was to be held by none other than Charles and that he would have it very soon. Charles was terror-stricken as the apparition clung to the house in which he was staying. He went into a church, but the Devil followed him in, and said: 'Why are you so frightened? And why do you run away? If I who foretell to you what is soon to happen had not come from God, I would not be able to follow you into this house of the Lord ' By these and other smooth arguments, the Devil persuaded him to receive from his hand the communion which [he said] God had sent him. Charles did so; and passing inside his mouth, Satan entered into him. Charles then came to his father, and was sitting in the council-hall with his brothers and the other faithful men, both bishops and laymen, when he leapt up, suddenly possessed, and said that he wanted to abandon the world and would not touch his wife in carnal intercourse. Taking his sword from his belt, he let it fall to the ground. As he tried to undo his sword-belt and take off his cloak, he began to shake violently. He was firmly held by the bishops and other men and, with his father much distressed and all present thunderstruck, he was led into a church. Archbishop Liutbert put on his priestly vestments and began to chant the Mass: when he got as far as the Gospel, Charles began to shout out with loud cries in his native language: 'Woe!Woe!'—like that, over and over again, until the whole of Mass was finished. His father handed him over to the bishops and other faithful men, and gave orders that he was to be led about from one sacred place of holy martyrs to another, so that their merits and prayers might free him from the demon and he might be able, by God's mercy, to recover his sanity. Then he planned to send Charles to Rome, but various other affairs intervened, and the idea of this journey was given up."

This opening section of the 873 entry in the *AB* will now be examined under three heads:

1. as a pair of historical narratives
2. as a literary text—a single tale—within the context of the 873 annal as a whole
3. as an ideological statement.

Historians have generally used only the first of these readings: I hope to show that the second and third can complement and inform the first.

I. Two histories.

The information on Carloman here is virtually the end of a story: the rest can be reconstructed from scraps of evidence, including some earlier entries in the *AB*.[6] Carloman was the third son of the West Frankish king Charles the Bald (840–877) and his queen, Ermentrude. He was born in 848 or 849, and given a name that marked him a full, throne-worthy member of the Carolingian family: hence a prince in the modern sense.[7] In 854 he was offered to the Church and

tonsured as a cleric—a new destiny for the legitimate son of a Carolingian king. Every dynasty sooner or later faces the choice of either
dividing the realm or shedding some of those eligible for the succession, or both.[8] The Carolingian Empire was divided in 843 among
three brothers. In the next generation—Carloman's generation—
options became more limited in the West Frankish kingdom: it had
two historic components, Neustria and Aquitaine. Charles the Bald
envisaged these as inheritances for his first and second sons: the
Church, previously the destination of illegitimate Carolingians, was
now to house the legitimate who were surplus to the supply of kingdoms. Carloman's three younger brothers all seem to have been
tonsured in their turn.[9]

Carloman was given the best-available education.[10] In 860,
he was consecrated to minor orders, as a deacon: half a century later,
with the benefit of hindsight, a chronicler claimed that Carloman had
been ordained "unwillingly and under compulsion"[11], but perhaps
his father's intention had been to open up prospects of a career for
him in the secular church. A precedent might have been seen in the
case of Carloman's cousin, Charles of Aquitaine, who after being
tonsured as a cleric in 850, was ordained a deacon in 854 and became
archbishop of Mainz in 856.[12] Carloman, aged perhaps fifteen, was
given the rich abbacy of St. Médard Soissons in 863, in 866 he
succeeded his younger brother as abbot of St Germain Auxerre, and,
about the same time, he acquired the abbacy of St Amand. Significantly, in none of these cases was Carloman the regular abbot: though
technically a cleric not a layman, and hence not strictly (like Charles
the Bald himself, and like a growing number of magnates) a lay-
abbot, Carloman operated just like one, administering, or exploiting,
the monasteries' economic resources, and leaving religious matters to
a regular abbot who held office in tandem with him.[13]

The death of Carloman's elder brother, the sub-king of
Aquitaine, in September of 866 caused his father Charles the Bald to
rethink the family's arrangements. There may briefly have been a
plan to deploy Carloman in Aquitaine; but in 867 Charles the Bald's
eldest son Louis was sent there as sub-king. [14] Perhaps Charles was
reconsidering the future of Neustria. In 868

> his son Carloman, deacon and abbot, was sent with a crack force of
> household troops, as [the Breton leader] Salomon had requested. . .
> across the Seine . . . to attack the Northmen based on the Loire.[15]

Carloman had a military following, like many other Carolingian pre-
lates—and like any king's son with aspirations to secular power. Some
of the lands of his monasteries were probably used to provide warriors with benefices. It is possible that Charles the Bald at this point
envisaged the return of Carloman to lay status. Again, there was a
recent precedent: Charles' nephew Pippin II of Aquitaine, forcibly
tonsured in 852 (like his younger brother in 850) to remove him from
the ranks of those eligible for kingship, had briefly been accepted
publicly in 858 as "a layman now" and given "some counties and
monasteries in Aquitaine."[16] But Pippin II had not been granted a
kingdom, or the title of king. Perhaps some similar deal was planned
for Carloman, who, moreover, unlike Pippin, had never taken monastic vows.[17]

In 869, however, two things dramatically altered Charles the
Bald's, and hence Carloman's, situation. First, Charles's nephew
Lothar II of the Middle Kingdom, died without a legitimate heir, and
Charles made a strong bid for the succession: at Metz on 9 September,
he had himself consecrated king of Lothar's kingdom. [18] On the same
day, he gave Carloman the abbacy (effectively the lay-abbacy) of St
Arnulf, Metz.[19] This was a significant grant, for Arnulf was an ancestor and patron of the royal family, his church the chosen burial-
place of Carloman's grandfather Louis the Pious, and Metz a center
of the Carolingian cult. [20] Now or soon after, Carloman was given
another major abbacy in the western part of the Middle Kingdom, the
rich royal monastery of Lobbes. He also received the abbacy of St.
Riquier in West Francia.[21] A second change in Carloman's situation
swiftly followed: his mother Queen Ermentrude died on 6 October.
Within days her place in the royal bed of Charles the Bald was taken
by Richildis, a young woman whose family had lands in the region of
Metz and powerful connexions elsewhere in the Middle Kingdom
too.[22] For Carloman, the first of these developments yielded welcome
new resources. The second threatened to foreclose the possibility of
Carloman's inheriting a kingdom: any son of Richildis would be
eligible for royal succession alongside Carloman's surviving elder
brother Louis.

In the course of the winter that followed, Charles the Bald
took steps to secure Lotharingia. After spending Christmas at
Aachen, he went to Nijmegen to meet the Viking lord of Frisia,
Roric, formerly the faithful man of Lothar II and hoped-for protector of the northern frontier of what had been Lothar's kingdom.[23]

But Charles's prospects of acquiring the whole of that kingdom were blighted. Many nobles in the area between the rivers Meuse and Rhine proved unwilling to accept Charles, while Louis the German, gravely ill the previous September and hence unable to forestall Charles's move into the Middle Kingdom, recovered and pressed his claims. In the early summer of 870, Charles held an assembly at the palace of Attigny, where negotiations began for a partition of the Middle Kingdom between himself and Louis the German. Carloman was there. [24] Perhaps he tried lobbying on his own account, having spent the previous months using the lands of Lobbes to win himself supporters in the region. His father reacted with characteristic decisiveness:

> Carloman . . . was alleged to have been stirring up plots against his father, in a faithless way. He was deprived of his abbacies and imprisoned at Senlis. [25]

The partition of Lotharingia proceeded. At Meersen in July, Charles's acquisitions north of the Rhone valley were limited to the lands west of the rivers Meuse and Ourthe: he lost Metz, but kept Toul, Verdun and Mouzon.[26]

Carloman won sympathy in high places. His imprisonment was brief: at St Denis on 9 October (St Denis' day), at the request of "the pope's envoys and some of Charles' faithful men," Charles decided to release Carloman on condition that he "stayed at his father's side."[27] But when Charles moved south to Lyons, against opponents in the Rhone valley,

> Carloman one night ran away from his father, and reached the Belgic province. Gathering around him many accomplices and sons of Belial, he wrought such cruelty and devastation at Satan's prompting that it could only be believed by those who actually saw and suffered that destruction.[28]

Carloman's base for these activities may well have been Lobbes, for the abbey's Annals imply that he retained control of it in 871.[29] Lobbes lay in the diocese of Cambrai in the ecclesiastical province of Rheims: hence close enough to Hincmar's heart to elicit the pained tone of the *AB* passage just quoted.

After a successful campaign in Burgundy, Charles moved north again to St Denis early in 871. Carloman went with his "accomplices" southwards to Mouzon and "laid waste that stronghold and the surrounding estates." He then sent envoys to his father, while he himself went to the Toul area. Charles, unimpressed by his son's tactics, ordered harsh reprisals against Carloman's supporters. Carloman fled across the Jura Mountains. In late summer 871, Charles "through the good offices of Louis the German" received more envoys from his son. In November, Carloman came to his father at Besançon

> with a show of humility. [Charles] received him, and ordered him to stay with him; and said that, when he had a chance to go to the Belgic province to speak with his faithful men there, he would decide with their counsel what honors he had best grant to Carloman.[30]

The reference to the "Belgic province" echoes the 870 annal, and gives a clue to what had been Carloman's intentions perhaps as early as 869, probably in early summer 870 (assuming the allegations had some basis), and surely by the end of that year. He had responded to the enlargement of his father's realm by staking a claim for a kingdom of his own in Lotharingia. In this context, the "Belgic province" should be understood to mean not only the area of modern Belgium[31], where Lobbes lay, but also the places where the *AB* locates Carloman's activities and supporters, namely, the regions of Toul and Mouzon. It may have been to forestall such a bid that Charles had, from the outset, made Carloman a sharer of the spoils—to the extent of giving him yet more abbacies in the newly-acquired lands. It was not enough; and Carloman seems to have been supported by some powerful men in the western part of the *regnum Hlotharii*—men who may have viewed with distaste the rise of Richildis' and her brother Boso's influence. Carloman may have hoped to work out from this base to attract more backers in the heartlands of the Middle Kingdom. There is evidence from the 860s that the "men of Lothar" were beginning to think of themselves as a group and sought to preserve "their" kingdom as a discrete bloc, against the ambitions of both East and West Frankish kings.[32] Carloman had a ready-made constituency. He failed because his father was determined to salvage as much of his Lotharingian acquisition as possible: for himself, in the short run, but in the long run for the new son he hoped Richildis would bear him.

Charles too could practise deceit: having promised Carloman some kind of deal involving "honors", perhaps including Lobbes, Charles:

> travelled to Servais. There he held an assembly with his counsellors, and on their advice he again consigned Carloman to prison at Senlis, while his accomplices he ordered to be bound by a solemn oath of fidelity, each in his own county; and on condition that each received a lord, whomever he wished, from among the king's faithful men, and that each expressed his willingness to live in peace, Charles allowed them to live in his kingdom.[33]

This passage again implies that Carloman's supporters were in Lotharingia: hence they had not yet got lords among the magnates in Charles's kingdom. Hincmar's first entry for 872 points in the same direction: in January, Charles went to Moustier near Namur "to speak with the Northmen Roric and Rodulf," presumably to secure their continued support for himself rather than his son. In October a further meeting ended in an open breach between Charles and Rodulf who, Hincmar says,

> had been plotting acts of unfaithfulness and making excessive demands.

From such strong language, it is tempting to infer that Rodulf had been intriguing with Carloman, or on his behalf. Eight years before, that same Rodulf had received a large payment, in cash and kind, from Lothar II for services rendered; and other Carolingian princes, including Charles the Bald, had found Viking allies and collaborators.[34] Charles, having sent Rodulf away empty-handed, knew that retaliation could be expected. But he may well have hoped that one particularly dangerous spin-off from Carloman's defection had been checked.

We hear no more of Carloman himself until the 873 annal (there is no mention of him under 872), which reveals that "evils were reviving." The same note is sounded in the capitulary that survives from the January assembly at Quierzy, reported in the annal: "evils still remained to be cut down."[35] The theme of this capitulary, not

new, of course, but notably insistent here, is the combatting of lawless-
ness: "the greatest effort" was called for. "Malefactors" who refused
to be brought to justice were to be outlawed. With c.4, giving point to
all this, came an explicit reference to "those who were with Carloman." Those of them who had not yet chosen a lord, "as ordered,"
were to have their allodial lands confiscated, i.e., taken into the royal
fisc. This was the most serious penalty, short of a death sentence, that
an early medieval ruler could impose. It was rarely threatened, still
more rarely demonstrably carried out.[36] In this case we do not even
know the names of the condemned, let alone how or if they were
punished. But the threat was symptomatic of the acute perception of
danger: Charles and his "counsellors" were very seriously worried. All
the gains of 870 may have seemed at risk. It can be no coincidence
that the capitulary went on to record that "male witches and female
witches are rising up in many places in our realm" and to recall, and
expand, Moses' injunction (*Exodus* xxii.18): "it is the king's office not
to permit witches and poisoners to live"; and finally to decree that,
should no firm evidence, or witnesses, be forthcoming in cases of
alleged witchcraft, then the accused should be put to the ordeal—the
"judgement of God."[37] This is the work of a jittery regime; and the
873 annal links the capitulary of Quierzy very firmly with the problem
of Carloman.

        The first solution was for the king to perform his royal office
(again the annal echoes the capitulary); the second was for the bishops
to perform theirs, by publicly trying and condemning Carloman. The
danger of Carloman's escaping was evidently so great that Charles did
not dare locate the synod anywhere else than his most secure stronghold: Senlis. Carloman, demoted from his grade of deacon, was left
merely with his clerial tonsure. Did Charles, and the bishops who
collaborated with him, intend Carloman to live out his days in prison
at Senlis, in an exact repeat of Pippin II's fate in 864? If that was their
plan, they would indeed have been shocked when Carloman and his
supporters, far from admitting defeat, were given new heart, arguing
now that Carloman as a layman was "freer" to "ascend to the title and
power of a king." The supporters, more enthusiastic than ever,
attracted recruits and planned to spring Carloman from jail. Their
aim, explicit and immediate now as apparently it had not been before,
was to "make Carloman their king" (*illum . . . sibi regem constituere*).

        The 873 annal presents this outcome as unforeseen by
Charles and his counsellors: a mess-up requiring hurried recourse to
a new tactic. Now a new secular assembly had to be convened to deal

with "the matters on which the bishopos had not judged" and Carloman, "according to the decrees of the sacred laws," i.e, the legislation of Roman emperors, was condemned to death.

Mess-up—or conspiracy? Could an experienced Frankish king like Charles the Bald, who had bound his son in clerical status precisely to render him unkingworthy, or experienced Frankish bishops, who had used precisely the same bonds for both Pippin II of Aquitaine and his brother, and for Carloman's brother too[38], really have failed to foresee the consequences of undoing the knot? Such carelessness is, frankly, incredible. What we should see here is a series of legal procedures adopted, quite deliberately, to result in the death sentence, which only a secular court, not an ecclesiastical one, could pass: this could then be commuted to the "gentler" one of blinding, though such commutations often brought death in any case[39].

The rest of Carloman's story is predictably brief.[40] Once blind, he could be transferred to a more open monastic prison at Corbie. From there he was rescued a few months later by "former supporters," and taken to Louis the German "in order to harm Charles' interests." Charles was "not greatly upset" by the news of his escape: he may have presumed a blind man to be disqualified for kingship, or may simply have known the extent of Carloman's injuries.[41] Louis the German consigned Carloman to monastic care, but, according to the *AB*, did not disguise his disapproval of Carloman's misdeeds. Louis accepted the *fait accompli*. Carloman's career was finished, its poignant epilogue the provision made by his lone surviving brother, Louis the Stammerer, for his posthumous liturgical commemoration at St Medard, Soissons.[42]

*   *   *   *   *   *

If Carloman was a king's son whose father may never have intended him to become a king, and whom the sources accord no titles other than "deacon and abbot," Charles the Fat was a real prince.[43] Born in 839, the third and youngest son of Louis the German, king of the East Frankish realm, Charles was marked out for a royal future, along with his brothers, almost as soon as he came of age. For Louis the German, unlike his West Frankish brother Charles the Bald, seems consistently to have planned to partition his lands into three, so that each son could succeed to a kingdom. Perhaps Louis was lucky, in having as many *regna*—Bavaria, Alamannia and Franconia—as he had legitimate sons. But the signs are that all his sons would have been consid-

ered kingworthy, and hence shared the succession, however many
there had been of them: not until the tenth century would an East
Frankish king put his son into the church. In 859, Charles the Fat was
assigned the county of Breisgau in Alamannia; but he appears in
documents with the title of, not "count," but *princeps:* "prince." (The
existing count seems to have stayed on as his subordinate.)[44] The
implications for his royal future became clear in 865 when his father
formally announced a prospective division of his kingdom among his
sons, assigning Alamannia and Rhaetia to Charles. The eldest, Karlmann, was to get Bavaria, and Louis, the second son, Franconia. The
plan was to come fully into effect after the father's death: meanwhile
each son was to hold certain royal lands in his future kingdom, and
judge minor cases, with major cases, control of the fisc, and appoint-
ments to bishoprics, abbeys and countships, being retained by Louis
the German.[45]

      The East Frankish king has been much praised by modern
historians for this sensible arrangement. But it did not prevent filial
resentment and rebellion. Adult sons, with their own followings
generating demand for loot and lands, inevitably had priorities of
their own. Karlmann had rebelled already in 861–2, seeking allies on
the eastern frontiers of Bavaria. Lothar II's continuing lack of a
legitimate heir, making the future of the Middle Kingdom uncertain,
tempted the East Frankish king's sons to look westwards. When Karlmann rebelled again in 863–4, he seems to have prodded an arch-
enemy of Lothar II, his erstwhile brother-in-law Hubert, into seizing
the abbey of Lobbes in the west of Lothar's kingdom.[46] In 865, soon
after the succession-plan was announced, Louis the Younger got
betrothed without his father's consent to the daughter of a magnate
with important holdings in Lotharingia and connexions also in West
Francia. Only under the combined pressure of his father and Charles
the Bald was Louis made to give up the match. [47] By comparison with
these unruly brothers, Charles the Fat has been seen as the "good
boy" of the 860s. Yet his marriage in 860 or 861 to Richgard, daughter of an influential count in Alsace, could suggest his own initiative,
hence his own perception of prospects in the Middle Kingdom, rather
than, as generally asumed, his father's. [48] If Louis the German was
interested in Alsace (he had, after all, extracted a grant, or promise,
of some kind of authority there in 860 from Lothar II), so too was his
son Charles, whose position in Alamannia would be strengthened by
contacts west of the Rhine. True, Louis stumped up the lavish morn-

ing-gift for Charles's bride; but he did so at Charles's request.[49] Perhaps this signified the father coming to terms with the son's bid.

Lacking an eastern frontier against the Slavs, Charles had less opportunity than his brothers to exploit the frontier's potential as a source of plunder and warlike renown, or of political allies. But in 869, when Louis the German himself was too ill to campaign, "compelled by necessity" he put Charles in charge of the army of Franks and (significantly) of Alamans which had already been collected. "The youngest son," as the Annals of Fulda call him—though he was now thirty—won a great victory over the Moravians, and carried off a good deal of loot.[50]

Charles certainly did rebel against his father in 871, when, in alliance with his brother Louis, he reacted fiercely to a rumor that their father was planning to give to Karlmann "parts of the kingdoms he had agreed they should have on his death."[51] The rebellion was serious, not least because it was encouraged by Charles's and Louis's uncle, Charles the Bald, and perhaps, too, by their mother.[52] According to the *AB*, they embarked on a "devastation of the realm."[53] But their father Louis the German was old—nearly 60—and for most of 870–1, seriously ill. His sons could hope soon to come into their inheritance. When the father made them an immediate grant of "benefices," they agreed to a reconciliation.[54]

There was another factor: Louis the German's nephew, the Emperor Louis II of Italy, was sonless and nearing fifty. In late summer 871 a rumor of his death spread north of the Alps. According to the East Frankish *AF*, Louis the German was "sad": the West Frankish *AB* report a different reaction:

> he despatched his son Charles [the Fat] to the territory [which Louis II] used to hold beyond the Jura Mountains, to bind as many men as he could to his allegiance with solemn oaths: and this young Charles duly did.[55]

The move fitted into Charles's planned future as king of Alamannia and Rhaetia: the "territory beyond the Jura" had been transferred by Lothar II to the emperor Louis back in 859, but real control of the region had been disputed between rival magnates.[56] Charles the Fat was to try to make a reality of royal power in this region contiguous to his own prospective realm, perhaps by allying with his mother's relatives, the grandsons of Count Welf. But the resentments of Louis the German's younger sons had only been soothed, not healed. At Forchheim in March 872, the reaffirmation of the 865 division-plan produced only sham submissions from Charles and his brother. [57] Plots were rife: if the succession to Lothar II had been the great open question of the 860s, in the early 870s Caroling-ian rivalries focused on the future of Louis II's Italian realm. And here, it was Charles the Fat rather than his brother Louis the Younger who had real prospects: he also had most cause for jealousy of his eldest brother Karlmann, whom he rightly suspected of aspiring to the imperial inheritance for himself.

In this atmosphere of tension and intrigue, Louis the Ger-man summoned the assembly at Frankfurt where took place the events recorded in the *AB* as a second item for 873. The *AF* give a rather different account of what happened when Charles the Fat came into the royal council-meeting on 26 January:

> a wicked spirit entered into him and tortured him severely, so that he could scarcely be held down by six of the strongest men . . .And justly so: for he who had wished to deceive the king chosen and ordained by God was himself deceived: he who had treacherously set traps for his father fell himself into the snares of the Devil. . . . When he was led into a church . . . he screamed, sometimes weakly, sometimes at the top of his voice, and threatened with open mouth to bite those who were holding him. The king [Louis the German] then turned to the young Louis and said: 'Don't you see, my son, whose lordship you accepted, you and your brother [Charles], when you thought to carry out wickedness against me? Now you may understand . . . that, as the saying of Truth has it [Matt.10.26]: "Nothing is hidden that is not laid bare". Confess your sins, there-fore, and do penance and pray humbly to God that they may be forgiven you. I also, as far as lies in me, grant you forgiveness.' After the attack of the Devil was over, Charles said aloud in the hearing of many, that as many times as he had plotted against his father, just so many times had he been delivered into the power of the Enemy.[58]

The *AF*'s account is paralleled in another contemporary report: according to the *Annals of Xanten,* Charles's aim was "to deprive his father of the realm and to imprison him"; Charles's possession by the malign spirit was 'a great miracle' which moved young Louis to fall at his father's feet and confess all.[59] The contrast between the *AB* version, and that of the other two annalists, will repay further attention.

Charles did "recover his sanity": the role of the clergy's exorcisms and ministrations in his recovery can only be surmised. Three months after his attack, he was judging disputes, under his father's eye; in 874 he was acting as his father's envoy to the West Franks; in 875, when the emperor Louis II died, he was sent on campaign to Italy to oppose Charles the Bald—unsuccessfully, as it proved; and in 876, when Louis the German died, the 865 plan finally came into effect, and Charles received his kingdom.[60] A reputation for incompetence has been cast over Charles's whole career by hindsight focussed on his last years from 885 onwards; but it is worth noting that contemporary writers of the early 880s record an able and assertive ruler.[61] There is no justification for regarding Charles as psychologically unstable then or in the 870s. His experiences in 873 ought not to be dismissed as symptoms of permanent mental disorder. More light is thrown on them by two further pieces of information about Charles's private life. The first is that, in 887, according to Regino, Charles summoned his wife Richgard before an assembly to answer charges of adultery with the arch-chancellor Bishop Liutward: Charles publicly alleged, *mirabile dictu*, that "in more than ten years' legitimate marriage," he had not had intercourse with his wife. Richgard's response was that she had not had intercourse with anyone, and was indeed still a virgin. She offered to prove this by ordeal of hot ploughshares, and, apparently having done so successfully, was permitted to retire to a convent.[62] The second significant fact is that in 880 or 881, Charles became the father of an illegitimate son, Bernard, and in 885 tried unsuccessfully to enlist papal help in having the boy recognised as *haeres regni*.[63]

*   *   *   *   *

The histories of Carloman and Charles the Fat that culminated in the episodes of 873, have been told separately; in fact they are connected in several ways. First, both princes were affected by the configuration of the Carolingian family at a particular point in time: for both, crises resulted from the conjunction of long reigns in two of the Carolingian

kingdoms with problematic successions in the other two. The sons of
Charles the Bald in West Francia and of Louis the German in East
Francia were both frustrated by their fathers' longevity, and both sons
responded with a new assertiveness to new dynastic openings in
Lotharingia and Italy. The two-way division of Lotharingia in 870
reaffirmed the older generation's control and blasted the hopes of
both younger men. Both princes sought new fields "across the Jura
Mountains," but with limited success. The coincidence of princely
rebellion in East and West Frankish kingdoms was therefore not
fortuitous.

The second connection between the princes' stories lay in the
encouragement given to their rebellious nephews by both the East
and West Frankish kings. Charles the Bald went eastwards to meet his
namesake in 871, and helped arrange a reconciliation between
Charles the Fat and Louis the German later in the same year. At the
same time, Louis the German appeared as a "go-between" for his
brother's rebellious son Carloman, and had evidently responded to
Carloman's request for moral support. After Carloman's blinding, his
supporters still looked to Louis the German for help. Axes of solidar-
ity between uncles and nephews crosscut the tense relationships between royal fathers and sons.

The stories of the rebel princes are linked in a third way,
revealing the tensions in Carolingian family politics from another
angle. Each story is documented largely by a single annalist writing in
the kingdom affected by the rebellion and clearly hostile to the rebel.
Thus the *AB* writer condemns Carloman and affirms Charles the
Bald's authority, while the *AF* writer affirms Louis the German's
authority and condemns Charles the Fat. But each writer, while
within his own kingdom firmly siding with father against son, shows a
sympathy for the rebel prince in the other kingdom. Both writers, in
other words, when not constrained by their own personal allegiances,
recognise the inevitability of conflict within the royal family; both
writers, while identifying their own interests with those of their respective kings, can share a prince's point of view. This dual perspective is at least hinted at in the *AF*'s brief reference to Carloman's fate:
"Charles, the tyrant of Gaul, put aside his paternal feelings and had
his son Carloman, who had been ordained deacon, blinded."[64]

But the development of a true counterpoint between paternal and filial themes is to be found in the *AB*, in the 873 annal, to
which we must now return.

II The 873 annal as a literary text.

It is already clear from the accounts of Charles the Fat's experience that even in what is often considered the dry–as–dust genre of annalistic writing, presentations of the same event can differ significantly. In this section I want to explore the *AB* passage I began with, as a text within a literary context. I shall argue that the two stories, of Carloman and Charles the Fat, can be construed as a single tale, and that the tale must be read in the setting of the 873 annal as a whole.

The question of authorial intention is fundamental. Archbishop Hincmar of Rheims took over the writing of the *AB* in 861, and continued it till his death in 882.[65] He had known of the existence of a continuation of the *Royal Frankish Annals,* kept up from 835 to 861 by Bishop Prudentius of Troyes. Hincmar borrowed the manuscript from King Charles the Bald, into whose hands it had come when Prudentius died. Hincmar made his own copy and kept it at Rheims where he added to it year by year. Modern historians (insofar as they have shown any interest at all in Hincmar as a historian) have commented on the wealth of historical material in Hincmar's annals.[66] They have also lamented his bias and selectivity: it has been noted, for instance, that in 873 his relations with Charles the Bald were very close—an entente born of a common interest in preserving for the West Frankish kingdom the territorial gains of 870 and hence in blocking Carloman's ambitions—and that his eventual role in Carloman's condemnation may explain why he made no mention in the *AB* of his involvement in attempts to reconcile Carloman with his father in 872.[67] But Hincmar's literary method in the *AB* has scarcely been studied. The following examination of the structure of a single annal will, I hope, help in evaluating its historical data, and also, perhaps, open up the rest of the *AB* to similar analysis.

The 873 annal, like most of the annals after 870, is relatively short: roughly half the length, on average, of the annals in the 860s. Though some topics are still dealt with quite lengthily, there are relatively fewer items of information per year. The 873 annal illustrates this. It consists of four quite long episodes, plus four smaller items inserted at intervals into the last and longest of the episodes:

1. Carloman
2. Charles the Fat
3. the political difficulties of the emperor Louis in southern Italy

4. the political and military success of Charles the Bald against the
   Northmen in the Loire valley, plus
   (a) the blinded Carloman's escape from Corbie to Louis the
       German
   (b) the death of the Northman Rodulf in East Francia
   (c) a plague of locusts (or grasshoppers)[68]
   (d) Louis the German's activities including his treatment of
       Carloman.

Items 4. (a) and 4. (b) are presented as news that reached Charles in
the course of his campaign.[69]
        All these items are also documented independently of the
AB; and the examples of items (1) and (2) have already suggested
comparisons between the treatments of material in the *AB* and in
other sources. In the Carloman case the close similarities of wording,
and of stance, between the *AB* and the Quierzy capitulary strongly
support the hypothesis that Hincmar wrote at least parts of the
capitulary.[70] Other contemporary annalists record Carloman's sentence laconically, but with evident disapproval of Charles the Bald's
action.[71] Hincmar's presentation in the *AB* is designed wholly to
condemn Carloman and in various ways to justify Charles the Bald's
response. Again, other evidence on item (4) shows that the successes
against the Northmen on the Loire owed a good deal more to Charles
the Bald's Breton allies than the *AB* account implies. The taking of
Angers may indeed have been a Breton rather than a Frankish
victory.[72] Item 4b identifies Rodulf in terms of the "many evils he had
inflicted on Charles' realm," and notes his death "in the realm of
Louis [the German] along with 500 of his accomplices"; the *AF* (dating
the appearance of Rodulf's fleet to June) tells a much fuller story, in
which 800 Northmen are slain, and the rest are said (twice) to have
departed from Louis's realm swearing never to return.[73] As for the
locusts (or grasshoppers), the *AB*'s reference is brief and un-
emotional: for Hincmar, it is only the *scale* of the attack that invites
comparison with the plague of Egypt (Exodus x.12–15.), whereas the
AF give a long and lurid account (". . . they had a wide mouth and a
long stomach and two teeth harder than stone . . ."etc.) and like the
Annals of Xanten, interpret this plague as a divine punishment for
"our sins."[74] Further, where the other contemporary witnesses say
that Gaul, or "the Franks," bore the brunt of the attack, Hincmar,
uniquely, claims not only that the insects went on to Spain, but that

Spain was the place worst-affected. If the plague was a sign of God's anger against sinners, Hincmar implied that those sinners were not the Franks of Charles's kingdom.

One phrase in the *AB* for 873 strikes the reader forcibly: Charles the Bald besieged the Northmen in Angers *viriliter ac strenue* ("manfully and energetically"). Such language applied to this king is unprecedented in Hincmar's section of the *AB*. It is a clue to the theme of the whole 873 annal—in what we call the *AB* but Hincmar called *The Deeds of Kings*.[75] The annal begins with "the king's office" embodied in legislation: the long description of the Angers campaign shows the king actually doing the job. The Northmen have been "ravaging towns, razing fortresses to the ground, burning churches and monasteries and turning cultivated land into a desert."[76]

Charles besieges them. The Bretons collaborate—on Charles's terms: Duke Salomon's own son swears an oath of fidelity. Charles "thoroughly tames" the Northmen: their leading men come over to him, swear "exactly the solemn oaths he ordered" and hand over "as many, and as important, hostages as he demanded"; finally, they agree either to leave Charles's realm forever, or to become Christians.[77]

> After all this, Charles, together with the bishops and people, with the greatest demonstration of religious fervour restored to their rightful places, with rich offerings, the bodies of SS Albinus and Licinius, which had been disinterred from their graves through fear fear of the Northmen.

Angers, its saints returned to it, could be left in safe hands. The annal ends with a description of Charles's route northwards to Francia: "via the city of Le Mans, and the town of Evreux, and passing close to the new fortress at Pîtres," and after hunting on the royal estate of Orville, "he reached St. Vaast where he celebrated Christmas."[78] The listing, with its careful gradation of settlements, is far from haphazard: Charles's royal journey signifies a direct inversion of the Northmen's activities—evoking patronage of urban life, responsibility for fortress-construction, devotion to the church, and (where the summertime cultivation of crops would be inappropriate) the hunting economy of winter.

The fourth episode, devoted to Charles's actions against the

Northmen, is neatly offset by the third, devoted to Louis II's difficulties in dealing with the Beneventans. Those old enemies of the Franks posed a new threat when sent help by "the emperor of the Greeks": against them, the "emperor of Italy" (Hincmar's use of this imperial title is tinged with irony) now had to mobilise the pope as a conciliator, cloaking his dependence by a show of deference to the vicar of St. Peter. [79] Louis, according to Hincmar, had sworn to capture the Beneventan duke Adalgis, "but in reality he was incapable of achieving this by his own strength."[80] Louis's lack of *virtus* contrasts with the very qualities Hincmar· goes on to attribute to Charles the Bald: "manliness and energy."

The smaller sections of (4) are woven into its main story. In (4a) Charles is *en route* for Angers when he hears of Carloman's escape, "with the connivance of two false monks," allegedly "as a result of the scheming of . . . Louis king of Germany," and "with the object of harming Charles's interests."[81] There can be no doubt of where the reader's sympathies are being led. In (4b) Charles has begun the siege of the Northmen in Angers when he hears of the death of his old enemy, the Northman Rodulf. But this item resonates with the preceding one: Rodolf had very probably been suspected of colluding with Carloman.[82] In (4c) while the fact of the plague of locusts is not suppressed, it is implicitly attributed to the sins of others, and especially of pagans. This points forward to Charles's ensuing success. In (4d) Louis the German's activities in fact mirror those of Charles—naturally, on a lesser scale. Louis's pagan enemies are the Wends. He heads for the frontier and, through envoys, wins over some of them; then he receives envoys of the Bohemians who plan to deceive him, and flings them into prison. As for Louis's reception of Carloman, it turns out that, though showing pity, Louis totally condemns "the evil deeds committed by Carloman against the holy church of God, against the Christian people, and against his own father."[83]

This brings us back to the episodes we began with. The stories of Carloman and Charles the Fat belong together. Both deal with the fraught relationship between a royal father and his son. Both show how the breakdown of the relationship endangers the right order of things. Carloman's rebellion and the acts of violence that accompany it threaten "the church of God and the Christian religion in Charles's realm": sacred laws (that is, the laws of Christian emperors) and sacred canons alike condemn Carloman. Despite being degraded from clerical rank, he remains bound by the canonical rules: the "ecclesiastical tonsure" has irreversible consequences. But Carloman is a criminal who persistently refuses to accept the restraints of law. Set apart from the world, he wilfully attempts to reenter it, fleeing from the church. Having been forbidden kingship, he seeks royal title and power. Where tonsure failed, blindness must ensure his ineligibility.

Charles the Fat, in Hincmar's presentation here, makes a comparable, yet contrasting case. As a king's son he is wide open to the temptation to rebel: so far the sources agree. But where the other sources go on to tell the story of a rebel unmasked, getting his just deserts, Hincmar in the *AB* depicts Charles the Fat as hardly responsible for his own actions. Tempted, the king's son is "terror-stricken" and flees to a church. When, possessed by the devil, he confronts his father, has action is the opposite of Carloman's: he seeks to abandon the world, renouncing the two kinds of activity, sex and war, that differentiate the worldly from the spiritual order.[84] This is madness. The royal father is acutely distressed; the attendant faithful men are "thunderstruck."

I shall return in section IV to the implications of these contrasting modes of filial defiance. For the present, I want to establish the link between the two within the structure of the 873 annal. They are parts of a single story: a tale of two princes. Each is an implicit comment on the other, just as the impotent Louis II is a foil to the manful Charles the Bald. Thus the whole annal forms a coherent whole. It opens with Charles the Bald, "in the manner of his ancestors," discharging the office of king, ensuring through law the peace of the church and the internal strengthening of the realm. Two princes are shown subverting this right order. Both fail, and two king-fathers reaffirm both that order and their own authority. Far away to the South, in Italy two emperors squabble over the Beneventans' allegiance, owed in the past to the emperors of Francia. Even the Carolingian Louis II lacks the strength to punish the faithless duke of a people once subject to the Franks. We return to Francia and the kings with strength. One asserts his authority over peoples on the eastern frontier. The other, with yet more conspicuous success, extracts due fidelity from the Bretons in the West and tames the men from the North. He restores the saints to "their rightful places." Amid images of re-established order, the annal ends with the calm resumption of royal routine.

III Ideology

Historians who have tried to extract from Hincmar's works a consistent political theory, whether of royalism or hierocracy, have been consistently unsuccessful. [85] The annals that Hincmar wrote from 861 to 882 have scarcely been considered at all in the context of political ideas. Yet they represent more clearly and consistently than do any of his other works, a set of ideological statements: responses to observed uses (and abuses) of power that attempt to accommodate these within the framework of heterogeneous beliefs and values which made up Carolingian culture.

Power is the central theme of the 873 annal; but Hincmar's concern here is not simply with the triumphant affirmation of patrimonial regalian authority. Power, for Hincmar, is complex and problematic. It has multiple sources, hence can be legitimized in more than one way. Kingship, its dominant secular form, may be "a scarce resource" but given partible royal succession, not as scarce as all that. [86] The transmission of royal power between generations is as negotiable as its distribution within each generation. The interests of individual royals crosscut those of the royal family; and are crosscut, in turn, by the interests of individual nobles and groups (often family-groups) of nobles. Already there exists a courtly society; but by no means all transactions of power are conducted at court. Hincmar would have agreed with his contemporary Notker (and both learned it from Augustine) that amidst all such uncertainties, only one thing was certain: "Nowhere and never is anything safe in this world of space and time (*in saeculo*), but always and everywhere is security an illusion."[87]

The tale of two princes highlights, first, the problem of power's recreation in space: how and when could a new king be validly made, to rule alongside his father? Within an existing kingdom could lie a potential one: what modern historians term the "sub-kingdoms" of this period were, for contemporaries, kingdoms whose noble families only awaited suitable princes for their distinctive political identity to be resumed. [88] The map could be redrawn with each generation. No Carolingian division, certainly not Verdun, had foreclosed subsequent rearrangements. Even if, as in Charles the Bald's case, the number of king's sons exceeded available kingdoms, (hence Carloman's tonsuring), kings had nephews as well as sons; and if a nephew himself died sonless, his uncle could validly claim a residual right to the orphaned kingdom. Hincmar presents the intended setting-up of Carloman by a group of Lotharingian nobles as invalid, not because of the incapacity of the would-be kingmakers but because of their candidate's personal ineligibility. In the *De Divortio* Hincmar considered the three ways that a man could "be set up in rulership" (*principatus* covers holy men as well as kings[89]): through the intervention of God, through God via men, or through men acting of their own choice (though always, Hincmar believed, with God's permission and foreknowledge). In the third and last category, a further distinction could be made. Men might collaborate with "angels," that is, with divine ministers—as when David ordered Solomon to be consecrated by Zadoch the priest and Nathan the prophet; or the king might be set up directly by men—and Hincmar was clearly thinking of the contemporary category of laymen: "by the support of citizens and soldiers," "by the succession of son to father," or through an individual's "tyrannical usurpation."[90] Solomon's inauguration was the prototype of the kind of procedure that Hincmar himself pioneered in Francia: where consecration by God's ministers operated in conjunction with the decision of a royal father (or in Queen Ermentrude's case, a royal husband) and the consent of the king's faithful men, the "people."[91] With the remaining man-made settings-up of kings, Hincmar evidently had in mind both Frankish (as well as Roman and Biblical) history and contemporary experience. For all his disctinction between angels and men, reflecting that between priesthood and laity in the Frankish world, and for all his preference for angelic participation, Frankish kingmakings, as Hincmar well knew, had been, and in the main still were, the work of laymen. And as such, he acknowledged, they were perfectly legitimate. Carloman was debarred from accepting "the support of citizens and soldiers" because of his clerical status: his crime turned potential kingmakers into "accomplices."

The story of Charles the Fat explores the problem of the timing of royal succession. Charles, validly designated to succeed his father, was tempted to jump the gun. Where other sources make it clear that there was a plot to remove Louis the German from his kingship, and present Charles's horrific experience as God's means of at once exposing and punishing him, Hincmar neither accuses the prince of actual rebellion, nor does he mention the unveiling of the plot as the sequel to Charles's fit. Instead, Hincmar repeats the claim, mentioned in the 870 annal, that Charles's eldest brother was being

given unfair preference, threatening Charles's own promised in-
heritance.No doubt Hincmar's presentation reflects his bias in Charles's favor: Hincmar's closeness to Charles the Bald in 873 prejudiced
him against Louis the German, who had so recently thwarted the
West Frankish king's hopes of acquiring the whole Middle Kingdom.
Hincmar hints, without perceptible disapproval, at Charles the Bald's
encouragement of Louis's sons in their rebellion against their father.
It is even possible that Hincmar retouched the 873 annal years later,
when he had come to view Charles the Fat as a potential ally against
his own rivals for influence in the West Frankish kingdom.[92] But as
the foregoing discussion of the annals' form has suggested, Hincmar
here intended more than a display of personal feeling. In juxtaposing
the very different outcomes of the two princes' filial misbehavior,
Hincmar contrasts the incorrigible with the contrite. At the same
time, he seems to invite sympathy for the temptation that inevitably
beset an adult king-to-be. Recent Frankish history could offer parallels: Hincmar had the evidence under his nose in the shape of the
Royal Frankish Annals and the earlier sections of the *AB*.

   The tale of two princes has another theme: the bringing out
into the open of dangerous secrets. To make such things public was to
allow them to be defused, bad power to be replaced by good. In
Carloman's case, all the criminal charges against him had to be re-
hearsed, by implication, before a court of Charles the Bald's faithful
men. This is reminiscent of the legislation of 873, requiring the
prosecution of witches before Frankish courts. In the case of Charles
the Fat, the means of exposure was an agonising seizure which happened "in the council-hall, before the king, Charles's brothers and
all their faithful men." The rebellion of Carloman, and the seizure of
Charles both constituted intrusions of wild power into the ordered
structures of a kingdom. Both had to be tamed and held within those
structures: hence the king used assemblies, and the counsel of faithful
men, to reassert control. Hincmar emphasises here the efficacy of
kingship working through consensus politics.[93]

   But all this would not be enough: "man-made" remedies
could not cope with threats that were in fact diabolical. Twice, and in
phrases that are not mere formal expressions of disapproval, Hincmar attributes Carloman's actions to the devil's instigation. Indeed
Carloman and his supporters, "sons of Belial," replicated the action of
that archetypal son of pride, Satan himself: in a capitulary only ten
years before, Hincmar had castigated contemporary Frankish mag-

nates for being the Devil's imitators in refusing to subject themselves
to the power constituted by God or to acknowledge others as their
"fellows and equals in the kingdom."[94] The annal's reference to Belial
is as precisely apt: Deuteronomy xiii linked sedition with sin against
God:

> If thou shalt hear say in one of thy cities, which the Lord thy God
> hath given thee to dwell there, saying,
> Certain men, the children of Belial, are gone out from among you,
> and have withdrawn the inhabitants of their city, saying, Let us go
> and serve other gods which ye have not known;
> Then shalt thou inquire, and make search, and ask diligently; and
> behold, if it be truth, and the thing certain, that such abomination is
> wrought among you;
> Thou shalt surely smite the inhabitants of that city with the edge of
> the sword, destroying it utterly, and all that is therein . . .
> And thou shalt gather all the spoil of it into the midst of the street
> thereof, and shalt burn with fire the city, and all the spoil thereof
> every whit, for the Lord thy God . . .
> And there shall cleave nought of the cursed thing to thine hand:
> that the Lord may turn from thee the fierceness of his anger, and
> shew thee mercy, and have compassion upon thee, and multiply
> thee, as he hath sworn unto thy fathers.[95]

Carloman too had attempted to withdraw the inhabitants of
cities from their allegiance; the people had suffered divine wrath; so
had the king, who now urgently sought the multiplication of his seed.
For men who knew their Old Testament, and believed themselves
part of the new Israel, such parallels did not need laying on with a
trowel. The Lord would be appeased only by the exposure and total
extinction of "the cursed thing."

Satan reappears in the story of Charles the Fat. What makes
this story so terrifying is the way in which evil is disguised as good.
The prince's supplanting of his father is presented to him by the
"angelic" apparition as reasonable and morally justified, his self-
interest coinciding with God's decision: since Louis the German
favors his firstborn unfairly, denying Charles what has been promised
him, God, offended, will remove power from Louis and transfer it to
Charles. Indeed the decision has already been made: the transfer is
imminent, and inevitable. This is the most insidious form of tempta-

tion: Satan looks like an Angel of Light. Charles's response does him
some credit. He mistrusts what he sees. The projection of his own
ambition produces not assent but terror—presumably the terror of
guilt. He links danger with his secular environment, his house; he
seeks safety in a church. But a second time, appearances deceive: the
"Angel" pursues him in, confronting Charles with an argument that
seems irrefutable in terms of the prince's own faith: "If I hadn't come
from God, would I have been able to enter?" This time the prince is
persuaded: understandably so, for the church is a consecrated place,
fortified against the Devil's attacks. Where if not in a church can
asylum be found? But the third and worst deception is to come: the
"Angel" now offers Charles the Host from his own hand. With the
prince's acceptance of that mouthful, the Devil is in him. It is impossible to imagine a more complete inversion of right order, a more
cruel denial of devout expectations: what looked like the sacrament,
the means of God's salvation, turns out to purvey the Devil instead.
"Nowhere and never is anything safe. . . ."

   Here too Hincmar had a Biblical model: the terrible story of
Judas in John xiii.27, where after the very mouthful of bread that
Christ gave him, Satan entered into the false disciple. [96] Hincmar
more than once used this text to convey a warning: to the *simplices* to
alert them to the dangers of predestination to damnation; to the
evil-living palace clergy to warn that the very act of taking the sacrament "into a stomach full of sin" could rebound against the
recipient.[97] The apparent contradiction, the fatal consequence of
taking what gave life, could in fact be resolved: the wicked already
belonged to Satan, so for them, as for Judas, taking the sacrament
only confirmed his grip. Bede in his *Commentary on John* had wrestled
with the problem, and offered such an explanation.[98] Hincmar's
return to the text on several occasions suggests its significance for
him, and helps to explain why he evoked it in trying to make sense of
Charles the Fat's experience.

   But, in the tale of two princes, Hincmar assaulted false
confidence, in order to restore true faith. God had appointed
mediators of the means of salvation, genuinely "angelic" ministers.
They were the ordained priests of the Church's hierarchy, and speci-
fically the bishops. The efficacy of their services could be relied on;
the laws they observed were fixed beyond dispute. In the thirty-six
lines of Latin text covering the Carloman story, Hincmar mentioned
the bishops and their functions four times, the Church three times,

the canons and holy orders twice each. This insistence has a crucial function in the text, and in the elaboration of an ideology. Hincmar wanted to show that the denial of Carloman's kingship was righteous. In practice, Hincmar knew, a secular penalty—blinding—ensured that no one would ever again support Carloman for king. That penalty followed Carloman's condemnation for his crimes by a secular court. But Hincmar sought to establish a prior ineligibility, and this could be done by invoking the immutable rules of canon law. At one level, this was a test case, which proved the effectiveness of Charles the Bald's putting his son into the Church as a means of extinguishing the young man's king-worthiness. At another level, the strategy work-ed by removing Carloman from a secular area of confliction and uncertain claims to an ecclesiastical area where clear-cut rules applied. The strategy could only work because laymen were willing to collude with it, recognising these rules, and their purview, absorbing the message of men like Hincmar that there were two orders, priestly and lay, mutually dependent, mutually supportive, each with its own rules, both within one Christian people: it was the old teaching of Gelasius, and it had a long run ahead of it.[99] But the scene was not just one of active clerics and passive laity. If churchmen knew that in the *saeculum* there was no doing without secular power, laymen—beset by uncertain and conflicting secular loyalties, by guilt, by fears of enemies within—sought from the Church a power without ambigu-ity. In the fraught divisions of the Carolingian Empire, they looked to the advice of bishops and priests "as if to a divine presence" to supply "a solution and an authoritive judgment." This is not Hincmar speak-ing, but the layman, Nithard.[100] And it was laymen who wanted, and accepted, the Church's lead in judging Carloman.

The denouement of Charles the Fat's story makes sense as part of the same bipartite ideology. Hincmar noted the involvement of the two orders, that is, of bishops and laymen together, in all three stages: they witnessed the prince's fit in the council hall; they held him firm and got him into a church; they took charge of him on the road to recovery. Charles's behavior during his fit was a kind of confound-ing of the orders: he tried to renounce his functions as husband and as warrior, and to take off his cloak *(vestimentum)*, the clothing that marked his status. The sequel reversed this violation of categories: the archbishop put on his priestly vestments *(vestes sacerdotales)* and began to perform Mass, the defining function of the priesthood. While he "chanted," that is, intoned in Latin, Charles "shouted out in the language of his ancestors." The ritual performance presented and reestablished the duality of orders and, implicitly, of functions. Charles would recover by following a sacred itinerary, defined by local cult-centers. The story, like the annal as a whole, after its dramatic climax ended on a quiet note. The restoration of right order had been possible, thanks to the Church's mediation of sacred power.

Hincmar and his contemporaries have been accused of blurring and softening Augustine's sharp vision of a violent and confused world in which no regime could be called just.[101] Of course, texts can be cited that seem to support this judgement. But it is both one-sided—for no Carolingian thinker consistently advocated mere facile conformism (though many had occasion to flatter royal patrons); and unhistorical—for it ignores the changes of the ninth century, and hence the variability of responses to them. Among those changes was the internalisation by at least some members of the literate lay elite of the essentialy monastic spirituality preached by the leaders of the Carolingian Reform. I do not think Charles the Fat's dilemma was Hincmar's invention.[102] It was not Charles's alone: from within a few years of 873 comes evidence of two other young men who shared it. Gerald of Aurillac and Alfred of Wessex, though born to secular power, and perhaps ambitious for it, rejected the carnality it required.[103] Hincmar took the dilemma seriously. He unmasked "angelic" temptation: lay power required and hence legitimised marriage and weapons.

The tale of two cities affirmed royal and paternal authority: the kings' triumph over filial rebellion was the triumph of God over the Devil, and the Church with law and ritual served the kings' interests. But in the annals that were perhaps not quite such a private work as has recently been claimed, Hincmar was no mere apologist for kings.[104] To "the historian's instinctive control of material"[105], Hincmar added the writer's conscious control and the statesman's recognition of the gulf between writing and reality. Hincmar the annalist, like Hincmar the draftsman of capitularies, recognised the ambivalence of human power. Alongside law and ritual, as forms of power, was coercion. When consensus failed, force was necessary: it was the king's job to wield it and so thwart the Devil and give "peace to the Church and Christendom in the realm." The order of the pure, the priesthood, required the exercise of impure power as a condition of its existence in the *saeculum*. The dilemma could not be evaded, as Charles the Fat had sought to evade it. Marriage and weapons had their uses—and kings had to use them. Worldly power would always be flawed, uncertain; but it acquired a conditional value. This had been Augustine's view: the judge conscious of his fallibility, of the necessary evil inherent in judging, had to get on with the job: "he must serve."[106] Hincmar's tale of two princes was also a tale of two cities. As such, it was realistic about power, but it was uncompromising about duty—and not without hope.

NOTES

[1] My thanks are due to Stuart Airlie, John Gillingham, Timothy Reuter, Richard Unger, and Patrick Wormald for help and criticism, and to Janos Bak for his patience and encouragement.

[2] Accusation and defence of Augustine are to be found in P. Brown, 'Saint Augustine', in B. Smalley, ed., *Trends in Medieval Political Thought* (Oxford, 1965), pp. 1–21, at p. 8 (reprinted in Brown, *Religion and Politics in the Age of St. Augustine* (London, 1972), pp. 25–45). *v* R. Markus, *Saeculum. History and Society in the Theology of St Augustine* (Cambridge, 1970).

[3] Hincmar of Rheims, *De Persona Regis et Regio Ministerio*, c. 5, ed. J. -P. Migne, *Patrologia Latina* (hereafter PL) 125, cols. 839–40.

[4] Critical, on the whole, of Carolingian political thought are R. W. and A. J. Carlyle, *A History of Medieval Political Theory*, 4th. ed. (Edinburgh, London, 1950) I; H. X. Arquilliere, *L'Augustinisme politique* (Paris, 1934). More sympathetic, yet also critical, are J. M. Wallace-Hadrill, "The *Via Regia* of the Carolingian Age," in Smalley, ed., *Trends*, pp. 22–41 (reprinted in Wallace-Hadrill, *Early Medieval History* (Oxford, 1975), pp. 181–200), and H. H. Anton, *Fürstenspiegel und Herrscherethos in der Karolingerzeit* (Bonn, 1968).

[5] *Annales Bertiniani*, ed. (F. Grat as *Annales de Saint Bertin*), J. Vielliard and S. Clemencet (Paris, 1965), hereafter referred to as *AB*. I use my own translation, to be published along with Timothy Reuter's translation of the *Annales Fuldenses* (hereafter *AF*), ed. F. Kurze, *Monumenta Germaniae Historica* (hereafter *MGH*), *Scriptores rerum Germanicarum in usum scholarum* (hereafter *SS rer. Germ. i.u.s.*) 7 (Hannover, 1891). *v* H. Lowe, "Geschichtschreibung der ausgehenden Karolingerzeit," in *Deutsches Archiv* 23 (1967), 1–30, at p. 3, 7–11; M. McCormick, *Les Annales du Haut Moyen Age* (Turnhout, 1975), pp. 18, 41, 46; J. L. Nelson, "The Annals of St. Bertin," in M. Gibson and J. Nelson, eds., *Charles the Bald: Court and Kingdom*, B.A.R. International Series 101 (Oxford, 1981), pp. 15–36 (reprinted in Nelson, *Politics and Ritual in Early Medieval Europe* (London, 1986), pp. 173–94). Hincmar's life and works are sensitively discussed by Wallace-Hadrill, "History in the mind of Archbishop Hincmar," in R.H.C. Davis and J. M. Wallace-Hadrill, eds., *The Writing of History in the Middle Ages* (Oxford, 1981), pp. 43–70; idem, *The Frankish Church* (Oxford, 1983), pp. 292–303. Interesting new perspectives on Hincmar's thought are opened up by K. F. Morrison, *Unum ex multis:* Hincmar of Rheims' medical and aesthetic rationales for unification," in *Nascita dell'Europa ed Europa Carolingia: un'equazione da verificare.* Settimane di Studio del Centro Italiano di Studi sull'Alto Medioevo 27 (Spoleto, 1981), pp. 583–712, esp. pp. 674ff. (reprinted in Morrison,

Holiness and Politics in Early Medieval Thought [London, 1985], no. II). For a first-rate critical survey of recent literature on Hincmar, *v* N. Staubach, *Das Herrscherbild Karls des Kahlen. Formen und Fulktionen monarchischer Reprasentation im fruheren Mittelalter,* diss. Munster, (1981), pt. II, with notes at pp. 366ff. The *AB* are scarcely mentioned in the otherwise exhaustive account of J. Devisse, *Hincmar, Archeveque de Reims (845–882),* 3 vols. (Geneva, 1975–76); nor by Nelson, "Kingship, law and liturgy in the political thought of Hincmar," *EHR* 363 (1977), pp. 241–79 (reprinted in Nelson, *Politics and Ritual,* pp. 133–71). For an excellent survey of Hincmar's life and works, with an up-to-date bibliography, *v* "Hinkmar von Reims," by R. Schieffer, *Theologische Realenzyklopadie,* 15, pp. 355–60.

⁶ *AB,* s.a. 873, pp. 189–92.

⁷ Since E. Dummler, *Geschichte des ostfrankischen Reiches,* 3 vols. (Leipzig, 1887–88, repr. Darmstadt, 1960), II, pp. 320–23, 337–38, 356–59, there has been no adequate treatment of Carloman's revolt. But *v* P. McKeon, *Hincmar of Laon and Carolingian Politics* (Urbana-Chicago-London, 1978), ch. 7; and, for brief accounts, K. Brunner, *Oppositionelle Gruppen im Karolingerreich* (Wien-Köln-Graz, 1979), pp. 134–35; and K. Bund, *Thronsturz und Herrscherabsetzung im Fruhmittelalter* (Bonn, 1979), pp. 466–67. In the title of this paper, I use the term "prince" in the modern sense of king's son, though I am aware of the variety of meanings of *princeps* in the Carolingian period: *v* K. F. Werner, "Les principautes peripheriques," in Werner, *Structures politiques du monde franc (VIe–XIIe siecles)* (London, 1979), ch. 2; H. Wolfram, "The shaping of the early medieval principality," *Viator* 2 (1971), pp. 33–51; *idem, Intitulatio I: Lateinische Konigs- und Furstentitel bis zum Ende des 8. Jhdt.* (Wien, 1967), pp. 148–51; K. Brunner, "Der frankische Furstentitel im neunten und zehnten Jhdt.," in Wolfram, ed., *Intitulatio II* (Wien, 1973), pp. 183–85. Special "family-names" were used to indicate the status and throneworthiness of kings' sons: Carloman was such a name for the Carolingians. Stuart Airlie will discuss the evidence in a forthcoming paper.

⁸ Cf. J. Goody, *Succession to High Office* (Cambridge, 1966), pp. 29–39.

⁹ For details, *v* Nelson, *Politics and Ritual,* pp. 81–82.

¹⁰ On Carloman's tutor, Wulfad, *v* J. Marenbon, "Wulfad, Charles the Bald and John Scottus Eriugena," in Gibson and Nelson, ed., *Charles the Bald,* pp. 375–83, at 375.

¹¹ Regino of Prum, *Chronicon,* ed. F. Kurze, *MGH SS rer. Germ. i.u.s.* 50 (Hannover, 1890), s.a. 870, p. 101.

¹² *v* T. Schieffer, 'Karl von Aquitanien. Der Weg eines karolingischen Prinzen auf den Stuhl des heiligen Bonifatius', in L. Lenhart, ed., *Universitas. Festschrift fur A. Stohr,* 2 vols. (Mainz, 1960), II, pp. 42–54.

¹³ For Carloman's lay abbacies in the 860s, *v* G. Tessier, ed., *Receuil des Actes de Charles II le Chauve,* 3 vols. (Paris, 1943–55), II, nos. 303, 338; J. Wollasch, "Das Patrimonium Beati Germani in Auxerre," in G. Tellenbach, ed., *Studien und Vorarbeiten zur Geschichte des grossfrankischen und fruhdeutschen Adels* (Freiburg, 1957), pp. 185–224, at pp. 215–7. W. Wattenbach and W. Levison, *Deutschlands Geschichtsquellen im Mittelalter,* 5, rev. ed., H. Lowe (Weimar, 1973), pp. 548, n. 224, 552, 563. The monks of St. Medard complained to Charles the Bald about the violence done to the monastery's resourced by their lord (*senior*) Carloman and his following (*sequaces*): *MGH Epp.* 6, pp. 179–80.

¹⁴ *AB,* s.a. 866, p. 130; 867, p. 135.

15 *AB*, s.a. 868, p. 151. F. Prinz, *Klerus und Krieg* (Stuttgart, 1971), p. 124, treats Carloman as a typical example of the military service of the higher clergy of this period.

16 *AB*, s.a. 852, pp. 64–65; 858, p. 78.

17 *AB*, s.a. 853, pp. 66–67; "*Pippinus . . . habitum monachi suscipit requlaeque observationem more monachis solito promittit*"; cf. 854, p. 69. Later Pippin was accused of being an "apostate," i.e., runaway monk: *AB*, s.a. 864, p. 105; Hincmar, Ep. 170, *MGH Epp.* VIII, p. 163. This charge was never levelled against Carloman. The difference between his status and Pippin's is ignored by Devisse, *Hincmar*, vol. 2, p. 752 ("*moine gyrovaque*").

18 *AB*, s.a. 869, pp. 157–64. *v* W. Schlesinger, "Zur Erhebung Karls des Kahlen zum Konig von Lothringen, 869" in Metz', in *Festschrift fur F. Petri* (Bonn, 1970), pp. 454–75; Staubach, *Herrscherbild*, pp. 239–71; Tessier, *Actes de Charles le Chauve*, II, no. 328, pp. 224–6.

19 Tessier, *Actes de Charles le Chauve*, II, no. 333, pp. 236–38; Folcuin, *Gesta Abbatum Lobbiensium*, ed. G. H. Pertz, *MGH Scriptores* IV (Hannover, 1841), p. 61.

20 O. G. Oexle, "Die Karolinger und die Stadt des heiligen Arnulf," *Frühmittelalterliche Studien* 1 (1967), pp. 250–64.

21 A. Dierkens, *Abbayes et Chapitres entre Sambre et Meuse (VIIe–XIe siècles)* (Sigmaringen, 1985), pp. 110, 130; *Carmina Centulensia*, no. 105, ed. L. Traube, *MGH Poetae Latinae* (Berlin, 1896), III, pp. 336–37.

22 *AB*, s.a. 869, p. 167; 870, p. 169. On Richildis and her family, see Brunner, *Oppositionelle Gruppen*, pp. 134, 137–40; J. Hyam, "Ermentrude and Richildis," in Gibson and Nelson, ed., *Charles the Bald*, pp. 153–68; S. Airlie, *The Political Behaviour of Secular Magnates in Francia*, unpub. D. Phil. (Oxford), 1985, ch. 5.

23 *AB*, s.a. 870, p. 168. *v* W. Vogel, *Die Normannen und das frankische Reich* (Heidelberg, 1906), p. 235.

24 J.-D. Mansi, ed., *Sacrorum Conciliorum Nova et Amplissima Collectio*, 31 vols. (Florence, Venice, 1758–98), XVI, col. 860. The implication that Carloman was taken by surprise is noted by McKeon, *Hincmar of Laon*, p. 121 and n. 15.

25 *AB*, s.a. 870, p. 171.

26 *AB*, s.a. 870, pp. 172–74. *v* Map. Cf. H. Henze, "Zur kartographischen Darstellung der Westgrenze des deutschen Reiches in karolingischer Zeit," *Rheinische Vierteljahrsblättër* 9 (1939), pp. 207–54, at 219–21, 236–43.

27 *AB*, s.a. 870, p. 177; cp. ibid. p. 179: Pope Hadrian II's envoys came with envoys from Emperor Louis II of Italy. Hadrian had written to Charles the Bald and Louis the German taking the emperor's part in protesting against the two kings' appropriation of the Middle Kingdom: *MGH Epp.* VI, no. 21, 25, pp. 724, 730. Hadrian protested to Charles about his treatment of Carloman: ibid., no. 31, pp. 735–36; perhaps again the emperor was involved in an attempt to embarrass Charles. I am not sure who else McKeon, *Hincmar of Laon*, p. 157, had in mind in referring to "influential parties in Italy" as among Carloman's sympathisers.

28 *AB*, s.a. 870, p. 178: '*Karlomannus . . . in Belgicam provinciam venit, et congregatis secum plurimis satellitibus ac filiis Belial, tantam crudelitatem et devastationem secundum operationem Satanae exercuit ut non possit credi. . . .*'

29 *Annales Laubienses*, s.a. 870, 873, ed. Pertz, *MGH Scriptores* IV, p. 15.

30 *AB*, s.a. 871, p. 179.

[31] So, Devisse, *Hincmar*, vol. 2,, p. 787, n. 497; McKeon, *Hincmar of Laon*, p. 123; R. McKitterick, *The Frankish Kingdoms under the Carolingians* (London, 1983), p. 186; and by implication Brunner, *Oppositionelle Gruppen*, pp. 134–35. Both McKeon and Brunner assume that the men on whom Charles the Bald and Hincmar of Rheims relied to deal with Carloman were in fact Carloman's supporters: assumptions that seem to depend, respectively, on a mistranslation of *AB*, s.a. 871, p. 179 (McKeon, pp. 121, 124, has Baldwin of Flanders as an envoy of Carloman's, where the *AB* clearly name him as an envoy of Charles the Bald to Carloman), and on the unsupported assertion (Brunner, p. 135, n. 85) that Charles's chamberlain Engilramn was Baldwin's brother. Carloman's supporters seem to have been active in the ecclesiastical province of Sens as well as those of Rheims and Trier: *v* Tessier, *Actes de Charles le Chauve*, II, no. 368, pp. 320–21, where the king complains about attacks on the see of Meaux.

[32] E. Hlawitschka, *Lotharingien und das Reich* (Stuttgart, 1968), pp. 15–19; Airlie, *Political Behaviour*, ch. 4.

[33] *AB*, s.a. 871, p. 184.

[34] *AB*, s.a. 872, pp. 184–85 (January), 188 (October); cf. the payment of Lothar II to Rodolf, s.a. 864, p. 105. For the alliances of Lothar II with Roric, see *AF*, s.a. 857, p. 47; of Lothar I with Harald, *AB*, s.a. 841, p. 39; and of Pippin II of Aquitaine with unnamed Northmen, *AB* s.a. 857, 864, pp. 74, 105. For the probable alliance of Charles the Bald with Ragnar, perhaps in 840, *v Vita Anskarii*, ed. G. Waitz, *MGH SS rer. Germ. i.u.s.* (Hannover, 1884) c. 21, p. 46; and for Charles's alliance with Weland, *v AB* s.a. 862, p. 89. *AF* s.a. 883, p. 100 and Regino, *Chronicon*, s.a. 885, p. 123 show Hugh, son of Lothar II, allied with the Viking Godfrid. A shrewd appraisal of the context of such relations is provided by Ian Wood, "Christians and Pagans in Ninth-century Scandinavia," in B. Sawyer, P. Sawyer and I. Wood, eds., *The Christianization of Scandinavia* (Alingsås, 1987), pp. 36–67. I am very grateful to Ian Wood and Simon Coupland for helpful discussion of the *AB* evidence.

[35] *MGH Capitularia Regum Francorum*, eds. A. Boretius and V. Krause (Hannover, 1897), II, no. 278 (Quierzy, 4 Jan., 873), c. 1, p. 343.

[36] Ibid., c. 4, pp. 344–5. For confiscation as a penalty, *v* Nelson, " 'A King across the Sea': Alfred in Continental Perspective," *Transactions of the Royal Historical Society* 5th. ser., 36 (1986), pp. 45–68, at 53–4.

[37] *MGH Capit.* II, no. 278, c. 7, p. 345:"Et quia audivimus quod malefici homines et sortiariae per plura loca in nostro regno insurgunt, quorum maleficiis iam multi homines infirmati et plures mortui sunt, quoniam, sicut sancti Dei homines scripserunt, regis ministerium est impios de terra perdere, maleficos et veneficos non sinere vivere, expresse praecipimus, ut unusquisque comes in suo comitatu magnum studium adhibeat, ut tales perquirantur et comprehendantur. Et si iam inde comprobati masculi vel comprobatae feminae sunt, sicut lex et iustitia docet, disperdantur. Si vero nominati vel suspecti et necdum inde comprobati sunt vel per testes veraces comprobari non possunt, Dei iudicio examinentur; et sic per illud Dei iudicium aut liberentur aut condemnentur. Et non solum tales istius mali auctores, sed et conscii ac complices eorum, sive masculorum sive feminarum, disperdantur, ut una cum eis scientia tanti mali de terra nostra pereat." On the significance of this as the first Carolingian legislation specifying the death-penalty for witchcraft, *v* J. B. Russell, *Witchcraft in the Middle Ages* (Ithaca, 1972), pp. 72–73, noting the influence of late Roman models.

38 Above, nn. 9, 12, 16.
39 Examples include Bernard of Italy, *Annales regni Francorum*, ed. F. Kurze, *MGH SS rer. germ. i.u.s.* (Hanover, 1895), s.a. 818, p. 148; the Breton *dux* Salomon, *AB*, s.a. 874, p. 196; and Lothar II's son Hugh, *AF*, s.a. 885, p. 103. H. Schaab's dissertation on blinding as a penalty in the early Middle Ages has unfortunately been inaccessible.
40 *AB*, s.a. 873, pp. 192–3. Cf. *Annals of Xanten*, ed. B. v. Simson, *MGH SS rer. Germ. i.u.s.* 12 (Hanover, 1909), p. 32. (On these annals, see below, n. 59.) Regino, s.a. 870, p. 102, adds that Carloman died not long after. McKeon, *Hincmar of Laon*, p. 158 and n. 17, cited evidence for 887.
41 McKeon, *Hincmar of Laon*, p. 158, mistranslates in suggesting that Charles the Bald "learned with alarm" of Carloman's rescue. But Brunner, *Oppositionelle Gruppen*, p. 135, notes that Charles could have been worried by Adalard's role here. Serious physical handicap seems to have been considered a bar to kingship: hence the noting of the lameness of Charles the Bald's son Lothar, tonsured in 861, in *AB*, s.a., p. 84. Cf. Charlemagne's eldest son Pippin, a hunchback, according to Einhard, *Vita Karoli*, ed. G. Waitz, *MGH SS rer. Germ. i.u.s.* (Hanover, 1911), c. 20, p. 25, and also a dwarf, according to Notker, *Gesta Karoli*, ed. H. F. Haefele, *MGH SS rer. Germ. i.u.s.*, n.s. 13 (Berlin, 1959), II, c. 12, p. 72. The Franks may have found this a useful criterion for dynastic shedding. Cf. P. Wormald, "Celtic and Anglo-Saxon Kingship: Some Further Thoughts," in P. E. Szarmach, ed., *Sources of Anglo-Saxon Culture*, Studies in Medieval Culture 20 (Kalamazoo, 1986), pp. 151–83, at 160, 162.
42 R. H. Bautier, ed., *Receuil des Actes de Louis II le Begue* (Paris, 1978), no. 30 (8 February, 879), p. 91.
43 For Charles the Fat's early career, *v* Dummler, *Geschichte*, vol. 2, pp. 36, 352–55; G. Eiten, *Das Unterkonigtum im Reiche der Merowinger und Karolinger* (Heidelberg, 1907), pp. 158–65.
44 M. Borgolte, *Die Grafen Alemanniens in merowingischer und karolingischer Zeit* (Sigmaringen, 1986), p. 162.
45 Dummler, *Geschichte*, II, p. 119. The *AF*, s.a. 865, do not mention this division, but the 866 entry, p. 64, assumes it.
46 This is implied in a charter of Arnulf, ed. P. Kehr, *MGH Diplomata regum Germaniae ex stirpe Karolinorum*, III (Berlin, 1955), no. 64 (15 November, 889). *v* Dierkens, *Abbayes et Chapitres*, pp. 109, 112–13.
47 Karlmann: *AF*, s.a. 861, p. 55; 863, pp. 56–57; Louis the Younger: *AB*, s.a. 865, pp. 123–24; *AF*, s.a. 866, pp. 64–65. *v* J. Fried, *Konig Ludwig der Jungere in seiner Zeit* (Lorsch, 1984), pp. 8–11.
48 Brunner, *Oppositionelle Gruppen*, p. 145; Borgolte, *Grafen*, p. 106.
49 *MGH Diplomata Regum Germaniae*, I, ed. P. Kehr (Berlin, 1937), no. 108 (1 August 861 or 862), pp. 155–56.
50 *AF*, s.a. 869, pp. 68–69.
51 *AF*, s.a. 871, pp. 72–73.
52 *AB*, s.a. 870, p. 176: "[Louis the German] suosque filios Hludouuicum et Karolum ad se venire praecepit. Qui sentientes. satagente matre, inclinatiorem esse voluntatem patris erga Karlomannum quam erga se, ad illum venire detrectaverunt". I take this to mean that the princes' mother sided with her two younger sons; Fried, *Konig Ludwig*, p. 8, that she encouraged her husband to favor their first-born.
53 *AB*, s.a. 870, p. 176.

54 *AF*, s.a. 871, p. 74.

55 *AB*, s.a. 871, p. 183. Cp. *AF*, 871, p. 74.

56 *AB*, s.a. 859, p. 82. *v* Brunner, *Oppositionelle Gruppen*, p. 140, though he admits that the conflicts in this area cannot be reduced to a struggle between "Bosonids" and "Welfs."

57 *AB*, s.a. 872, p. 186 seems more plausible than the bland statement of *AF*, s.a. 872, p. 75. The *AF* at this point are virtually an "official" source, consistently favouring Louis the German.

58 *AF*, s.a. 873, pp. 77–78.

59 *Annals of Xanten*, s.a. 873, pp. 31–32. Written at this time in Cologne, these original- ly Lotharingian annals show a bias in the late 860s and early 870s towards Louis the German. *v* H. Lowe, "Studien zu den *Annales Xantenses*," *Deutsches Archiv* 5 (1950), pp. 59–99.

60 *AF*, s.a. 873, p. 78; *AB*, s.a. 874, p. 196; *AB*, s.a. 875, p. 198; *AF*, s.a. 876, p. 89.

61 Dummler, *Geschichte*, vol. 3, p. 291, n.2, points out that there is no evidence for the nickname "the Fat" before the twelfth century. I have followed Dummler in using it for convenience to distinguish this Charles from his uncle, the West Frankish king. For confusion in early medieval sources between the two Charleses, *v* K. U. Jaschke, "Die Karolingergenealogien aus Metz," *Rheinische Vierteljahrsblatter* 34 (1970), pp. 190–218, at 198, 214–27. For positive views of Charles the Fat's career down to 886, *v AF*, first continuator, pp. 107–14, and *Annales Vedastini* (Ann. St. Vaast), ed. B. v. Simson, *MGH SS rer. Germ. i.u.s.* 12 (Hanover, 1909), pp. 51–60. The main *AF* author is more critical, but does not disguise Charles's success in some traditional royal roles: s.a. 882, p. 98; 883, p. 100; 885, p. 103. It seems unreasonable to link the fact that Charles was trepanned in 887 after suffering headaches (*AF*, first continuator, s.a., p. 115), with his fit in 873, and conclude that he had suffered from a nervous disorder throughout the intervening period.

62 Regino, s.a. 887, p. 127, where, at n.5, the editor (Kurze) says that the imputation of "ten years" to Charles's and Richgard's marriage is an error for twenty-five years. But Regino (and Charles) may have been calculating from 873. The broader significance of Richgard's case is nicely brought out by P. Stafford, *Queens, Con- cubines, and Dowagers: The King's Wife in the Early Middle Ages* (Athens, Georgia, 1983), pp. 94–96.

63 *AF*, s.a. 885, p. 103; Notker, *Gesta Karoli*, II, c. 12, p. 74, c. 14, p. 78.

64 *AF*, s.a. 873, p. 78.

65 *v* Nelson, "Annals of St. Bertin," pp. 22–29.

66 Lowe, '*Geschichtschreibung der ausgehenden Karolingerzeit*', pp. 3, 7–10; Wallace- Hadrill, "History in the Mind of Archbishop Hincmar," pp. 52–54. By contrast, the *AB* are virtually neglected by Anton, *Furstenspiegel und Herrscherethos* (a fleeting mention, p. 285), and, more curiously, by Devisse, *Hincmar*, where the remarks at vol. 2, pp. 974, n. 34 ("*document officiel*"), and 1054 ("l'oeuvre la plus anonyme du prelat") betray a failure to give this text the same careful attention accorded Hincmar's other works.

67 Nelson, "Annals of St. Bertin," p. 27; Devisse, *Hincmar*, vol. 2, p. 787, n. 497.

68 *AB*, s.a. 873, p. 193, n. 2. the word *locusta*, with its obvious Biblical connotations, was also used for this pest in the 873 annals of *AF*, p. 79, *Annals of Xanten*, p. 83, and Regino, p. 105.

69 It is tempting to infer that Hincmar was with Charles the Bald on this campaign. Cf.

his insistence in 867 on the regularity with which he performed his due military service: v Nelson, "The Church's Military Service in the Ninth Century," *Studies in Church History* 20 (1983), pp. 15–30, at 29 (reprinted in Nelson, *Politics and Ritual*, pp. 117–32).

[70] For the manuscript evidence of Hincmar's involvement, see Nelson, "Legislation and Consensus in the Reign of Charles the Bald," in P. Wormald, ed., *Ideal and Reality. Studies in Frankish and Anglo-Saxon Society presented to J. M. Wallace-Hadrill* (Oxford, 1983), pp. 202–27, at 205–8, 225 (reprinted in Nelson, *Politics and Ritual*, pp. 94–97, 114).

[71] *AF*, s.a. 873, p. 78; *Annals of Xanten*, p. 32. Regino, s.a. 870, p. 102, is evenhanded.

[72] Compare the well-informed account of the siege by Regino, s.a. 873, pp. 105–7. v Werner, "Zur Arbeitsweise des Regino von Prum," *Die Welt als Geschichte* 19 (1959), pp. 96–116.

[73] *AF*, s.a. 873, p. 80. (The *Annals of Xanten*, s.a. 873, p. 32, like the *AB*, give the figure of 500 slain.)

[74] Cf. n. 68 above.

[75] *MGH Epp* VIII, i, ed. E. Perels (Berlin, 1939), no. 187, p. 194.

[76] *AB*, s.a. 873, p. 193.

[77] Ibid., pp. 194–95.

[78] Ibid., p. 195.

[79] Ibid., p. 192. Cf. *AB*, s.a. 864, p. 105, where Louis II is "so-called emperor of Italy" (*imperator Italiae nominatus*).

[80] Ibid., s.a. 873, p. 192: " . . . rem re vera virtute sua obtinere non posset."

[81] Ibid., pp. 192–93.

[82] v above, p. 113, and n. 34.

[83] *AB*, s.a. 873, p. 194.

[84] Cf. Notker, *Gesta Karoli* II, c. 10, p. 66: "[res et negotia] sine quibus res publica terrena non subsistit, coniugio videlicet usuque armorum."

[85] For some valiant attempts, v Anton, *Furstenspiegel*, pp. 281–355; Devisse, *Hincmar*, vol. 2, pp. 671–723; W. Ullmann, *The Carolingian Renaissance and the Idea of Kingship* (London, 1971), pp. 83–101; Nelson, "Kingship, Law and Liturgy in the Political Thought of Hincmar of Rheims," *EHR*, 92 (1977), pp. 241–79 (reprinted in Nelson, *Politics and Ritual*, pp. 133–71). All of these effectively ignore the *AB*.

[86] Cf. Goody, *Succession*, pp. 170–72.

[87] Notker, *Gesta Karoli* I, 22, p. 31: "[in cautelam] nusquam et numquam in hoc saeculo tutae sed semper et ubique vanae securitatis." For the central Augustinian concept here, v R. A. Markus, *Saeculum*, esp. pp. 101–2, 133–34, 150–53.

[88] Werner, "*Principautés peripheriques*," pp. 490ff; idem, "La génese des duchés en France et en Allemagne," in *Nascita dell' Europa ed Europa Carolingia: un'equazione da verificare, Settimane di studio del Centro Italiano di Studi sull'alto medioevo*, 27 (1981), pp. 175–207, at pp. 176–80.

[89] For non-royal *principatus* in the Frankish world, v the works cited above, n. 7.,

[90] Hincmar, *De Divortio Lotharii regis et Tetbergae reginae*, PL 125, col. 758. Anton, *Furstenspiegel*, pp. 295–96 (followed by Wallace-Hadrill, "History in the mind of Hincmar", p. 57), misleadingly says that Hincmar "lists six types of ruler." The sixfold classification is Anton's inference only: Hincmar seems (though without enumerating) to start with three types, and the third, when he reaches it, prompts

further sub-division. The whole passsage is a riposte to those who argue that Lothar "could be constituted king . . . by God alone." After considering the various ways in which men have in fact become kings, Hincmar concludes with filial succession, and comments: "The king ought rather to fear divine judgements and show respect for human judgements, than take vast pride in acquiring the kingdom, if he does not imitate his father's good behaviour . . . ." Note that human as well as divine judgment is here threatened as a sanction.

91 v Nelson, "Inauguration Rituals," in P. Sawyer and I. N. Wood, eds., *Early Medieval Kingship* (Leeds, 1977), pp. 50–71, at 61–63 (reprinted in Nelson, *Politics and Ritual*, pp. 283–307, at 294–96); idem, "Carolingian Royal Ritual," in D. Cannadine and S. Price, eds., *Rituals of Royalty* (Cambridge, 1987), pp. 137–80.

92 Devisse, *Hincmar*, II, pp. 982–83.

93 Cf. Hincmar's views in the *AB* and in the *de Ordine Palatii*: Nelson, "Legislation and Consensus," pp. 214–22 (reprinted *Politics and Ritual*, pp. 103–11).

94 *MGH Capit.* II, no. 272, pp. 305–6 (and, for Hincmar's authorship, the editor's note, ibid., p. 303).

95 Deuteronomy xiii, 12–17.

96 *John* xiii, 26–27: "Respondit Jesus: ille est [qui me tradet] cui ego intinctum panem porrexero. Et cum intinxisset panem, dedit Judae Simonis Iscariotae. Et post buccellam, introivit in eum Satanas."

97 *MGH Epp.* VIII, i, no. 37, p. 22; no. 127, p. 66. Cf. *de Cavendis Vitiis* (addressed to Charles the Bald probably in 869), PL 125, col. 925. Further references (though without details) ar indicated in Devisse, *Hincmar*, III, p. 1267.

98 Bede, *In S. Ioannis Evangelium Expositio*, PL 92, cols. 810–12. Cf. Walafrid Strabo, *de Exordiis et Incrementis* c. 18, ed. Krause, *MGH Capit.* II, p. 491, where the fate of Judas is cited to justify withholding the sacrament from those in a state of mortal sin.

99 Cf. Wallace-Hadrill, "History in the Mind of Hincmar," p. 56: "Hincmar remained a Gelasian"; also Anton, *Furstenspiegel*, pp. 319–55.

100 Nithard, *Historiarum Libri* IV, ed. E. Muller, *MGH SS rer. Germ. i.u.s.* (Hannover, 1907), IV, 1, p. 40: " . . . ut illorum [i.e., bishops and priests] consultu veluti numine divino harum rerum exordium atque auctoritas proderetur'. On Nithard's ideas, see Nelson, "Public *Histories* and Private History in the Work of Nithard," *Speculum* 60 (1985), pp. 273, 284–85 (reprinted Nelson, *Politics and Ritual*, pp. 217, 228–29); and idem, "Carolingian Royal Ritual" pp. 160–61.

101 v above, p. 105. Markus, *Saeculum*, p. 153, rightly notes that later developments were "scarcely in line with the grain of Augustine's own thought."

102 Hincmar's account of Charles's aspiration to celibacy in 873 is unique. But cf. Regino, s.a. 887, p. 127, cited above, p. 119 with n. 62. An important aspect of the context of Charles's behavior is explored by K. Leyser, "Early Medieval Canon Law and the Beginnings of Knighthood," in L. Fenske, ed., *Festschrift für J. Fleckenstein* (Sigmaringen, 1984), pp. 549–66 (with a reference to Charles's case at p. 563).

103 A comparison between Gerald and Alfred was suggested by Patrick Wormald in a lecture to the Anglo-American Conference of Historians, London, 1985. I hope in a future paper to consider Charles's case along with these.

104 He often criticises individual kings in the *AB* but never hints here at any hierocratic idea of episcopal jurisdiction over kings.

105 Wallace-Hadrill, "History in the Mind of Hincmar," p. 54.

106 Augustine, *De Civitate Dei* XIX, 6.

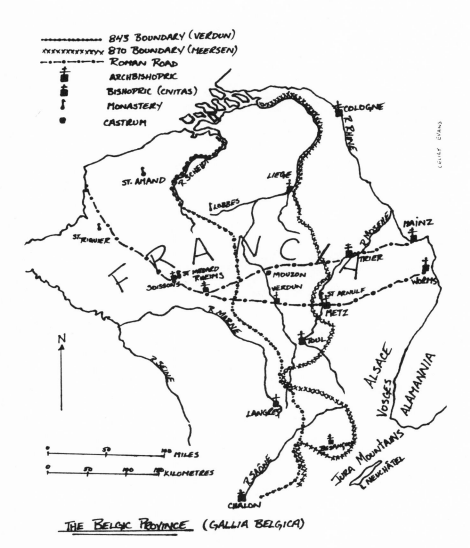

843 BOUNDARY (VERDUN)
870 BOUNDARY (MEERSEN)
ROMAN ROAD
ARCHBISHOPRIC
BISHOPRIC (CIVITAS)
MONASTERY
CASTRUM

CECILY EVANS

THE BELGIC PROVINCE (GALLIA BELGICA)

INDEX

Abbot of Saint Florent, 18, 42
Achilles, 78, 79
Adalard, 137
Adalgis, Duke, 124
Aeneas, 63
Agostino, see Antona
Agramante, 80
Agus, I. A., 51
Airlie, Stuart, 133–135
Alamanni, Luigi, 101
Albinus, SS, 123
Aldabella, 82, 83
Alexander the Great, 101
Alfred of Wessex, 132
Altobello, 82, 83, 99
Amin, 3
Anderson, P., 38
Angelieri, Carlo, 93
Anton, H. H., 133, 138, 139
Antona, Buovo (d'), 71–75, 79, 89, 95, 96, 99, 101
Aragona, Cardinal Luigi (d'), 84
Aragona, Tullia (d'), 84, 85
Arese, Felice, 91
Aretino, Pietro, 84
Ariosto, Ludovici, 59, 80–84, 87–89, 99, 100
Aristotle, 81, 84
Arquilliere, H. X., 133
Arraldus, 25
Artu, King, 63–65, 76
Arturo, 68
Artusius, 61
Ascoli, Albert R., 975
Augustine, 105, 126, 132, 133, 140
Aymard, O. 54

Bachrach, Bernard S., 38, 41, 42, 45–47, 49–55
Bak, Janos, 133
Baldus, 86, 87
Baldwin of Flanders, 136
Barberino, Andrea (da), 59, 66–76, 78, 82, 84, 85, 92, 93, 96, 97, 100
Barbicone, Ajolfo (del), 86, 99
Barini, Giorgio, 91,
Baron, Hans, 93
Battista, Appresso Gio., 99
Bautier, Anne-Marie, 46
Bautier, R. H., 137
Bayerle, R., 47
Beaulieu-les-Loches, 20, 48, 49
Bec, Christian, 99
Bede, 140
Beer, Marina, 95, 97, 100
Behm, Herbert, C., 97
Behrends, Frederick, 49
Belial, 129
Bello, Francesco, 98
Bernard, 119
Bernard of Italy, 137
Berta the Big Foot, 61, 76, 77, 96
Besly, Jean, 42, 52
Beumann, H., 39
Bienvenu, J. M., 39, 43, 44, 48, 54
Bindoni, Augustino, 98
Bindoni, Francesco di Alessandro, 86, 96
Binni, Walter, 97
Biondo, Flavio, 68
Bloch, Marc, 4, 36, 37
Boccaccio, 77, 84, 88, 96

Bongi, Salvatore, 97, 99
Boni, Marco, 92, 94
Bonnassie, 37
Boretius, A. 136
Borgo, 84
Borgolte, M. 137
Borromeo, Carlo, 88
Boso, 112
Bouchard of Broillay, 25, 28, 53
Boussard, Jacques, 39, 45, 48, 50,
    51, 53, 54
Boutruche, Robert, 39
Boyer, Marjorie Nice, 47
Bradmante, 80
Branca, Daniela Delcorno, 90–92
Brandoria, 71, 72
Braund, David, 49
Broussillon, Bertrand, (de), 39
Brown, P., 133
Brown, R., Allen, 55
Brucker, Gene A., 95, 96
Bruhl, Carlrichard, 41
Bruni, Leonardo, 67
Brunner, K., 134–138
Buchner, R., 47
Bund, K., 134
Bur, Michael, 37

Caesar, Julius, 79
Canavari, Romualdo, 98
Caponetto, Salvatore, 101
Carloman, 106, 108–114, 119–122,
    124–126, 128–131, 134–137
Carlyle, A. J., 133
Carlyle, R. W., 133
Cash, Annette, 92
Catalano, Michele, 100
Catarino, Ambrogio, 87
Cavalcanti, Giovanni, 70
Cavall, Luigi, 92
Charlemagne, 28, 59, 66, 67, 77,
    80, 83, 93, 96, 99, 100

Charles of Aquitaine, 109
Charles the Bald, 105, 106, 108–
    117, 119–126, 128, 131, 134–
    138, 140
Charles the Fat, 106–108, 115–121,
    124, 125, 127–132, 137, 138
Chateau–Gontier, 6, 25, 39, 125
Chatelain, Andre, 55
Cheyette, F. L., 38
Chickering, H., 49
Chiorboli, Ezio, 98
Ciggar, Krijnie, 55
Cinthio, Giovanni Battista Giraldi,
    62, 68, 91
Clark, Colin, 45
Clemencet, S., 133
Clio, 68
Collett, Barry, 101
Colonne, Guido Delle (of Messina),
    78
Commune of Osimo, 61
Commune of Siena, 61
Conamoro, 68
Constantine the Great, 67, 68, 70,
    73
Contreni, John, 55
Council of Rheims, 21
Coupland, Simon, 136
Croce, Benedetto, 98
Cutolo, Alessandro, 94–96, 98–102

Dagobert I, King, 52, 53
Danese, 99
Dante, 59, 80, 88
Daurellus, Aimo, 52
David, 127
Davies, R. W., 55
Davis, R. H. C., 133
Delatouche, R., 45
Denis. L. J., 52
Deuteronomy, 129, 140
Devaillly, Guy, 37

Devisse, J., 134–136, 138–140
Dhondt, Jan, 4, 37
Diaconus, Paulus, 68
Dido, 63
Dierkens, A., 135
Di Maria, Salvatore, 97
Dionsotti, Carlo, 90, 100
Dolce, Ludovico, 81
Doni, Anton Francesco, 84, 86, 98, 99
Drusiana, 71, 72–75, 89, 95
Dubled, Henri, 39
Duby, Georges, 37, 45
Dummler, E., 134, 137, 138
Durliat, Jean, 48

Ehler, S. Z., 38
Einhard, 137
Eiten, G., 137
Elisena, Princess, 81, 97
Engels, Donald W., 46, 50
Engilramn, 136
Esplandian, 82
Espinay, G. d', 39, 40
Ermentrude, Queen, 108, 110, 127
Eusebius, Bishop, 33, 49, 54
Evans, John, 46

Fabriano, Mambrino Roseo (da), 82
Falconetto, 99
Falerina, 68
Fanning, Stephen, 49
Felix, Pope, 68
Fenske, L., 140
Ferguson, F. S., 95
Ferrario, Giulio, 90
Finley, M. I., 3
Fiordispina, Queen, 83
Fiovo, 69
Florando, 68
Florisello, 68
Foffano, Francesco, 90

Folcuin, 135
Folengo, Teofilo, 86, 87, 101
Fossier, Robert, 37, 45
Francia, Reali di, 68
Frederick, (Abbot of Saint Florent), 31
Fried, J., 137
Fulbert, 49
Fulk, Count, 21
Fulk the Good, 29–31, 51–53
Fumagalli, Vito, 45, 97, 99

Gailone of Maganza, 72, 75, 95, 96
Gambarin, Giovanni, 91, 93
Ganshof, F. L., 39, 41, 43, 44, 53
Gardner, Edmund G., 91
Garin, Eugenio, 93
Garzoni, Tommaso, 68, 87, 93
Gasnault, P., 44,
Gaula, Amadis de, 68, 81, 82, 98
Gelasius, 105, 131
Gerald of Aurillac, 132, 140
Gibson, M., 133–135
Gilbert, Felix, 93
Gillingham, John, 133
Ginevara, Queen, 63–65, 82
Giodanengo, 37
Giussani, Gian Pietro, 88
Godfrid, 136
Goffart, Walter, 45, 55
Goody, J., 134, 139
Gorra, Egidio, 96
Gramain, 37
Grand, Roger, 42
Grandmaison, Ch. (de), 54
Grasilier, T., 41
Green, Louis, 93, 94
Gregory of Tours, 44, 554
Gregory VII, 105
Grendler, Marcella T., 93
Grendler, Paul F., 91, 96, 99

Greymantle, Geoffrey, 5, 28, 30,
    31, 33, 34, 39, 46, 48, 51–53, 55
Gualdo, Peitro Durante da, 87
Guadagnino, Giovanni Andrea
    Vavassore Detto, 99
Guerard, B., 44, 48
Guerrind, 97
Guido, Duke, 71, 72
Guillot, Olivier, 38–44, 49–51, 54

Hadrian II, Pope, 135
Haefele, H. F., 137
Halphen, Louis, 37–40, 43, 44, 46–
    51, 53–55
Hanawalt, Barbara, 46
Harald, 136
Hartley, Dorothy, 46
Haswell, Margaret, 45
Havinghurst, Alfred, 55
Hector, 79
Helen, 79
Henze, H., 135
(d')Herbecourt, Pierre, 54
Herbert, Count of Maine, 50, 51
Herlihy, David, 95
Higounet, 37
Hiller, Catharine M., 92
Hincmar, Archbishop of Rheims,
    105, 106, 111, 113, 121–128,
    130–135, 138–140
Hindess, Barry, 3
Hirst, Paul Q., 3
Hlawitschka, E., 136
Hogan, Richard M., 48, 52
Housseau, Dom, 40–42, 52, 53
Hubert, Abbot of Saint Aubin, 49,
    116
Hubert, Bishop of Angers, 21, 49
Hubert, Viscount of Vendôme, 53
Hugh (son of Lothar II), 136, 137
Hyan, J., 135
Hyde, J. K., 91

Irmino, Abbot, 19
Isanhard, 17, 47
Isola, I. G., 92
Isotta, 61, 63, 64, 65, 82

Jackson, W. A., 95
Jaschke, K. U., 138
Jason, 78
Jones, A. H. M., 40, 44
Jordan, Constance, 97
Judas, 130, 140

Karlmann, 107, 116, 118, 137
Kienast, Walther, 38
King of Armenia, 72
King of Gaul, 81
King, M., 38
Krause, V., 136, 140
Kristeller, Paul Oskar, 95
Krusch, Bruno, 45, 52
Kurze, F., 133, 134, 137, 138

Labande, E. R., 51
Lackner, B. K., 38
Lancilotto, Sir, 63–65, 68, 76, 82
Langdon, John, 47
Langeais, 22
Latouche, Robert, 37, 51
Leandra, 100
Leighton, A., 47, 50
Lega, A. Bacchi Della, 93
Lenhart, L., 134
Leo of Meung-sur-Loire, 25
Leo, Pope, 106
Lepeletier, L., 43
Levi, Ezio, 91
Levillain, Leon, 41
Levine, Lawrence W., 90
Levinson, W., 45, 134
Leyser, K., 140
Licinius, 123

Lisoius of Bazougers, 25, 26, 50
Liutbert, Archbishop, 108, 119
Liverani, Giuseppe, 101
Livy, 79
Lo Blanc, Tirante, 68
Lodovici, Francesco, 100
Longnon, A., 45, 48
Lothar, 107, 136, 137, 140
Lothar II, 110, 113, 116, 117, 136, 137
Louis II, Emperor, 117, 119, 121, 135
Louis the German, King, 106, 107, 111, 112, 115–120, 122, 124, 127, 129, 135, 137, 138
Louis the Pious, 45, 110
Louis the Stammerer, 115
Louis the Younger (II), 116–118, 124, 125, 137, 139
Lovato, Lovati, 61, 62
Lowe, H., 133, 134, 138
Lucian, 68
Lyon, Bryce D., 39, 54, 55
Lyon, M., 39

Mabille, E., 48
Magiabotti, Andrea, 66
Magnou-Nortieri, Elisabeth, 37
Mailfert, Yvonne, 39, 41, 42, 44, 48
Malatesta, Gioseppe, 97, 101
Mambriano, 98
Mangiabotti, Andrea, 66
Mansi, J. D., 135
Mantova, Benedetto (da), 101
Manyon, L. A., 37
Marchegay, Paul, 40, 43, 48
Marco, King, 63, 64, 76
Marenborn, J., 134
Margolana, 68
Margutte the half-giant, 80
Markus, R. A., 133, 139–40

Martel, Charles, 67, 93
Martel, Geoffrey, 5, 18, 27, 31, 33, 34, 43, 48, 51–55
Martindale, Jane, 42
Mattaini, Adelaide, 93
(de)Mause, Lloyd, 95
McCormick, M., 133
McKeon, P., 134, 135, 137
McKitterick, R., 136
Medea, 78
Melusina, 68
Meschino, Guerrin, 85, 86
Metais, Charles, 40
Metz, 135
Migne, J. P., 133
Milone, 61
Minnucci, Giovanni, 101
Montalvo, Garci Rodriquez (de), 81
Montanari, Massimo, 45
Montechiello, Domenico (da), 78
Montreuil-Bellay, 10
Montreuil, Lord of, 43
Morf, H., 96
Morgana, 68
Morgante the Giant, 80
Morrison, K. F., 133
Moses, 114
Muller, E., 140
Muller-Mertens, E., 38, 47
Murray, Alexander, 55
Musso, Cornelio, 102

(de)Narni, Cassio, 100
Nathan, 127
Neirmeyer, J. F., 40
Nelson, J. L., 133–136, 139–140
Nerra, Fulk, 5, 18, 21, 25, 26, 28, 31, 33–35, 42, 43, 48–55
Nithard, 131, 140
Noble, T. F. X., 55
Notker, 126, 137–139

O'Connor, John J., 98
Oexle, O. G., 135
O'Hagan, T., 38
Ordish, O., 45
Oriana, Princess, 81
Orlando, 61, 79, 80, 83, 87, 99
Osella, Giacomo, 92
Ovid, 78, 79, 87

Pallotta, Augustus, 98
Panigarola, Francesco, 102
Pantzer, Katharine F., 95
Paravicini, W., 50
Paris, 79
Parodi, E. G., 91
Pasini, Mapheo (Maffeo), 86, 96
Patourel, John Le, 39
Paul, Count, 35, 55
Pepin, King, 67, 74, 77, 96
Pepin the Short, 76, 93
Perels, E., 139
Pertz, G. H., 135
Petrarch, 80
Philp, K. R., 38
Picone, M., 90
Pierce, Frank, 98
Pierozzi, Antonio, 88
Pierrugues, Ant. Dom., 98
Piramo, 79
Pirenne, Henri, 35, 55
Pippin II of Aquitaine, 110, 114,
    135–137
Place, Edwin B., 97
Planchenault, A., 39
Plantagenet, Geoffrey, 34
Plantagenet, Henry, 34
Poirier-Coutansais, Mlle, 36
Polidori, Filippo-Luigi, 91
Politi, Lancellotto, 98
Pollard, A. W., 95
Possevino, Antonio, 88
Poly, 37

Polybius, 68
Postan, C., 45
Poulantzas, N., 38
Poupardin, R., 49, 50, 53
Powe, F., 38
Predelli, M. Bendinelli, 90
(del)Prete, Leone, 92
Primald, 49
Prinz, F., 135
Prou, M., 54
Prudentius, Bishop of Troyes, 121
Pulci, Luigi, 59, 79, 80, 85, 86, 89
Pulicane, 71, 94

Quaritsch, Helmut, 37
Quint, David, 90

Ragnar, 136
Rajna, Pio, 90, 93, 97
Rechin, Fulk le, 53
Redgrave, G. R., 95
Regino of Prum, 119, 134, 136–
    140
Renaud, Bishop of Paris, 25, 53
Renda, Umberto, 101
Renzi, Lorenzo, 91
Reuter, Timothy, 133
Reyerson, K., 38
Richgard, 116, 119, 138
Richildis, 110, 112, 113, 135
Rinaldo, 83, 87, 99, 100
Robert-Henri, 46
Robertis, Domenico de, 90
Robortello, Francesco, 68
Rodini, Robert, 97
Rodulf, 113, 122, 124, 136
Rois, Adene li, 67
Roland, 61, 66
Rolandus, 61
Rodulf, 113, 122, 124, 136
Rondello, 75
Roric, 113, 136

Roseo, Mambrino, 98, 102
Ross, James Bruce, 95
Rossi, Vittorio, 98
Ruggiero, Guido, 80, 96
Russell, J. B., 136
Russell, J. C., 46
Russo, Luigi, 90

Saint Amano, 109
Saint Antoninus, 88
Saint Arnulf, 110, 137
Saint Aubin, 10, 21, 25, 28, 49
Saint Felix, III, 68
Saint Florent de Saumur, 7, 13, 14, 18, 31, 48, 54
Saint-Georges-sur-Layon, 7, 18, 26, 42
Saint Germain Auxerre, 109
Saint-Germain-des-Près, 19, 45
Saint Hillary, 25
Saint Jouin-de-Marnes, 52
Saint-Julian-de-Tours, 54
Saint Leo I, 68
Saint Marcel, 25
Saint Martin of Tours, 44
Saint Mary, 30
Saint Medard Soissons, 109, 115, 134
Saint Nicholas, 20, 48
Saint Riquien, 110
Saint Serge, 30, 49
Salmon, A., 53
Salomon, Breton dux, 137, 109, 123
San Bernardino of Siena, 102
San Martino del Vescovo, 61
Sawyer, B., 136
Sawyer, P., 136, 140
Schaab, H., 137
Schieffer, R., 134
Schieffer, T., 137
Schlesinger, W., 135

Sessa, Melchior, 99
Shakespeare, William, 60
Shaver, Anne, 92
Sigo, Abbot of St. Aubin, 49
Simson, B. v., 137, 138
Smalley, B., 133
Snuggs, Henry L., 91
Solomon, 127
Sondheimer, J., 39
Soria, Francesco Ant., 98
Southern, Sir Righcar, 34, 53
Stafford, P., 138
Stauback, N., 134
Stevens, W., 38
Strabo, Walafrid, 140
Strayer, J. R., 38
Strevo, Manfrino (Bono) de (Monteferato da), 96
Sulpicius of Buzancais, 25
Sultan of Babylon, 75
Slyvester, Pope, 68
Szarmach, P. E., 137

Tasso, Bernardo, 81
Tasso, Torquato, 81
Tellenbach, G., 134
Terpening, Ronnie H., 97
Tessier, G. 134–136
Theoderic, Abbot of St. Aubin, 21, 49
Theodosius, Emperor, 68
Theodosius II, 68
Thomas, Henry, 98
Thomas of Loches, 29–31, 33, 53
Tinenti, Alberto, 94
Tinto, Alberto, 98
Tisbe, 79
Tonna, Giuseppe, 101
Tramezzino, Michele, 98
Traube, L., 135
Trinity of Vendôme, 20

Tristano, 61, 63–65, 76, 82
Troiano, Re, 82, 83

Uggieri, 100
Ugolini, Francesco A., 91, 97
Ullmann, Walter, 139
Unger, Richard, 133
Urseau, Charles, 40

Vaganay, Hugues, 98
Valentinian, Emperor, 68
Valentinian III, 68
Valerano, 83
Van Bath, B. H. Slicher, 45
Vandelli, Giuseppe, 91, 93
Varanini, Giorgio, 92
Vegetius, 33
Vegio, Leonardo de, 97, 99
Vergil, 79, 80, 86
Vezin, J., 44
Vielliard, J., 133
Villani, Giovanni, 71, 95
Vinaver, Eugene, 91
Viscardi, Antonio, 92
Vogel, W., 135
Volpicelli, Luigi, 102

Waitz, G., 136, 137
Wallace-Hadrill, J. M., 34, 55, 133,
    139, 140
Watson, Wendy M., 101
Watt, J. A., 38
Wattenbach, W., 134
Weinburg, Bernard, 97
Weland, 136
Welf, Count, 117
Werner, K. F., 38, 50, 51, 134, 139
White, K. D., 45
White Jr., Lynn T., 47
Wickham, Chris, 3, 4, 13, 20, 23,
    24, 27, 35–38, 40, 42, 44, 50, 55
Wilcox, Donald J., 93
William the Conqueror, 34, 55
Wolfram, H., 134
Wollasch, J., 134
Wood, Ian, 136, 140
Wormald, Patrick, 133, 137, 140
Wulfad, 134

Xanten, 122

Zadoch, 127
Zambrini, F., 93

CONTENTS OF
PREVIOUS VOLUMES

VOLUME I (1978)
ROSLYN PESMAN COOPER
Pier Soderini: Aspiring Prince or Civic Leader?

BERNARD F. REILLY
On Getting To Be a Bishop in Leon-Castile: The "Emperor" Alfonso
VII and the Post-Gregorian Church.

MICHAEL M. SHEEHAN
Choice of Marriage Partner in the Middle Ages: Development and Mode
of Application of Theory of Marriage.

RICHARD C. TREXLER
The Magi Enter Florence: The Ubriachi of Florence and Venice
INDEX, Volume I–X (Old Series).

VOLUME II (1979)
JERRY H. BENTLEY
New Testament Scholarship at Louvain in the Early Sixteenth Century.

LEROY DRESBECK
Techne, Labor et Natura: Ideas and Active Life in the Medieval Winter.

M. PATRICIA HOGAN
Medieval Villainy: A Study in the Meaning and Control of Crime in an
English Village.

BERNHARD SCHIMMELPFENNIG
Ex Fornicatione Nati: Studies on the Position of Priests' Sons from the
Twelfth to The Fourteenth Century.

VOLUME III (1980)
ERIC FÜGEDI
Coronation in Medieval Hungary.

ARCHIBALD LEWIS
Patterns of Economic Development in Southern France, 1050–1271 A.D.

MARY STROLL
Calixtus II: A Reinterpretation of His Election and the End of
the Investiture Contest.

M. F. VAUGHAN
The Liturgical Perspectives of Piers Plowman.

VOLUME IV (1981)
MARC GLASSER
Marriage in Medieval Hagiography.

ALBERT L. ROSSI
"A L'Ultimo Suo": *Paradiso* XXX and Its Virgilian Context.

RICHARD C. TREXLER
and MARY ELIZABETH LEWIS
Two Captains and Three Kings: New Light on the Medici Chapel.

VOLUME V (1982)
ALAN E. BERNSTEIN
Theology Between Heresy and Folklore: William of Auvergne on
Punishment after Death.

ROBERT D. STEVICK
A Formal Analog of *Elene*.

ARON JA. GUREVICH
On Heroes, Things, Gods and Laughter in Germanic Poetry.

PAUL C. BURNS
Beneventan Interest in Vergil.

VOLUME VI (1983)
RICHARD C. HOFFMANN
Outsiders by Birth and Blood: Racist Ideologies and Realities around the
Periphery of Medieval European Culture.

KATHRYN L. REYERSON
Land, Houses and Real Estate Investment in Montpellier: A Study of the
Notarial Property Transactions, 1293–1348.

D. L. FARMER
Crop Yields, Prices and Wages in Medieval England.

VOLUME VII (1986)
BERNARD S. BACHRACH
Geoffrey Greymantle, Count of the Angevins, 960–987: A Study in French Politics.

ROSLYN PESMAN COOPER
The Florentine Ruling Group under the "governo populare," 1494–1512.

JENNIFER L. O'REILLY
The Double Martyrdom of Thomas Becket: Hagiography or History?

VOLUME VIII (1987)
MAVIS MATE
The Estates of Canterbury Prior before The Black Death, 1315–1348.

SHARON L. JANSEN JAECH
"The Marvels of Merlin" and the Authority of Tradition.

M. PATRICIA HOGAN
The Labor of their Days: Work in the Medieval Village.

MARY ERLER and NANCY GUTIERREZ
Print into Manuscript: A Flodden Field News Pamphlet.

JAMES D. ALSOP and WESLEY M. STEVENS
William Lambarde and Elizabethan Polity.

VOLUME IX (1988)
CAROLA M. SMALL
Medieval Settlement in Basilicata

QUENTIN GRIFFITHS
The Capetian Kings and St. Martin of Tours

ROSALIND KENT BARLOW
The Rebels of Vézelay

CLAIRE WHEELER SOLT
Romanesque French Reliquaries